The ALL NEW Print Production Handbook

Published and distributed by
RotoVision SA
Route Suisse 9
CH-1295 Mies
Switzerland

RotoVision SA
Sales and Editorial Office
Sheridan House, 114 Western Road
Hove BN3 1DD, UK

Tel: +44 (0)1273 72 72 68
Fax: +44 (0)1273 72 72 69
www.rotovision.com

Revised edition copyright © RotoVision SA 2011
First edition copyright © RotoVision SA 2006

All rights reserved. No part of this publication
may be reproduced, stored in a retrieval system, or
transmitted in any form or by any means, electronic,
mechanical, photocopying, recording or otherwise,
without permission of the copyright holder.

While every effort has been made to contact
owners of copyright material produced in this book,
we have not always been successful. In the event
of a copyright query, please contact the Publisher.

10 9 8 7 6 5 4 3 2 1

ISBN:
13-digit: 978-2-88893-159-1
10-digit 2-88893-159-1

Editors: Chris Middleton and Steve Luck
Designer: Jane Waterhouse
Art Director: Tony Seddon

Reprographics in Singapore by ProVision Pte.
Tel: +65 6334 7720
Fax: +65 6334 7721

Printing and binding in China by
Toppan Leefung Printers Ltd.

The ALL NEW Print Production Handbook

David Bann

RotoVision

Contents

06. **Introduction**

08. **Print in the 21st century**
08. The historical perspective (the birth of print to digital printing and CTP)
18. Print on demand
20. New media
24. Print and the environment

26. **Origination and prepress**
26. The print production workflow
28. Editorial basics
30. Images for print production
34. Halftones
36. Color theory and color separation
44. Color management
46. Scanning
48. Typesetting
52. Typefaces and fonts
54. Page layout and design applications/suites
56. Computers and peripherals
58. File formats and digital workflow

60. **Proofing and platemaking**
60. Exchanging files electronically and on disk
62. Types of proof
68. Checking color proofs
70. Checking color on press
72. Imposition and platemaking
76. Computer to plate (CTP)
78. CTP and the PDF workflow
80. Platemaking for other processes

84. **Printing processes**
84. An introduction to the processes
88. Offset lithography
96. Digital printing
100. Gravure
104. Screen printing
108. Letterpress
110. Other processes

114. **Paper and Ink**
114. History of paper
116. How paper is made
126. Types of paper
130. Specifying papers
132. Potential problems with paper
134. Paper and the environment
136. Ink and toner

140. Finishing
140. Finishing processes
142. Folding
144. Binding types and materials
152. Other finishing methods
154. Stamping and embossing
156. Packing and distribution

158. Working with the printer
158. Print buying
164. International suppliers
168. Specifications
178. Quality control
180. Scheduling and print orders
182. Legal considerations

184. Endmatter
184. Glossary
214. International paper sizes
216. Paper usage
217. Book and paper sizes
218. Conversion tables
219. Select bibliography and picture credits
220. Index
224. Acknowledgments

Introduction

In the introduction to the first (1986) edition of this book I said that printing had been predicted to be largely replaced by electronic media, but that I thought that printing would be a prime means of communication for many years to come. Now, twenty-five years later, you are still reading this page printed in ink on paper. The printing industry is still relatively healthy, despite the presence of the Internet and the emergence of new electronic publishing platforms such as eBook and ePub. Why is this so?

There are many reasons. Books, magazines, posters, newspapers, brochures, leaflets, and other printed materials are technologies that work: they are portable, recyclable, do not need a power-supply to operate them, and are not prone to software crashes and system failures. Print can be read anywhere, and the reader can easily go back to check anything not clearly understood. Advertisers like the printed page, because it cannot be switched off in the way that a television, a computer, or a cellphone can—or blocked, as is the case with popup advertisements on websites. Beyond all these reasons, of course, the Internet has undeniably made it possible for us to buy books, posters, and magazines from all parts of the globe both instantly and cheaply. Furthermore, the very forces that are supposed to be killing print can actually nourish it—books thrive in the wake of TV series or movies; printed posters decorate the streets, and our food, technology, health, and beauty products come in beautifully printed packages which people want to own alongside the product.

Nevertheless, there are areas where print is being rapidly replaced by other media—for example, multivolume encyclopedias have been replaced by CD-ROMs, DVDs, editable online resources, and even podcasts; classified advertisers (particularly for recruitment) often use the Internet rather than newspapers; direct-mail volumes are in decline in the wake of emails and data collection via online portals; newspapers' online versions compete with the printed ones and are available to a global audience, although many news providers now charge a subscription fee to readers for access to some or all areas of their sites. Despite this, print is still holding its own in areas where other media cannot be as effective.

The developments in information and printing technologies since the late 1980s have reinforced print's position, by making it more accessible, quicker, less expensive, and of a more consistent quality. The client or designer now carries out work that previously could only be performed by craftsmen, skilled in a particular aspect of print. This applies particularly in the prepress area, which has seen the biggest amount of change over the years, and high-quality print can now be produced to near professional levels from the comfort of your own home office.

One thing that has not changed is the excitement of being involved in printing. Printed items have to be produced to a deadline, whether they are newspapers for tomorrow's breakfast tables, or a book to coincide with the launch of a new TV series. And the printed word has an authority, which other media still fail to emulate in quite the same way. Printers are usually obsessed with avoiding errors, because they remain on the printed page for the life of the book or magazine and cannot be edited out. It is said that printers "have ink in their veins," and it is certainly true that most people who start their careers in printing (or related fields) find their work exciting and fulfilling, and often work in print for the whole of their working lives.

David Bann

INTRODUCTION

7

The historical perspective

Printing has developed in fits and starts. There have been periods when centuries passed with no real progress—the Gutenberg of 1456 would have been quite at home in an 1850s print shop—and then several periods of just a few years, during which there were dramatic leaps forward in technology.

PRINT IN THE 21st CENTURY

Printing started in China in the 6th century with woodblock printing—in which the words and pictures were carved onto a wooden block. The world's oldest known printed book *The Diamond Sutra* was produced in 868—this too was printed from woodblocks. Printing from individual type characters made of hardened clay was carried out in China in the 11th century by Pi Sheng, and by the 13th century printing from metal type came into use in the Far East (China, Korea, Japan), but its development stalled as it was not suitable for the ideographic characters used.

The key development was the introduction of moveable type by Johannes Gutenberg, who invented a mold that could cast individual letters. He established a press in Mainz, Germany in 1444 and started work on the Gutenberg Bible (see fig. 1.1), published in 1456. Moveable type meant that a text could be proofread and corrected before printing. Each character was cut on a steel punch, from which a matrix (mold) was made in a softer metal, into which molten lead, mixed with tin and antinomy, was poured to create the character. The characters were then assembled, line by line, to make the page and, after printing, the pages were taken apart and the type could then be reused.

The wooden press Gutenberg used was based on the wine press and was of simple construction—the type was locked up in a frame on the bed of the press, inked with ink balls (sheepskin pads with wooden handles), the sheet of paper placed on top, and then a large handle was pulled to turn a wooden screw which pressed a thick sheet of wood against the paper to create the impression from the type. The paper was dampened before printing to achieve a better impression. It was 200 years before this basic press design was improved and the ink balls were replaced with rollers.

Printing, based on Gutenberg's invention, spread rapidly throughout Europe, reaching England in 1476, when William Caxton started his press. Stephen Daye brought printing to America in 1638. The printers in the various countries developed many different typefaces, versions of which are still in use today.

The next development was presses made of iron rather than wood and featuring a lever mechanism instead of a screw. The Earl of Stanhope built the first of these around 1800 and it was developed by George Clymer, whose Columbian press (of which many examples still survive) was easier to use. This was followed by a period of rapid innovation in press design and in 1814, *The Times* was printed on a steam-driven cylinder press, designed by Frederich Koenig. This printed sheets of paper and the first web-fed press (printing from a reel of paper) was introduced by William Bullock in America in 1865. The treadle platen (see fig. 1.3) handfed and operated by a foot treadle was used for small items of jobbing work.

1.1 Gutenberg Bible
printed in Mainz in 1456 by Johannes Gutenberg. This was one of the first books to be printed from moveable type. The rubrics (decorations and initial letters) in color were added later by hand.

PRINT IN THE 21ST CENTURY

1.2 Medieval printing office
This woodcut shows the printing office of Abraham von Werdt in Nuremberg, who printed there between 1640 and 1680. In the left foreground, paper is being dampened prior to printing; in the left background, type is being set by hand and, on the right, the type in the press is being inked using ink balls (eventually replaced by rollers).

9

1.3 Treadle platen PR
This press was used for small items of jobbing print and powered by the printer's foot. Rollers transfer the ink from the disk on the right to the type in the bed of the machine. Sheets of paper are fed in by hand and pressed against the type to make the impression.

1.4 Hand setting of type
The metal characters are in cases (trays) and the compositor assembles them in a composing stick a line at a time. After printing, the type is put back in the cases and reused.

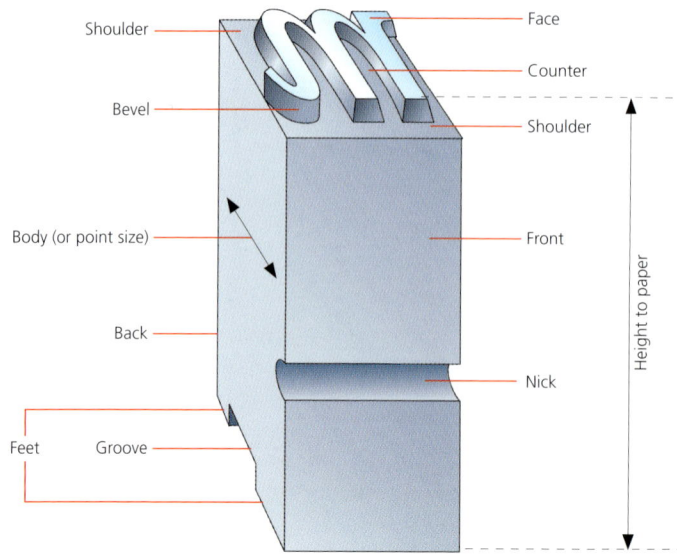

1.5 Metal type character showing the named parts. The nick is used to ensure that the character is set the right way up.

PRINT IN THE 21st CENTURY

10

Until the end of the 19th century, the growth of printing was held back by the slowness, and therefore cost, of setting type by hand. A hand compositor could set about 1,000 characters an hour, meaning newspapers and book printers needed scores of compositors to keep pace with their publishing requirements. This problem was resolved with Ottmar Mergenthaler's invention of the Linotype machine, which was installed at the *New York Herald Tribune* in 1886. The Linotype consisted of a keyboard which, when a character was depressed, caused a brass matrix of that character to drop into a channel and (with spaces inserted) form a line. When the line was complete, molten lead was pumped in to make a solid line of type. 1890 saw the arrival of the Monotype system, invented by Tolbert Lanston. This system consisted of two parts—a keyboard produced a punched paper tape, which was then fed into a caster, which cast individual pieces of type in the correct order. Corrections to Monotype setting could now be made by hand, whereas in Linotype setting the whole line had to be reset. With these two machines, type could now be set at typing speed, thereby transforming the economics of printing and publishing at that time. Amazingly, both machines were still being used commercially until the 1980s when filmsetting, and subsequently digital typesetting, came into cost effective general use.

Illustrations were printed from woodblocks and etchings until Alois Senefelder invented the lithographic printing process in Germany in 1796. Drawings were made on stone and rather than being in relief or recessed, were on a flat surface. The image was made to print by the mutual antipathy of oil and water. However, it was 1904 before the first lithographic press printing by the offset principle on paper was introduced (they were originally used in the late 19th century for printing on tinplate). Although offset lithography is now the predominant printing process, it did not become so until the mid-20th century, because prior to the development of filmsetting, type had to be photographed to make a lithographic plate and letterpress, and so printing directly from type was therefore cheaper. The photogravure process (with a recessed image) was developed in the late 19th century. The line block for letterpress printing made photographically was invented in France in 1850 and the first halftone (a photograph broken up into dots for letterpress printing) appeared in 1891. This led on to the development of the four-color process (where all colors are produced by making separation halftones of the original image into cyan, yellow, magenta, and black).

1.6 Typesetter
The skilled art of the typesetter is now the domain of the desktop software package.

PRINT IN THE 21ST CENTURY

PRINT IN THE 21st CENTURY

The first half of the 20th century saw the beginnings of the automation of finishing and binding, which had until then been entirely a hand operation. Guillotines, folding machines, and automatic binding lines were gradually introduced.

The Monotype Corporation started work on filmsetting (photocomposition) in 1944 and the Intertype Photosetter was introduced in 1945, but it was the 1960s before filmsetting started to be used commercially. As well as the Monophoto, early machines included the Lumitype (Photon), Linofilm, Monotype Lasercomp (see fig. 1.8), Linotype VIP, and Compugraphic. These were much faster than their hot-metal counterparts and avoided the storage of tons of metal type which had to be kept for reprints, taking up a great deal of space—plus the money tied up in the cost of the metal. Filmsetting also had the first page-layout program, which would eventually lead to desktop publishing in the late 1980s and early 1990s. Filmsetting depended on the first simple computers to deal with the spacing and layout requirements. Most filmsetters were standalone units driven by paper tape or floppy disks produced on separate keyboards. Up to this point everything had been "typed" twice—once by the original author, and again by the typesetter's keyboard operator. As well as doubling the work, this also meant that the text had to be checked carefully as the keyboard operator could introduce errors. It was at this stage that the idea of the "single keystroke" was introduced, when authors started using simple wordprocessors and supplied floppy disks rather than typed manuscripts.

Filmsetting helped to establish offset lithography as the main printing process, at the expense of letterpress. Offset presses became faster and more sophisticated and web-offset presses (printing from reels of paper rather than sheets) were used for long-run products, such as magazines and newspapers. These types of presses run at up to 50,000 impressions an hour compared with sheet-fed speeds of 15,000 an hour.

Alongside the developments in filmsetting, new techniques were developed for color separation and page makeup of film. The electronic color scanner developed in the 1960s enabled the high-speed scanning of transparencies and flat artwork, producing four-color separated film in minutes rather than the hours it had taken previously using process cameras. Electronic airbrushing and color correction techniques also greatly enhanced the quality of many illustrations. Increasingly, fine screen and stochastic screening (see p. 39) have allowed tremendous improvements in color reproduction.

1.7 Handbinding
It was only in the 20th century that binding started to be automated. In this Victorian bookbindery, all the operations are carried out by hand.

12

1.8 Monotype Lasercomp
Monotype Lasercomp (in the right of this picture) was an early filmsetting system. Keyboarding was done separately and a magnetic tape drove a laser that imaged the film. The machine here was at Oxford University Press. On the left is a Monophoto 400/8.

The next major developments in printing, in the 1980s and 1990s, had their origins in the office. The introduction of the personal computer (PC) and the first Apple Macs gave birth to desktop publishing, which started in the office before being taken up by printers. The photocopying machine fathered today's digital printing presses, while email, text files, hypertext, and transfer protocols (which came into use during the 1990s) enabled fast communication of information and the transmission of files over long distances.

Probably the most significant event in printing in recent years was when desktop publishing started to be used for commercial design and printing, rather than just being used in the office for internal documents. The two main applications initially were QuarkXPress (see p. 54) and PageMaker (the forerunner of InDesign [see p. 54]) and initially these were just used for text, with illustrations and tints dealt with by conventional means, but soon desktop publishing applications were able to produce a file of the complete job. Scanners became much cheaper and more sophisticated, and for the first time the client or designer could scan less demanding pictures. When Quark or PageMaker files were sent to a prepress house or printer, these were output to film on an imagesetter and a lithographic plate prepared from the film, but by the beginning of this century most work was being produced by CTP (computer to plate [see p. 76 and *passim*]), cutting out film and subsequent expensive film storage altogether.

The last decade has seen the arrival of several new versions of QuarkXPress and the Adobe Creative Suite, with the Design Premium version consisting of InDesign, Photoshop Extended, Illustrator, and Acrobat as well as Dreamweaver, Flash and Fireworks. InDesign has long replaced PageMaker and has steadily added many new features. QuarkXPress was at one time the predominant program, but InDesign has rapidly gained ground, offering greater integration with the industry-standard Photoshop and other applications within the suite. Some designers, particularly freelancers, use both, depending on the nature of the job or their clients' requirements, but InDesign is now the more dominant of the two. Scanners, especially flatbed versions, and ink-jet and laser printers have become cheaper and give ever higher quality, and each year brings ever more powerful Macintoshes and PCs. Storage media such as external hard drives have fallen drastically in price while providing massive storage potential.

Where designers used to send application or PostScript files to prepress suppliers, files are now supplied in the form of cross-platform PDFs (Portable Document Format). This has greatly simplified the workflow so that, for example, a designer can design a job, turn it into a PDF and email it to the client for approval—Acrobat Reader (which allows the user to view and comment on PDFs) is widely available as a free download, whereas many clients don't have access to InDesign or QuarkXPress. On approval, the job can then be supplied to the prepress supplier as a PDF.

The advantage of a PDF is that it is not easy to edit the file without specialist knowledge, making it rare for mistakes to be introduced at prepress or printing. However, this does mean that the designer will have to create a new PDF in order to amend any corrections. However, if you work with a trusted supplier many adjustments or amendments can be made without the need to create completely new PDF files. Bear in mind that significant changes should always be introduced to the original application files as well as the PDFs.

1.10 Adding notes to PDFs Designers and editors can attach interactive text notes to PDFs, which can save massive amounts of time and avoid the need for expensive and wasteful laser printouts and postage costs.

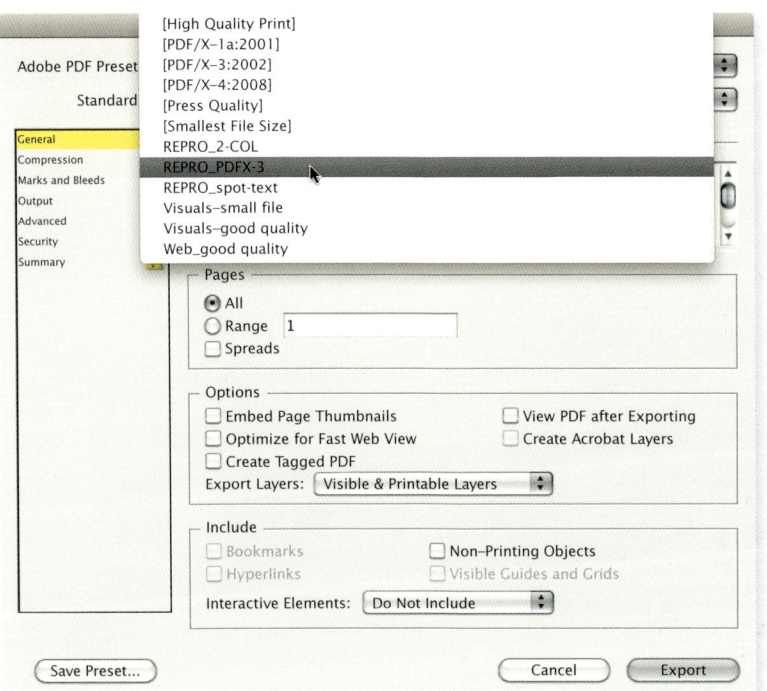

1.9 Creating a PDF
Here is the PDF dialog in Adobe InDesign, where designers and editors can make PDFs from the layout—for example, at high resolution for printing out, and at low resolution for emailing and checking on screen. The screen grab shows both built-in presets and custom presets created by the user.

PRINT IN THE 21st CENTURY

15

PRINT IN THE 21st CENTURY

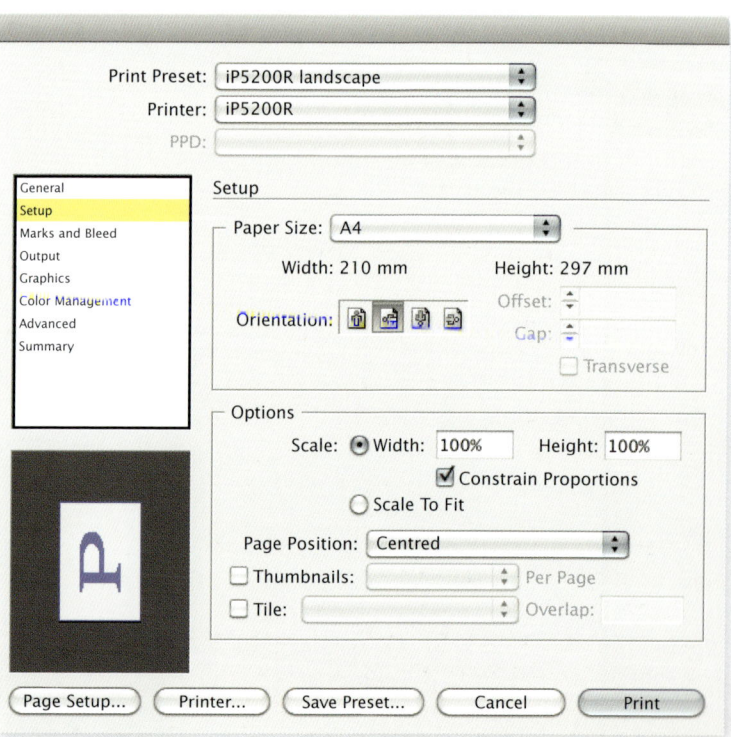

1.11 Large format printing
The Canon iPF8300 can produce high-quality images up to 44 inches wide, using its 12-color pigment ink system. Printers of this quality can produce material suitable for use in both production applications and proofing environments.

1.12 Setup presets
All printers come with their own driver software, which will be loaded into your system when you select the printer on the network. It is simplest to create print presets for regular types of job.

16

The common use of broadband for Internet access means that all but the very largest files can be practically sent by email or FTP (file transfer protocol), locally or internationally, rather than having to be burned to CD or DVD. This avoids the delay and cost in sending files to the printer by courier, particularly when sending files to overseas suppliers. A file can now be with a printer in the Far East, or anywhere in Europe, as quickly as one in the next town.

Digital color proofs have come down in price and show improved quality. "Contract" proofs conform to commonly agreed standards, enabling the printer to achieve a better match on press. "Remote" proofing (see p. 66) is now common practice, where the client checks the proof on screen (although this requires higher quality monitors, calibrated to the same color space as the vendor's monitor), again saving time and cost in physically sending proofs to the client and returning them. Computer to plate (CTP) working has replaced film, resulting in lower costs and improved quality with a more accurate image and reduced ink use. A new generation of color presses have controls that automatically adjust inking and register. Press data from the initial print run is stored for close matching in the event of a reprint.

Digital printing is now widely available, allowing very short runs and also personalized printing (variable data printing). This has enabled Print on Demand (P.O.D., see p. 18) whereby a publisher can economically print as little as one single copy, rather than having to print hundreds and store them in a warehouse, where the paper may begin to age visibly. All these developments combined have greatly simplified and speeded up the design, printing, and publishing processes and made them more accessible.

Doing it yourself

All the developments in desktop publishing and prepress have made it much easier for an individual or company to save time and money by doing many of the operations themselves, rather than using outside sources. An individual or company with a personal computer, scanner, and printer can produce simple items at home or in the office, rather than having to use outsourced designers and printers. Obviously, someone without design training will not be able to create sophisticated layouts, but simple newsletters, menus, or posters can be produced. In companies, staff can be trained in page layout applications (such as InDesign or QuarkXPress) or use templates which have been designed professionally. Printing itself can be done in-house on office ink-jet or laser printers, if the run is fairly short and the quality requirements are not too demanding. Anything more than a few hundred copies will be cheaper to outsource to a print shop than to print in-house because of the cost of consumables (such as toner) or the click-cost, where an office printer is paid for based on usage. Most office printers won't give the same quality as high-end digital or offset printing, particularly when printing illustrations and using coated paper.

However, even when using an outside printer, if the design is not too demanding, it can be done in-house and supplied to the print shop as a PDF. This cuts out both cost and time in the approval and correction of proofs.

Print on demand

Print on Demand (or P.O.D.) is a logical evolution of storing text and images digitally; rather than storing books as physical items in warehouses and risk them lying unsold or decaying, they can be printed as and when someone wants even a single copy. This has revolutionized publishing in the 21st century as it slashes wastage and losses, and can make even very short-run or niche publications profitable.

The term P.O.D. is mainly, though not exclusively, used in relation to book publishing and printing. Traditional book publishing suffers from the problem that it is uneconomical to print short runs. This is because the preparatory costs (prepress, platemaking and make-ready on the printing press) are spread across the quantity printed, meaning that runs of a few hundred result in a high production cost and therefore a prohibitive retail price. This is usually more of a problem on reprints rather than new titles. To take an example—a new higher education text book might be first published in a run of say 20,000 copies, which would give both a reasonable retail price and a reasonable profit, even allowing for the fact that as well as the printing preparatory costs, the writing, editorial, design/typesetting, and distribution costs have to be recovered. Typically, the new book will sell a lot more in the first year of publication than subsequent years and the 20,000 copies might last two years, after which the publisher has to decide whether it is economical to print a few hundred to cover likely orders over the following year or so, or to let the book go out of print, despite there being an ongoing market. This problem is compounded by the fact that the printing cost has to be paid at the time and won't be fully recouped until the last copy has sold. In addition, there are the costs of storing the books.

This problem has been largely solved by the development of digital printing and specialist offset litho equipment designed for short runs, backed up by suitable finishing and binding equipment. Now, it is possible to print very short runs (tens rather than hundreds) or even just a single copy at a realistic price. True print on demand is where the publisher holds no stock at all and the book is printed in response to a customer order, even if only one copy is required. To achieve this, the publisher supplies the printer with digital files (usually PDFs) of the cover or jacket and text and these are held on the printer's database to be retrieved immediately when required. Where digital files aren't available, the printer can scan the text and cover/jacket to digitize it, a one-time cost to the publisher. Orders are placed electronically, so that an order from a consumer, bookseller, or wholesaler can trigger the printing automatically and produce invoices (to the customer and publisher), minimizing administration costs. Most specialist short-run printers offer fulfillment services, meaning once the publisher has put the book on the printer's database, orders can go direct to the printer and the publisher simply receives a statement each month from the printer detailing the receipts and production costs, along with any necessary payments.

This model doesn't work for every type of book—a mass-market paperback book would have too low a retail price to justify printing on short-run equipment. However, for academic, legal, technical and reference books, the concept has revolutionized the economics of the business and brought back into print hundreds of thousands of titles, which would previously have been unavailable. Some out-of-print popular fiction authors from previous decades are also available to devotees using this model. It's also possible for students to have books individually compiled for them, consisting of chapters selected from different books combined to suit the course being taken.

Printing on demand has also enabled much more accessible "self-publishing." Before short runs were economical, someone who wanted to publish a book that wouldn't be accepted by a conventional publisher had to go to a "vanity publisher" who would print several hundred copies in order to reduce the per unit cost, even though these might not all sell, and charge a fee for the editorial and design work—all of which made self-publishing an expensive exercise. Now, several companies enable authors to put their book on a Web site and will fulfill orders for as few as just one copy, at a reasonable price. A telling statistic is that 50% of all published books with an ISBN (International Standard Book Number) sell fewer than 250 copies, so the potential market for short-run printing is vast. Internet booksellers such as Amazon make these books easily available, whereas the larger bookstores wouldn't normally stock such titles. However, there may be a role for the conventional bookseller in print on demand—machines which print and bind single copies are being developed, which may be installed in bookshops to print on-demand copies of out-of-print books, thus cutting out shipping and warehousing costs. Apart from books, other printed items can use P.O.D.—art galleries can supply prints or posters printed at the time of purchase. Newspapers can be printed on demand and made available remotely in international locations.

PRINT IN THE 21st CENTURY

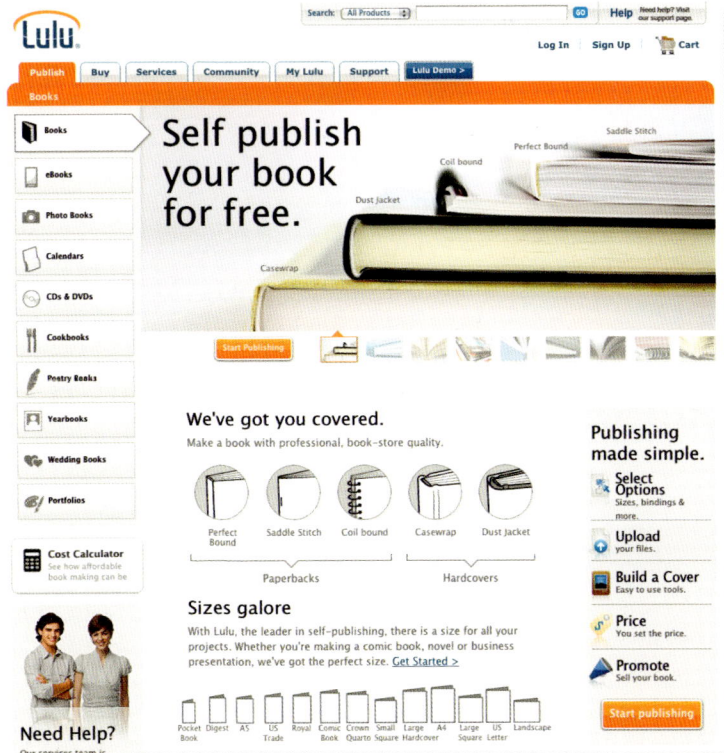

1.13 P.O.D. online
Numerous companies are now offering P.O.D. services via the Internet. Publishers include those of niche books and publications; formerly out-of-print popular authors; and even "vanity" publishers, allowing people to publish and sell their own work.

New media

For many years, the four main media were print, television, cinema, and radio. All of these have been affected dramatically by the development of new media in the last twenty years, particularly the Internet and mobile technologies.

Today, print certainly has company and the Internet, together with the growing use of broadband has had far-reaching effects on all the "old" media and print has had to fight to retain its share of the global communication market. Most forms of print (excepting possibly posters and packaging) have been affected. Newspapers are under threat from two directions—they are losing classified advertising to recruitment and general "for sale" websites on the Internet (a particular problem for local newspapers) and also readers are reading the on-line version of their newspapers and other news websites and possibly ceasing to buy a newspaper. This may change now that some news corporations are beginning to introduce subscription charges to view their syndicated online content. Direct mail marketing volumes are declining but this may be because more personalization of direct mail has made it more targeted to likely consumers, through use of databases and digital printing.

The Internet has also changed the face of book and journal publishing—although trade books (such as bestselling novels) continue to thrive, reference books (particularly encyclopedias) and learned journals have suffered the competition of a medium that has very low delivery costs and can be updated instantly if required. Magazines have been less affected; as for most of them the consumer still wants the convenience of viewing the content in the form of a printed magazine, rather than on screen—indeed, the Internet has added communities of interest, discussion boards, and privileged content to regular readers or subscribers of the printed article.

Podcasting (including video podcasting), audio books, and eBooks also pose a threat to magazines and books, as content can be listened to or viewed on an MP3 player or iPad. For example, travel guides are particularly well suited to an electronic format, giving a real-time accompaniment, complete with Google Map directions, to sightseeing. Podcasts also have a useful role in education and training, particularly in areas such as language learning and revision aids. It goes without saying that developments in mobile phone technology and the advent of the smart phone have made them yet another competitor to the printed word.

eBooks are books in digital form. The book exists as a file that can be read on any PC or suitable handheld device. Furthermore a book in electronic form can be coded to facilitate instant searches of various kinds—a limitation of books with a conventional index. A conventional book's main advantages over an eBook are portability and legibility. The first handheld devices for eBooks were launched in the late 1990s, but were not commercially successful, as they tended to be too large and heavy and the type was difficult to read on the screen. This has all changed with the release of devices such as Amazon's Kindle (pictured on page 7) or Apple's iPad (see fig. 1.14). The latest Kindle, known generically as the Kindle 3 by users, is equipped with 3G technology and displays text and images using an improved, high-contrast E Ink screen. Books can now be purchased and downloaded directly to the device, whereas older models had to be connected to a PC to access and load new material. These features obviously make the device a much more attractive and flexible proposition for readers prepared to ditch the traditional paperback in favor of the digital reading experience. Apple's iPad is quite different in that it is a fully featured tablet computer, marketed as the perfect portable device for accessing audio and visual media, as well as for surfing the Web and gaming. Books are read using the iBooks application which can be downloaded from the App Store, and a number of major book and magazine publishers have committed to publishing for the iPad.

eBooks are cheaper than their printed versions and, as the price of newer devices becomes more affordable—as has already happened with the iPod for example—eBooks will certainly increase their share of the market. Books can be published simultaneously as a printed book and an eBook, but it is important to be clear about the suitability of the book for the new media publication. Not all printed titles will naturally lend themselves to the new formats and may need a good deal of remedial work to transform them successfully. It is for the individual publishers to decide how to form their publishing strategies, based on their own lists.

Blogging and vlogging (the self-publishing of online journals and video logs) are also threatening traditional publishing models, as they exist outside of the editorial control and filtering process of traditional media.

PRINT IN THE 21st CENTURY

1.14 Apple's iPad
Apple have once again revolutionized the way we view content with what is arguably the world's first truly usable tablet computer. Released in April 2010, 3 million were sold in just 80 days.

Courtesy of Apple.

PRINT IN THE 21st CENTURY

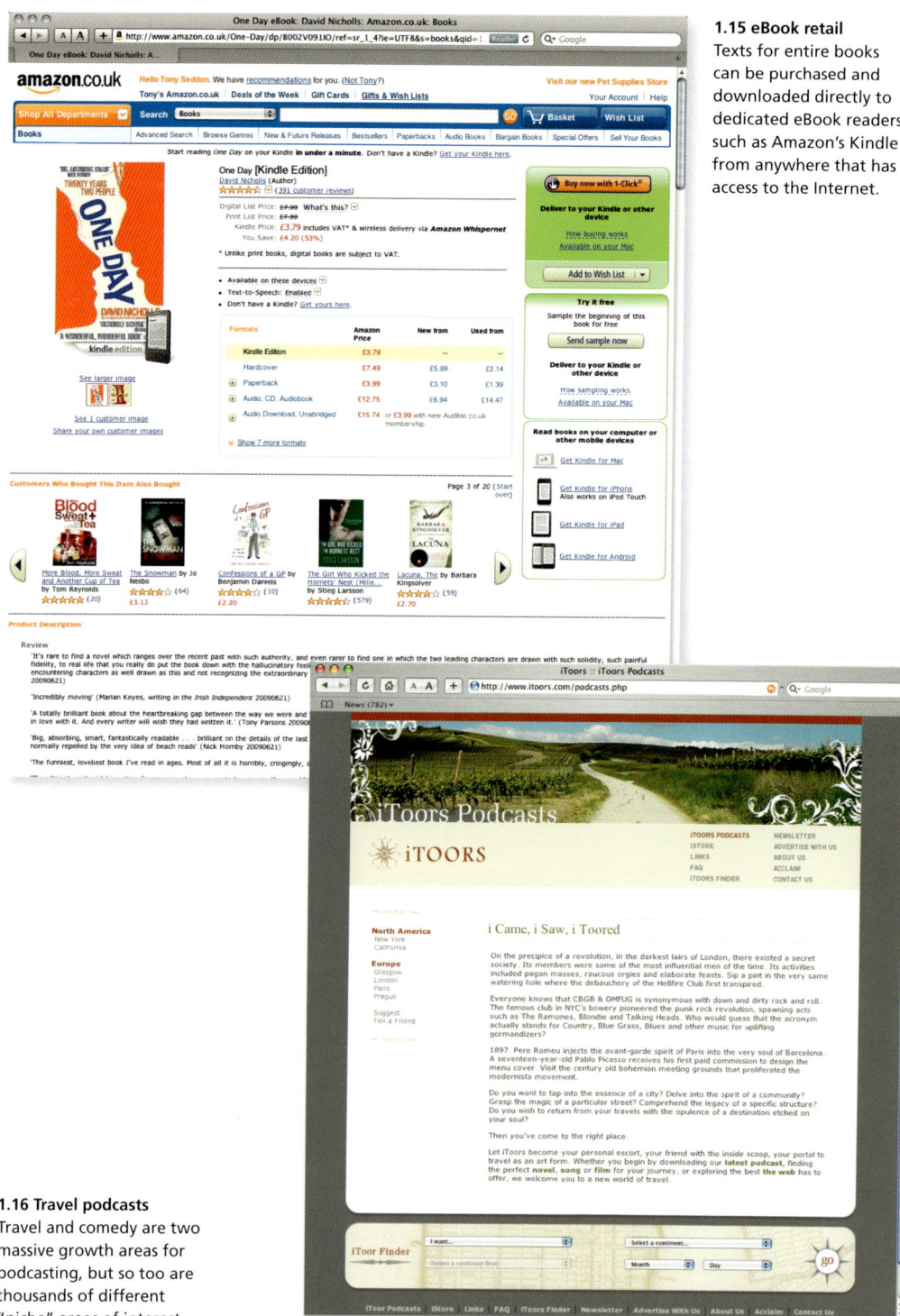

1.15 eBook retail
Texts for entire books can be purchased and downloaded directly to dedicated eBook readers such as Amazon's Kindle from anywhere that has access to the Internet.

1.16 Travel podcasts
Travel and comedy are two massive growth areas for podcasting, but so too are thousands of different "niche" areas of interest.

Design for non-print media

The requirement for cross-platform design is essential today, and practically all companies have online presences that complement their print-based visual identities. However, this should not be at the expense of mimicking a print design and failing to make the most of a Web site's interactivity and ability to link to other pages and websites. XML (eXtensible Markup Language) is the key to cross-platform working. This programming language has been designed to be flexible and enables jobs to be written in other languages, but the use of XML enables different programming languages to work together. XML's predecessor is SGML (Standard Generalized Markup Language), which was used for structuring different types of electronic document (including text for books and other printed products). XML is a public format owned by the World Wide Web Consortium (W3C). XML tags (adds a descriptive identity to) headlines, body copy, and other elements, and enables easy transfer of content within a medium and from one medium to another.

To give an example, in a print document a caption might be specified as 10pt Helvetica in the page layout application, but XML would just tag it as "caption," so that when the document is displayed on the Web, the tag "caption" will follow the style for the Web document—which may be a different type size and typeface. This avoids having to reformat a document from scratch when publishing it in another medium.

PRINT IN THE 21st CENTURY

1.17 Cross-platform design
Designers who work with text and images today work in a cross-platform, multichannel media, where the same words and images can be consumed from the printed page, websites, and portals.

23

Print and the environment

In the 21st century, the environment has become an issue of global debate and controversy. However, there is a huge amount that printers, publishers, designers, and everyone else in the print-production chain can do to minimize the environmental impact and wastage associated with their work.

Printing of all sorts impacts on the environment in countless ways. Many companies, for example, make their CDs and DVDs "carbon neutral," which means planting trees or replacing natural resources to a degree equivalent to the environmental cost of their production. But clearly, the most important area is paper, its content and pulping; the chapter on paper and ink (see p.114) deals with the effects of the use of these raw materials on the environment and how they can be minimized. Here, we will deal with other ways that publishers and printers can use more sustainable ways of working. Many companies will want to do this voluntarily, but this may not be a choice as many large client companies and government agencies insist on certain environmental standards, as a condition of working for them. Often, sustainable initiatives (as in reducing energy costs) will also save money.

In printing, the introduction of digital printing and the CTP method of working—particularly where used with processless plates—has dramatically reduced the use of raw materials (film and chemicals) in prepress. CTP presswork has reduced the number of wasted sheets in the make-ready stage of a job. Remote proofing cuts out both the raw materials used for conventional proofs and the energy used to transport them. Printing, however, still has issues with solvents used in the process, and energy used for drying and fume extraction, although all of these are being addressed and processes improved. One of the main ways to save energy is to control the energy used in a factory or office, for heating, lighting, air-conditioning, and so on. Most equipment such as computers, photocopiers, and printers can be switched off overnight. Increasingly, manufacturers will introduce technologies that have no "standby" mode to avoid wasting electricity.

At the buyer's end of the equation, the way you design and specify a print job affects the ability for it to be recycled, so wire-stitching (page 144 onward) and lamination (page 152-153 make it more difficult to recycle the product after use. Another area to look at is transport—are the ways you deliver goods, be they proofs and layouts or the finished job, as energy-efficient as they could be?

There are international standards for environmental management where companies' procedures are audited for environmental impacts and a certificate granted for compliance. Compliance with these standards may be difficult and expensive for smaller companies, but the lack of a certificate doesn't prevent them from doing business in a sustainable way.

Environmental issues also include the human impacts of working methods. Most large multinational companies have codes of conduct for their suppliers, covering health and safety, hours of work, trades union recognition and so on and these are used in particular to ensure that printing factories in developing countries have good working conditions and employment practices.

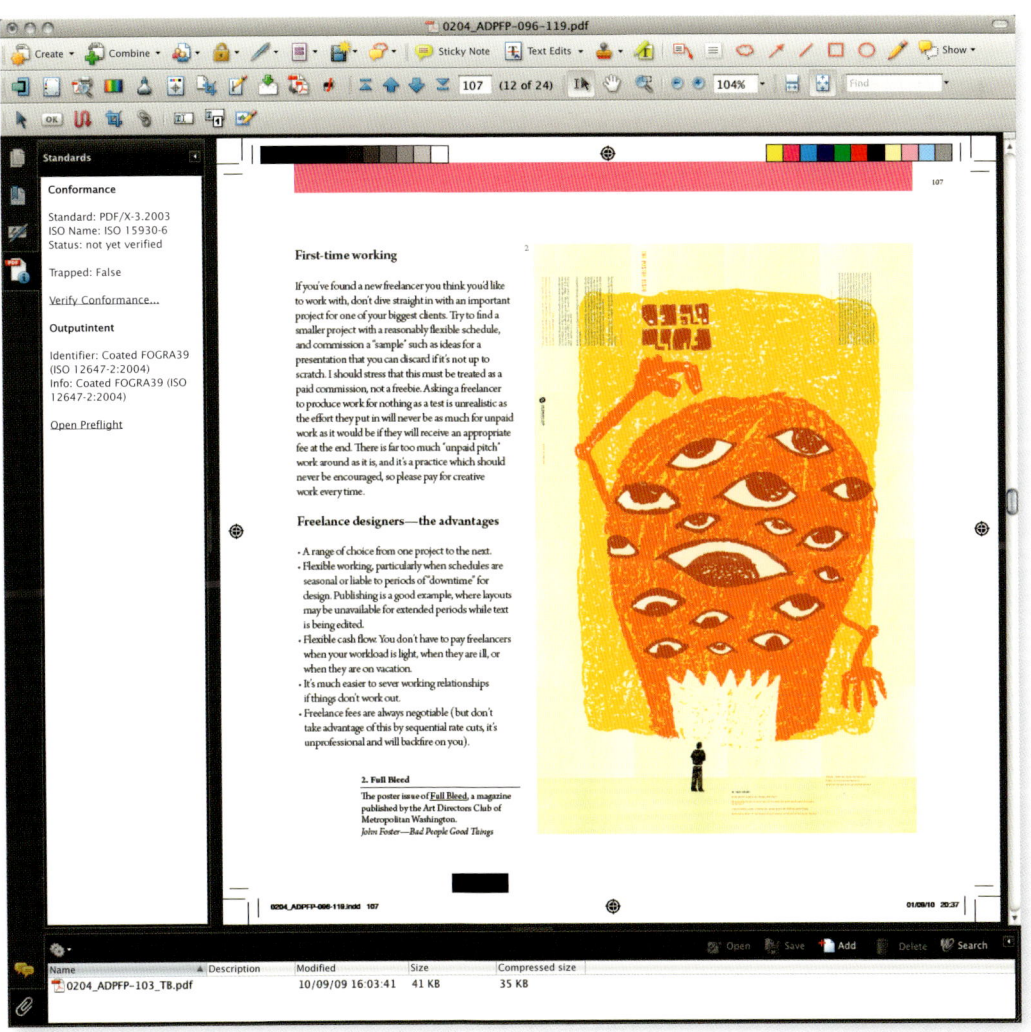

1.18 PDF proof
PDF proofing avoids the need for wasteful laser printouts, and can also prevent waste in transport by avoiding the need for proofs to be sent through the mail. The saving in time also ameliorates environmental impact.

The print production workflow

This describes the path of the job between all the people involved in the production of a printing job. These include: client, designer, prepress house, printer, and finisher/binder. Each party supplies an output, which becomes the input for the next party involved in the workflow. However, rather than each just doing the work and passing it on to the next, the workflow also involves files, proofs, and information being passed back and forth as the job progresses.

ORIGINATION AND PREPRESS

You can see from the chart, opposite, that even a simple printing job will involve several different parties and operations, and these need to be carefully planned and controlled, and the responsibilities of each of the parties made clear from the outset.

Job Definition Format
Job Definition Format (JDF) is a way of linking every stage in the production of a printed job electronically, dispensing with unnecessary paperwork and (as a by-product) supplying a lot of useful information and statistics. It can be seen as an electronic "job ticket," which can be used to specify all the information needed about a job, starting with estimating and going through to delivery of the finished job. It is a system based on a standard, rather than a product you can purchase, and anyone can use it without payment. It is administered by the independent CIP4 organization, whose members are the leading companies in the graphic arts sector.

JDF operates by breaking down all the stages in producing print into separate processes, each of which is defined in terms of inputs and outputs. As an example, the inputs for a printing press are paper, plates, ink, and quantity, and the outputs are the printed sheets from the press, which then become inputs for the finisher/binder.

The important thing about JDF for the client or designer is that it is a tool that can be used by them from the beginning of a job, rather than just being something used by the printer. When you first ask a printer for an estimate, you will be able to do so on an electronic form that is JDF compliant. That information is then used to create the estimate and, after acceptance of the estimate and any subsequent changes to the specification, it is used to create the order. At the design stage, the JDF information is attached (using Acrobat) to the PDFs supplied to the prepress house or printer, enabling all the production details of a job to be combined with the job itself, when it goes in hand. JDF can then be used in the digital workflow (see p. 59). As the job progresses, Job Messaging Format (JMF) allows messages to be passed up and down the workflow, supplying information and reporting problems. For example, if a job is running late at printing stage, a message is automatically passed back up the workflow to inform the client of the delay and down the workflow to tell the finisher/binder that the sheets will not arrive on time. This exchange of information can be done over the Internet in a variety of ways, as we will see.

JDF has been written with XML metadata, meaning that users can write their own tags (descriptions) for any job in hand, knowing that it can be read by anyone else using XML. JDF eliminates double-handling and mistakes due to human error and gives all parties more up-to-date information. For the printer, this information enables higher productivity through less downtime.

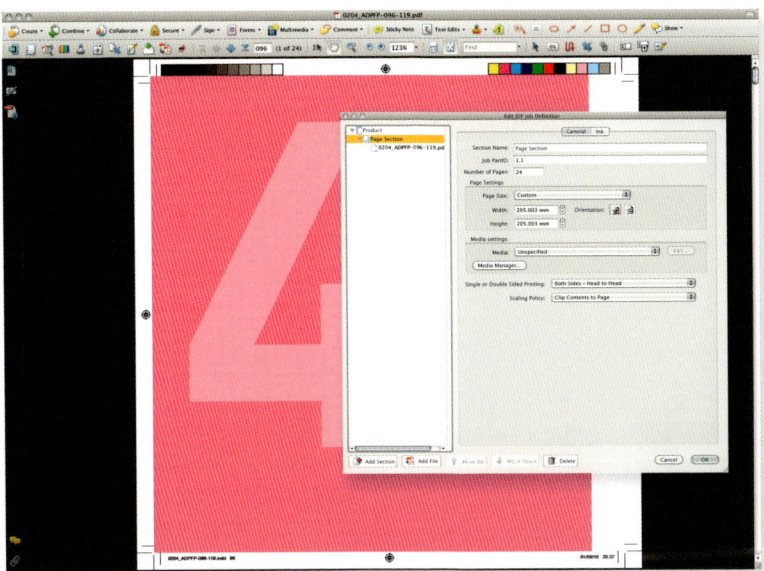

2.1 Acrobat's JDF (Job Definition Format) panel, where JDF information can be added and edited.

2.2 JDF (Job Definition Format) logo

ORIGINATION AND PREPRESS

CLIENT	Supplies →	Specification, copy, design brief, order
	← Receives	Estimate, roughs, layouts, proofs, dummy, finished job, archive files
DESIGNER	Supplies →	Roughs, layouts, application files or PDFs, archive files
	← Receives	Copy, design brief, proofs
PREPRESS	Supplies →	Estimate, proofs, printing plates or PDFs
	← Receives	Specification, order, application files or PDFs
PRINTER	Supplies →	Estimate, proofs, printed sheets
	← Receives	Specification, order, printing plates or PDFs
FINISHER/ BINDER	Supplies →	Estimate, dummy, finished/bound job
	← Receives	Order, printed sheets

27

Editorial basics

Copy will normally follow a "house style" which the client asks the writer to follow. House style deals with spelling, punctuation, abbreviations, and other style issues, and how the wordprocessed file should be supplied to suit the subsequent editorial and design processes. This may include structuring text and headings rather than just supplying raw copy to be formatted by the designer. Copy may then be copy-edited; both to check that it conforms to the house style, and to identify any text that needs revision.

The copy-editor may also assemble the other elements of the job, if not provided by the client or author, which can include photographs, commissioned illustrations, maps, captions, and so on, and ensure the appropriate permissions have been acquired to reproduce text or images. The editor ensures consistency between these elements and the text before the job is handed to the designer along with the design brief.

The designer will then lay out the pages and supply the editor, author, or client with proofs for checking. Corrections to proofs are best made using the standard proof correction marks (see opposite). Rather than making handwritten corrections on the hard copy, proofs can be emailed as PDFs and these can be annotated on the file itself and returned. Software exists to add proof-correction marks to PDFs on screen. Many editors today working on illustrated books or magazines work in layout software, principally QuarkXPress or Adobe InDesign, proofreading and editing straight into the designer's layouts—or within Word and reimporting the text—cutting their copy to fit the space set by the designer. In magazines, production editors are a bridge between copy editors and designers, fitting text to available space and images.

Once the pages are laid out an index can be prepared. The editor will see the proofs of the index and revised proofs of any corrected pages before the job is sent to the prepress house or printer. The printer may supply a plotter proof (see p. 76) as a final check before printing. Corrections become more expensive the further production progresses.

Optical Character Recognition (OCR)
Where text exists only on paper, rather than as a wordprocessed file, you can use OCR software (such as OmniPage), which will scan the text and create an editable file. It can read only clean text and cannot deal with handwritten corrections on a typescript. Text should be carefully proofread before subsequent use. Text can also be double-keyboarded (keyed twice and compared to ensure accuracy) inexpensively in countries such as India.

Casting off and copy fitting
Casting off is estimating the number of words in a manuscript. Before wordprocessing was used, this was a tedious manual task, but all wordprocessing software now includes a word counter. Copy fitting is working out the space that the text and images will occupy in the final printed job. The easiest way to do this is to do some sample setting in the chosen typeface to assess how much space the text will occupy in that font. If a job is determined to be over or under the required length, it is a fairly easy job to alter typeface, type size, leading, line length, and so on using page layout software.

Proof correction marks
Opposite are the standard proof correction marks used by editors and authors when correcting a manuscript or typeset artwork. We have shown them in a tint of black but it is standard practice to use a red pen so the corrections can be seen easily on a layout.

2.3 Proof correction marks
Different countries have their own standard proof correction marks, but those shown here are in common use.

MARK IN TEXT	INSTRUCTION	MARK IN MARGIN
ta‸king or ∧ or >	Insert text or character	⋏
⟋take⟋ or take⟍	Delete text	↗ or ⨯ or ⌇
a⟋	Delete character	↗ or ⨯ or ⌇
under͡neath	Close up	⌒
under⫶neath	Delete and close up	↗ or ⨯ or ⌇
underneath⟋	Full stop	⊙
here⟋or here	Comma	∧
see below⟋	Semicolon	⨤ or ⁏
underneath⟋	Substitute colon for semicolon	⊙ or :
undern⟲a⟲th	Reverse order of letters	underneath (write correctly)
⟨out⟩⟨walk⟩	Transpose	tr or ts
underneath	Set in italics	or ⫽
here or _here_	Set in roman	rom
underneath	Set in bold	bold or bf or ⌇
⟨underneath⟩	Set in light face	l.f.
⟨H⟩ere or ⟨H⟩ere	Set in or change to lower case	l.c. or ≢
october	Set in or change to capitals	caps or ≡
october	Set in or change to small capitals	sm. caps or ═ or s.c.
octo⟋ber or ∧	Insert hairline space between characters	Y or hr #
under⟋here	Insert space between words	Y or #
here⟋Start	Start new paragraph	⌐ or ¶
here.⤴ ⟨Start⟩	Run on (no new paragraph)	⌒
stop. ⟨Talking	Indent text	⌐

MARK IN TEXT	INSTRUCTION	MARK IN MARGIN
stop. ⟨Talking	Cancel indent	⌐
⟨h⟩ere	Wrong font	⨯ or
here∧or∧here ∧or⏜	Space evenly	eq# or
A tall man	Let it stand	stet
⌐ lets walk out	Set to left	⌐
lets walk out ⌐	Set to right	⌐
effect	Set as ligature	⌒
walk⟋out	Align horizontally	═
⟨The bath is full	Align vertically	⫼
walk 200⟨ft.⟩	Spell out	(sp)
turn⟋in	Hyphen	− or −/ or ⌒ or
2000⟋2001	En dash	$\frac{1}{N}$ or en or
underneath⟋but	Em dash	$\frac{1}{m}$ or em or
E=mc⟋2	Superscript	⌇ or E=mc²
H⟋2O	Subscript	⌒ or
I can⟋t do it	Apostrophe	∨
⟋Really?⟋he said	Quotation marks	⁇ ⁇ or
the number⟋one⟋	Parentheses	(/)
the number⟋one⟋	Brackets	[/] or [/] or
⟨born in 1966⟩	Query to author	au/? or
⟨5xt=t5x⟩	Query to editor	ed/? or
here.⟋Start	New paragraph flush with previous line	¶
this⟋is what	Three-dot ellipsis	⊙/⊙
the end⟋	Four-dot ellipsis	⊙/⊙/⊙

ORIGINATION AND PREPRESS

29

Images for print production

Images are a vital tool in printed media, and in magazines they are preeminent. In today's multimedia world it's easy to source images from digital cameras, online resources, CDs and DVDs, but also from line or painted originals, prints, transparencies, and a variety of other sources. This poses a production challenge.

Digital images and other artwork

With few exceptions the image workflow for publishers is now exclusively digital. Images can come from a number of different sources but most newly commissioned material is now shot on digital cameras, which have largely replaced film for most kinds of professional work. For photographers, the advantages are legion, in that the prohibitive cost of shooting and processing dozens of rolls of film per job are avoided; work can be previewed with the client on camera, or on computer in situ, and workflow is dramatically speeded up. Digital files are also easily shared, archived, and published online, and custom image libraries can be produced swiftly if metadata is logical and well managed.

For the commissioner of the work, the challenge is predominantly one of image management and archiving, ensuring that images are logically and intuitively labeled, and collected for output (to print). If it offers a practical benefit, digital images can be replaced with low-resolution positional copies to avoid slowing down computers during the text-editing stage. This is becoming less of an issue now as processor speeds increase and large storage solutions become much cheaper.

One of the problems of receiving digital scans of prints or transparencies, is that to a certain extent it needs to be taken on trust that it is a good reproduction of the original. This is where profiles are extremely important as they enable the person viewing the scan to know that they are seeing it the way the person who scanned it intended it to be viewed. Designers and production staff are also learning repro skills, enabling them to check digital images in Photoshop (see p. 54) to ensure that they are of appropriate quality, and to specify any correcting or retouching that might be needed. Checks should include sharpness (it is often necessary to sharpen digital images); that they have reasonable contrast (without highlights burning out or dark areas filling in); and that they do not have an overall color cast from different lighting sources. If preferred, it is easy enough to include such corrections as part of the repro instructions accompanying a job and have the images corrected. Bear in mind that this will increase your overall repro costs, and that it may be more cost effective to train someone in-house to carry out many of the basic corrections that digital images require.

Many illustrations are also now created using applications such as Photoshop, Illustrator (see p. 55), CorelDRAW, or a 3-D drawing package, and supplied as digital files. Where images are supplied in physical form, rather than files, these can come in various ways. **Line originals** are often specially commissioned. The original should be black, and may be drawn larger than the finished size, as reduction can help to sharpen the image and minimize slight inaccuracies. Care also has to be taken to prepare the original in proportion to the final reproduction size. **Black-and-white photos** to be reproduced as halftones should have as wide a tonal range as possible. Image-editing can be done using Photoshop or similar applications, particularly by using the Levels and Curves tools to correct any tonal inadequacies.

2.4 Correcting with Curves
Here the tonal range of an image is improved using Photoshop's Curves control to improve shadows, contrast, and even correct the white balance by removing color casts. In this example, a selection has been made before applying the Curve adjustment, limiting the changes to certain highlighted areas.

2.5 Line original
This illustration is by R. Kikuo Johnson from the book, *Night Fisher*. The line original has been saved as a bitmap, which is two-color black and white, as opposed to a grayscale image (like fig. 2.6). Line work should always be saved at high resolution to retain crispness of image.

2.6 Black-and-white photo
This black-and-white portrait by Chris Middleton has been scanned from a print, taken from a high-speed black-and-white negative, and saved as a high-res grayscale TIFF. Using the image smaller on the page than the original scan improves definition.

ORIGINATION AND PREPRESS

31

2.7 Color transparencies
Color "trannies" were once the professional medium of choice until the uptake of digital photography. They remain popular with some for certain types of work, such as landscape and fashion photography. These may need to be scanned by the prepress or repro house, using a positional scan as a guide.

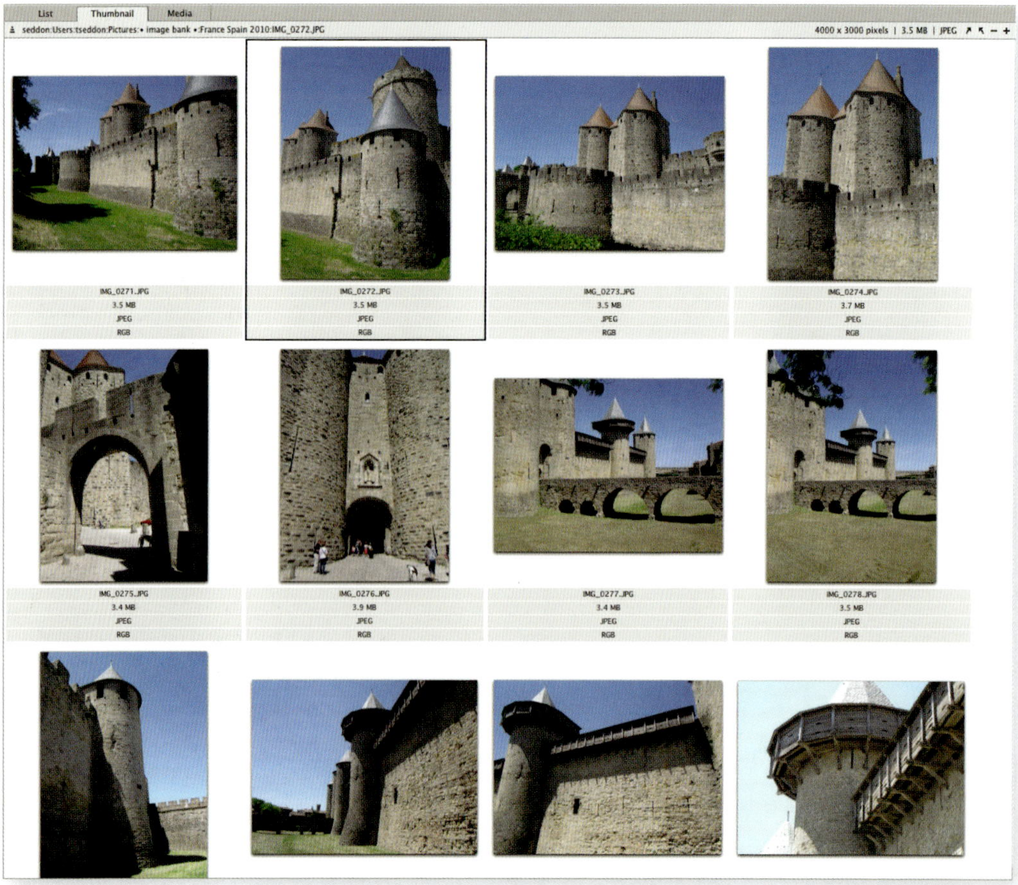

ORIGINATION AND PREPRESS

Color photographs

These originals can be either transparencies (also known as transmission copy, or colloquially, as "trannies"), or color prints; the former give a brighter, sharper result and remain popular with some photographers for landscape work and high-fashion portraits. The original should have reasonable contrast and there should not be an overall color cast. Excessive grain (normally from fast films) should be avoided, as this will reproduce, particularly when the picture is enlarged. Original transparencies are preferred to duplicates, as the duplicating (or "duping") process can add to the density of the original—high quality photo-labs can make acceptable quality duplicates. Although 35mm transparencies can stand a fair amount of enlargement, where the printed result is to be large (for example, a double-page spread in a magazine), better results are obtained from larger transparencies, such as 5 x 4in (102 x 107mm). Again, any retouching required can be done using Photoshop, or similar applications.

When a physical original is to be scanned by a prepress or repro house, rather than the designer, an important point is that the repro house will, unless instructed otherwise, attempt to reproduce the transparency exactly as it stands. If you want the final result to be different (for example, losing a color cast), the relevant instructions must be given at the outset. This will avoid the time and expense of later retouching and reproofing.

2.8 Cataloging images
Digital imaging enables the easy cataloguing of images in searchable, low-res image libraries that relate to high-res originals stored on a central server. Software shown: Microsoft Expression Media, on the Apple OS X platform.

Color flat artwork (reflection copy)

Smaller originals can be scanned by the designer or repro house on a flatbed scanner, but originals larger than 11 x 8 ½in (or European A4) may have to be scanned on a drum scanner or large flatbed scanner at a repro house. For this, the board used by the artist should be flexible, enabling it to be wrapped around the scanner's drum. If rigid board is used, either the artwork has to be reproduced by first photographing it (as a transparency or digital photograph), or the top surface of the board has to be stripped off—which can cause damage and is to be avoided unless the board is made for stripping. It is also possible to scan a large artwork on a smaller scanner in sections and join the sections together.

Digital asset management

Any organization involved in design, advertising, publishing, or related fields will soon build up a huge archive of images and application files. If data is stored logically from the outset, then such a repository of data can become a searchable, creative asset. Files may be stored on CDs, DVDs, Blu-Ray disks, on detachable hard drives, DAT tapes (in terms of end-of-day backups), or, during the course of a job, on a central, networked server containing each element of the job.

A digital asset management strategy is essential to control access, management responsibility, and accessibility. It is vital to evolve a way of storing all the files that need to be kept for reuse in one place and in such a way that the latest versions can easily be found and retrieved. This can be done either by using asset management software and storing archives in-house, or by having the storage done by an outside specialist (some printers and prepress houses offer this service). It is advisable to have the files stored in more than one location as a backup in the event of loss or damage.

ORIGINATION AND PREPRESS

Halftones

Unlike a line original, a black-and-white photograph does not consist only of areas that are either black or white; instead it is made up of an almost infinite number of shades of gray. These cannot be printed as such by offset lithography (or most of the other printing processes) and so the grays have to be simulated by breaking the picture up into small dots; the dots are largest in the dark areas and very small in the pale areas so that the printed effect is shades of gray, although only black ink has been used.

This halftone effect used to be obtained by placing a "screen" in the back of a process camera, between the lens and the film. This screen carries a fine grid of lines to break the image up into dots, thereby producing a halftone negative. Color originals are also converted into halftones, with each of the four process colors broken up into dots, which, when printed, give the effect of full color. Converting the continuous-tone image into dots is now done electronically at the film or platemaking stage, but the term "screen" is still used to describe the size of the halftone dots. Screens range from coarse to fine, depending on the printing process and the paper that is to be used—the rougher the paper, the coarser the screen required. The offset process can print very fine screens, whereas screen printing requires a coarse screen.

The numbers used to describe screens represent the number of lines per inch or, in metric, lines per centimeter on the screen; for example, 133 screen (per inch) is 54 screen (per centimeter). In the UK and USA screens are normally described in lines per inch—the higher the number of lines in the screen, the finer the dot size. Most commercial, magazine and book printing on reasonable papers uses at least 150 screen (per inch), but newspapers on coarse paper can use halftones as low as 65 screen. The "dot gain" caused by the absorption of ink (as on a sheet of blotting paper) can make images appear bolder (and type seem heavier. See p.40.)

Improvements in platemaking, printing, paper and inks have led to the use of finer screens and 175 and 200 are common, with 300 screen being used for particularly demanding work. In black-and-white reproduction, the halftone screen is usually placed at an angle of 45 degrees to the horizontal, as this makes the rows of dots less obvious to the eye.

Most pencil drawings are treated as halftones in order to reproduce the subtle shades of gray, something line origination cannot do. Often the backgrounds of such halftones are "dropped out," so that in these areas there are no dots, just unprinted paper. A line and tone combination is used, for example, where solid type is to appear superimposed on a photograph or for an ink-and-wash illustration. Here, the artwork is scanned twice and combined.

Duotones

A variant of the halftone process is the "duotone"—a two-color halftone, with the second color often being black. Today this is achieved from a single scan by creating a Photoshop duotone (you can also make tritones or quadtones to make three- or four-color images from a black-and-white original). Duotones can be particularly effective when photographs are printed with gray as the second color; many high-quality photographic books are printed using this technique.

2.9 Halftones
To make halftones from an original, it is broken up into dots. If the image is enlarged, as shown in the right-hand example, the halftone dots can be clearly seen. The lightest areas are made up of small black dots on white, the dark areas from larger black dots.

2.10 Halftone dots
These are placed at an angle of 45° for single color printing, this being the least noticeable to the human eye. At 90° the obvious rows created by the halftone dots draw attention away from the image detail to the dots themselves.

Screen angled at 90°   Screen angled at 45°

2.11 Duotones
The same original is reproduced as a duotone with the second color originated as a full-value halftone.

ORIGINATION AND PREPRESS

35

Color theory and color separation

Color originals have to be "separated"—that is, the visual effect to the human eye of full color is achieved in printing by breaking the original picture down into four components, corresponding to the three basic print colors—magenta, cyan, and yellow—plus black, added to give finer detail and greater density in dark areas. The shorthand for this is CMYK with K (key) standing for black, although it also avoids confusion with blue. This separation process, known as the "four-color process," results in four printing plates, one for each color.

Virtually any color can be reproduced from combinations of these four colors; for example, greens are produced by combining a certain amount of yellow with a certain amount of cyan.

To explain this, some understanding of the nature of light is required. "White" light from the sun or an artificial source is formed by a combination of all the colors of the spectrum, and these can be broken down into three "primary" colors—red, green, and blue (RGB). Since these three colors, when added together, create white light, they are known as the "additive" primaries (see fig. 2.12). Where any two of these colors overlap you get the secondary primaries, known as "subtractive" primaries. The combination of red and blue together produce magenta; red and green give yellow; and green and blue give cyan. The additive primaries (red, green, blue) can be used only with transmitted light (e.g. a monitor). When printing we start off with white paper and white light being bounced off it. What we need to do here to see the full spectrum of colors is to use ink colors that will subtract the light wavelengths and so show us colors. Cyan for instance is the red subtracting (or absorbing) color, magenta is the green subtracting color and yellow is the blue subtracting color. Where all three of the subtractive colors C, M, Y are added together, a dirty brown is produced. Because of the imperfections of the pigments it is necessary to add in black to get a clean solid black. Subtractive primaries don't give as wide a range in the color gamut as additive primaries, but give an acceptable printed result, within the confines of the CMYK color space.

In the design/printing process, most image files start off as RGB—digital photographs are RGB, as are the initial color files produced by applications such as Photoshop. The designer's monitor will also be showing the colors in RGB, because here we are dealing with qualities of light. In drawing applications, such as FreeHand and Illustrator, imported Pantone (color ink system) colors should be converted to CMYK. When a job is ready to send to the reproduction house or printer, all files should be converted to CMYK, preferably based on an ICC profile (see p.44) provided by the printer, or the conversion can be done by the printer.

Before the advent of scanners, imagesetters, and platesetters, separation could only be done photographically. In this process, the negative for each of the process colors (subtractive primaries) required the use of a filter of the respective additive primary color. For example, to make a negative record of the yellow component of the original, a blue filter was used, the effect of which was to absorb all wavelengths of light reflected from the yellow components of the original, with the result that yellow was not recorded on the photographic emulsion. To separate black, either all three filters were used, or no filter at all. These negatives were screened and positives were made, which were then used to produce a printing plate for each color.

Additive colour

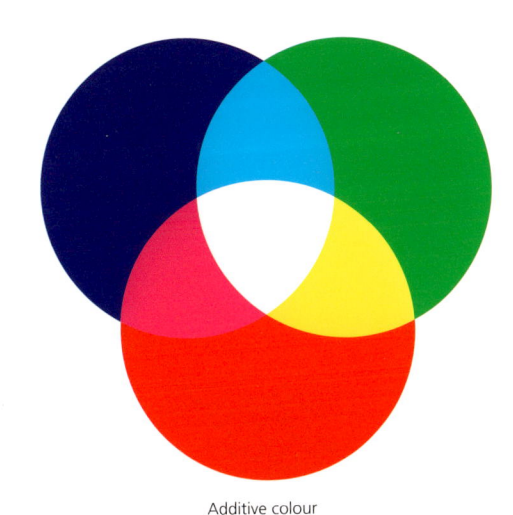

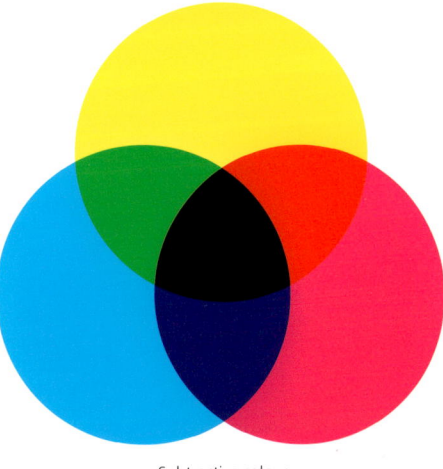

Subtractive colour

2.12 Additive and subtractive color
Knowing something of the color properties of light helps further an understanding of how the four-color printing process works. Red, green, and blue are called "additive primaries" because they produce white light when they are added together. The combination of two additive colors produces a third color, known as a "subtractive" primary. Red and green will produce yellow; blue and green will produce cyan; red and blue will produce magenta.

Two subtractive primaries mixed together will create an additive primary. In short, cyan and yellow make green; yellow and magenta make red; cyan and magenta make blue. Unlike the additives, which produce white light when combined, the three subtractives make black.

Full color

Black

Cyan

Magenta

Yellow

2.13 Color separation
The process colors used in four-color printing are yellow, magenta, cyan and black. Each color is printed as tiny dots and, because they are so small, the eye visually mixes the colors to reproduce all the colors of the original. Here you can see how the four process colors combine to give the full-color effect.

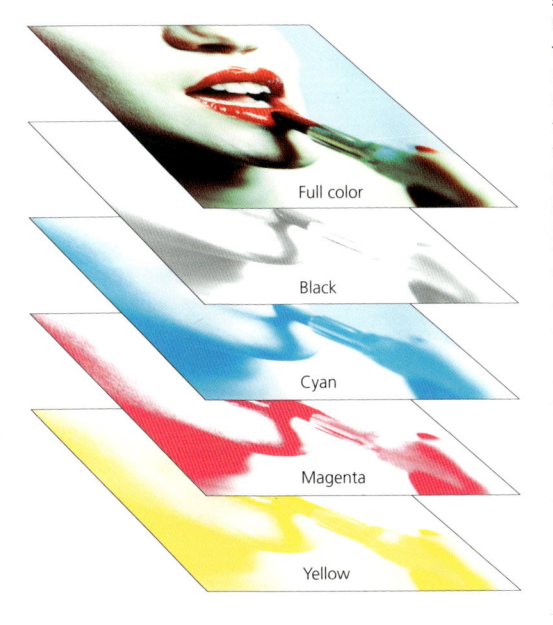

Yellow

Yellow plus magenta

Yellow, magenta plus cyan

Yellow, magenta, cyan plus black

ORIGINATION AND PREPRESS

37

2.14 Screen angles

At the stage of making film or plates, the rows of dots have to be positioned at the correct angles, otherwise moiré patterns can occur. When printing an image in two colors (**1**), the black dots need to be placed at a 45° angle (as this produces the least visible dots) and the second color should be at a 75° angle. For three-color printing (**2**) the same angles are used but the third color is placed at angle of 105°. In four-color printing (**3**), the black is placed at an angle of 45°, the magenta at 75°, the cyan at 105° and the yellow at 90°. This latter angle produces the most visible dots and this is why the yellow—the lightest of the process colors—is placed at this angle. The four process colors overlap to give full-color reproduction of the original image and this can be clearly seen (below). The dots have been greatly enlarged to show how the principle works, but at their normal size individual dots cannot be seen and merge to produce a full-color effect.

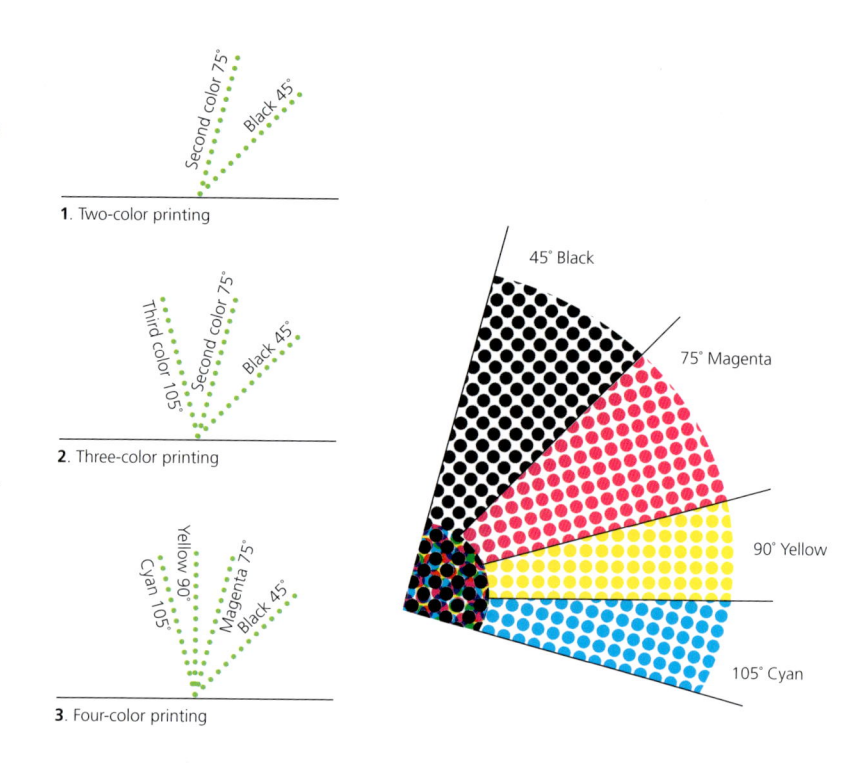

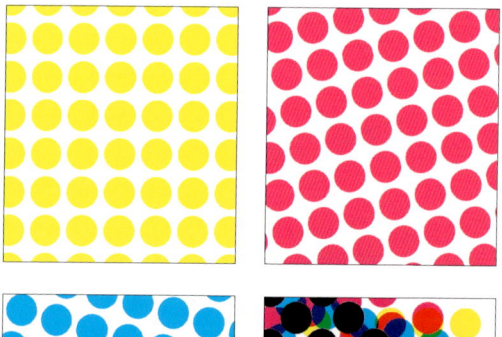

1. Two-color printing

2. Three-color printing

3. Four-color printing

2.15 Color screens

Halftone dots are used (left) to reproduce color originals for each of the process colors. The halftone dots form a rosette pattern, which can be clearly seen in the enlarged picture (right).

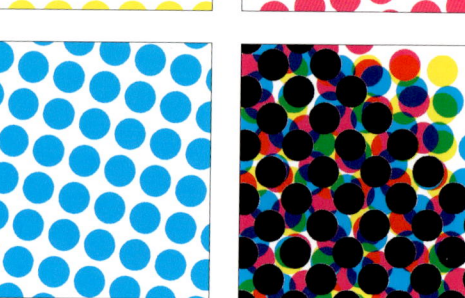

ORIGINATION AND PREPRESS

38

2.16 Moiré
This is the pattern caused when the screen angles of the dots clash. In four-color printing it is avoided by setting the screen angles to avoid it.

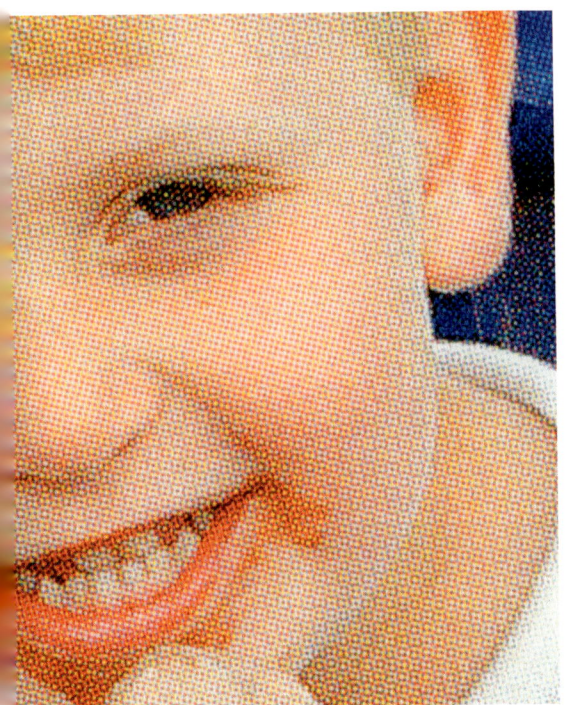

On modern equipment, the separation is done (using the above principles) on a scanner (see Scanning p. 46), where the original is laid on the flatbed or drum and a beam of light reads the original at high speed as a series of lines. Scans done on a flatbed scanner are scanned in RGB and then, in Photoshop, converted into CMYK after color correcting. On drum scanners the image is also scanned in RGB, but the proprietary software on the scanner converts it to CMYK so that the image file that comes from a drum scanner is in CMYK ready for printing. Before printing, the image will have to be broken down into halftone dots, but this is now done at a later stage (in the Raster Image Processor [RIP] on an imagesetter or platesetter), after the job has been designed and final files sent to the printer or repro house.

FM Screening
Normal screening is AM (amplitude-modulated), meaning that the dots are arranged in regular rows and columns, but vary in size. With FM (frequency-modulated) screening, which is also known as stochastic screening, the dots are scattered randomly, with a heavier concentration in the shadow areas and fewer in the highlights, but all dots are the same size. FM screening helps to achieve more detail in an image especially in the shadow and highlight areas—with AM screening this can be only achieved by having a very fine (say 200 line screen). Other advantages of using this technique are that it avoids the visible "moiré" pattern caused when the dots in conventional AM screening clash, and FM screening allows smoother vignettes. FM screening can be difficult to print unless a printer is using newer machines that can hold the very small dots. Hybrid screening is now available and this uses FM screening in the highlight (0% to 10%) and shadow (80% to 90%) areas and AM screening for the midtones.

ORIGINATION AND PREPRESS

39

Hexachrome

This is a development of the four-color process to six colors with orange and green being the colors added to CMYK. These four colors are brighter than standard four-color inks, enabling a superior matching of the colors in an image than the conventional four-color process. Hexachrome normally uses FM screening. Costs are higher than four-color process because as well as the cost of printing the extra two colors, proofing often has to be done in the form of press proofs, as digital proofs may not be accurate. However, there are printing jobs for which hexachrome is a good option, including art books, catalogs, and packaging work, where special colors can be matched out of the six colors, rather than having to be printed as a special Pantone color. This is also known as HiFi color.

Special colors

Where a color is required that cannot be well matched in the four-color process, it is printed as a separate color, normally using a Pantone ink reference. Special colors are required where companies or brands have a "house" color, which has to be consistent across a range of printed items; or in packaging that may carry large areas of a particular solid color. Many printing presses have five or six units, allowing the fifth to be used for a special color and the sixth unit for a seal (e.g. an aqueous coating) or varnish.

Tints

Where a flat area of color is required, this is normally produced using tints (see fig. 2.18) created in the layout software. A tint is not solid ink, but is made up of dots of one or more colors (normally the four process colors). The colors used to be screened in percentages, usually in increments of ten per cent, and each color was combined with one, or more, of the other colors. Now, in software, a color can be chosen by specifying the percentage tints of each of the four process colors. Another option is to pick a color visually on a color wheel and getting the software to produce that color in the CMYK model (showing the appropriate percentage tint for each color needed to make up that color).

Dot gain

The term "dot gain" describes an increase in the dot size that can occur when printing takes place. Normally the dot on the file can be reproduced at almost exactly the same size on the printing plate, but in the printed version the size may have increased. This is a result of various factors, including the offset blanket, the machine, the inks and paper being used. The designer, reproduction house and printer must therefore allow for dot gain in the reproduction and proofing process. This is achieved through purposely making the dot on the file or plate smaller than it "should" be so as to allow for the gain that will take place at the printing stage. The ICC profile of the press being used allows for dot gain, and ensuring use of the profile when creating the files and plates will result in the correct size dot on the printing plate.

2.17 Pantone sample book showing the range of solid colors available in the Pantone Matching System (PMS). These exact colors can be approximated in four-color printing but not matched exactly, so if the color is critical (as on a company logo), it must be printed as a special (fifth) color.

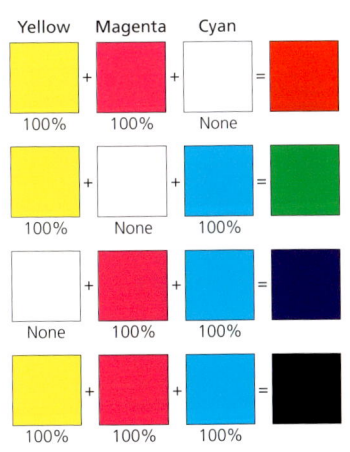

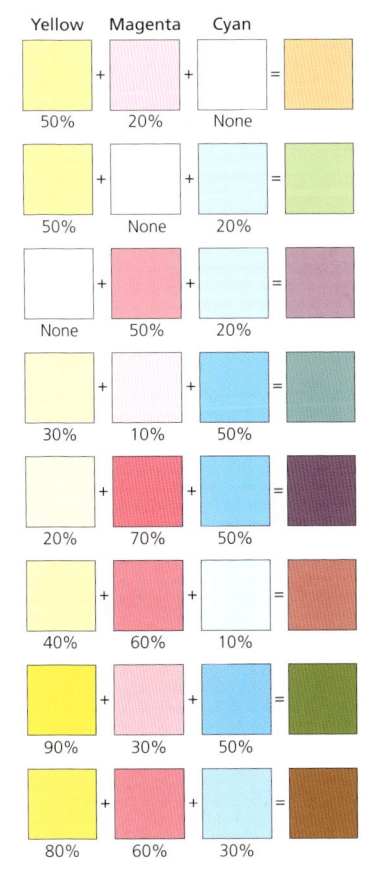

2.18 Tints
The four process colors (yellow, magenta, cyan and black) can be printed in various combinations of percentages to produce the appearance of flat colors. In the first four columns (far left), a few of these combinations and the colors they produce are shown. The columns on the right are illustrations of a few of the tints that are available and the combinations that produced them.

ORIGINATION AND PREPRESS

41

2.19 Registration
Poor registration (where different colors are "out of register") is when there is a visible, undesirable gap between adjacent areas of color. This will show up on proofs and can be remedied as below.

2.20 Trapping
Trapping is the kiss-fit between two colored items. The diagram (right) shows the white gap that can occur if register is not accurate. To avoid this, trapping (far right) gives a small overlap where two colors touch.

Before trapping

After trapping

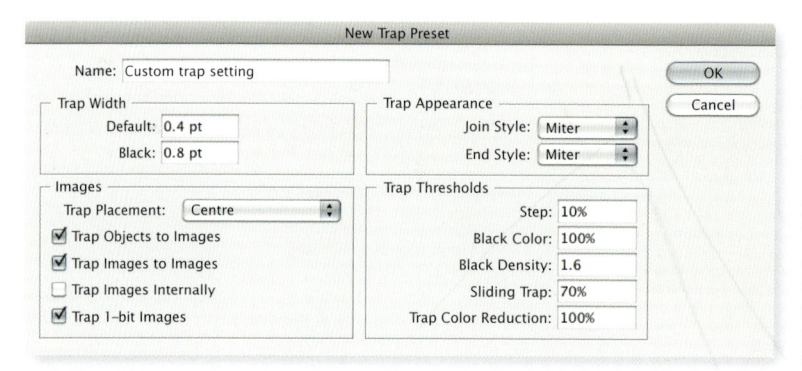

2.21 Setting traps (left)
Here color trapping presets are being established in the dialog with Adobe InDesign, part of the Creative Suite.

2.22 Densitometer (right)
This measures light absorption or reflection. In printing it is used to measure tint density against a reference source, to establish the level of dot gain. This can then be compensated for.

Undercolor removal (UCR)

This technique is used to save ink and avoid drying problems on the printing press. When a subject has a dark area, the four-color process will normally reproduce it using large dots of all four colors, whereas an identical effect can be achieved using only one or two colors. When heavy dots of all four colors overprint each other, there are drying and other problems, and more ink is used than is necessary. To avoid this situation, the scanner can be set to remove most or all of the magenta and yellow in the dark areas, leaving mainly black, sometimes with some cyan to improve the density.

Achromatic color removal

(Also known as gray component replacement [GCR]) This is a development of undercolor removal. In conventional reproduction, a gray component is formed when a hue containing a mixture of all three color primaries is printed on paper. This inherent three-color gray component is replaced with a corresponding amount of black. This results in stability during the run, reduced wastage, and thus increased savings.

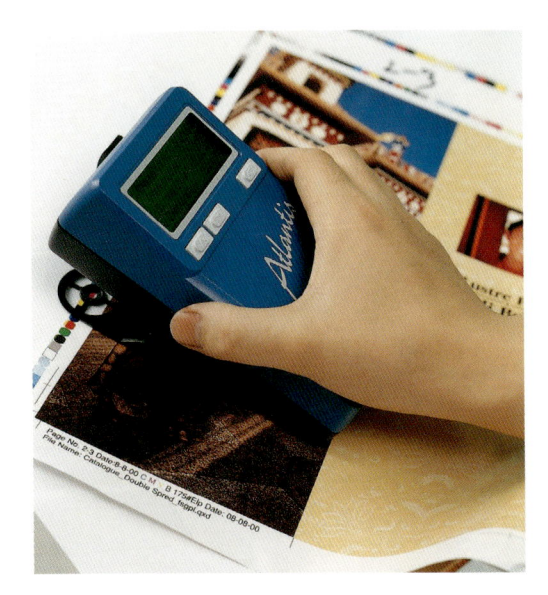

Trapping

This is the kiss-fit between two colored items. This fit cannot be guaranteed on press, because of misregister (printing slightly out of position). To avoid white showing between two adjacent areas of color, the two colors are made to overlap slightly—normally the lighter color extends into the area of the darker color. When the border is around a character or object, lighter colors are "spread" (made bigger) and darker colors "choked" (made smaller). This is done automatically in the printer's RIP (or prepress workflow). It is possible to use the built-in trap presets of your chosen layout software, but the best advice is to let your printer take care of the trapping for you. Settings will vary from machine to machine, and the printer is better placed to compensate for the inaccuracies of their own printing equipment.

Some confusion is created in that in the layout software (InDesign or QuarkXPress) "trapping" is also used to refer to "overprint" and "knockout" settings as well as to spreads (trap +) and chokes (trap -). The printer's software calls "overprint" and "knockout" prepress settings, not trapping, and these are shown as either overprint "on" or "off." As it is often a design decision as to whether type should be overprinting an image it is running across, or knocking out (where the type creates a white hole in the image and in effect sits directly on the white paper), the overprint settings are seen as the responsibility of the designer.

Another meaning of trapping is the degree to which an ink sticks to a previously inked image. If printing is on a four-color press, ink will be overprinting still wet ink and trapping will therefore be lower compared to wet ink overprinting already dry ink (as on a proofing press).

ORIGINATION AND PREPRESS

Color management

With so many links in the color printing chain, from shooting a color image all the way through preparing layouts and designs to proofing and printing the finished publication, it is essential to manage color consistency from device to device, to ensure that what you see on screen is as near as possible to the final printed article.

In the design, prepress and printing stages of a job, color will appear differently, depending on the device used to display it. These devices can include a monitor, a color laser or ink-jet printer, a high-quality digital proofer, and the printing press itself. To solve this problem and ensure that the color of the final printed job is as intended at the outset, color management is used.

The agreed standard in printing is that formulated by the International Color Consortium (ICC), which set up a universal platform-independent structure for color profiles enabling color from any input or output to be viewed or processed in a device-independent way. "Device profiles" contain information on the color space of each device and these are used to create CMMs (color-matching modules), which compensate for color variation or imperfections in a device and therefore allow that device to give the closest rendition of the color required within its limitations. ColorSync, for example, is the CMM used by Apple.

Digital image formats themselves—for printing, the common ones will be TIFF and high-res JPEG—may also contain embedded color profiles if that is intended by the photographer. However, this is not a requirement of the file format itself. On opening an image within an editing application, users are given the option to use the embedded profile, or to discard it in preference to their own. The ICC standard is there to facilitate the exchange of output device characteristics and color space metadata (tags, or data about data), to ensure consistency across each stage in the production up to and including the printing of the finished article.

ICC profiles are used extensively at prepress houses in their scanning and proofing devices and when converting from RGB to CMYK. Printers create ICC profiles of their presses and then either these profiles or international standards (e.g. SWOP or Europe ISO coated) are the ones used by the repro houses or designers when proofing or converting to CMYK. Recent versions of Photoshop and InDesign encourage designers to use color management and ICC profiles when working with digital images. Color management, in terms of the press profiles and controlling the output curves, is being used by most modern printers to achieve the correct dot size on the press.

Color management is particularly important if remote proofing (see p. 66) is part of your workflow, as the monitors used by you, your client, and the printer must all display colors identically. Color matching with ICC profiles helps to achieve this.

Colors perceived by the human eye: infinite

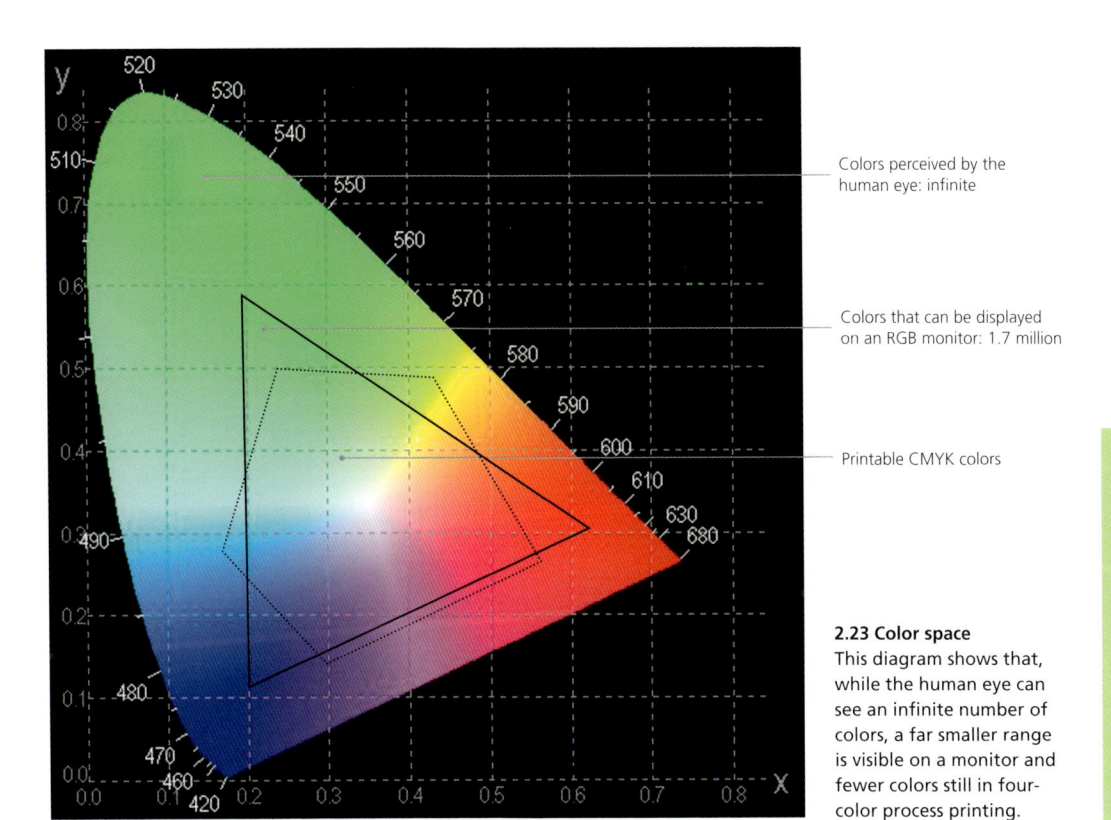

Colors that can be displayed on an RGB monitor: 1.7 million

Printable CMYK colors

2.23 Color space
This diagram shows that, while the human eye can see an infinite number of colors, a far smaller range is visible on a monitor and fewer colors still in four-color process printing.

ORIGINATION AND PREPRESS

2.24 LaCie blue eye
This monitor calibration and automatic ICC profiling tool will help ensure accurate color rendering across different monitors as part of a color managed workflow.

45

Scanning

Scanning used to be the preserve of prepress houses on expensive drum scanners operated by skilled craftsmen who were typically scanning six or so subjects an hour. Most scanners are now inexpensive flatbed devices used in-house by clients or designers. They can scan 20 to 30 images an hour, and need limited skill to operate them. Digital photography means that many images arrive ready to be imported straight into the layout application, but prints, transparencies, and flat artwork all still have to be scanned to provide a high-resolution file for use in the layout.

Most flatbed scanners use charge-coupled devices (CCDs) to record the image. Scanners need to be calibrated regularly and zeroed to white light. The image must be scanned at the correct resolution to be detailed enough when appearing printed to its eventual size. A rule of thumb is that it should be scanned to give a file whose resolution will provide double the screen ruling being printed. In printing, 150-line screen is typical, which would require a 300 dpi (dots per inch) file from the scanner. That applies if the printed image is to be the same size as the original, but where the image is going to be enlarged, the resolution will need to be higher, so that if an image is going to be printed at twice the size of the original, it will need to be scanned at 600 dpi. Scanning in-house will normally be done as RGB and only converted to CMYK at the last stage, when preparing files for the printer. Black-and-white originals are scanned as grayscale or line, because they will print just in black, or any other single color—not all four colors.

In-house desktop scanners can now deal adequately with most images, but where particularly high quality is needed or where the original is too large for the desktop scanner, originals are sent to a prepress house for scanning on a drum scanner or high-resolution flatbed scanner. These can be supplied back to the designer as high-res scans or as low-res versions (FPO—for position only), which can be used in the page layout application. When the designed job goes back to the repro house, the software substitutes the high-res scans for the low-res, known as OPI (Open Prepress Interface). Scanning done at a prepress house can be done as either RGB or CMYK. Some prepress houses have copy-dot scanners, which can scan existing screened film separations and converts the image to a file (e.g. TIFF) that can be used with page layout applications. If no film exists, a printed version of the image, halftone or four-color, can be scanned with dot-for-dot pickup and a new file created for the page layout. This process is known as descreen/rescreen and avoids the creation of a moiré pattern.

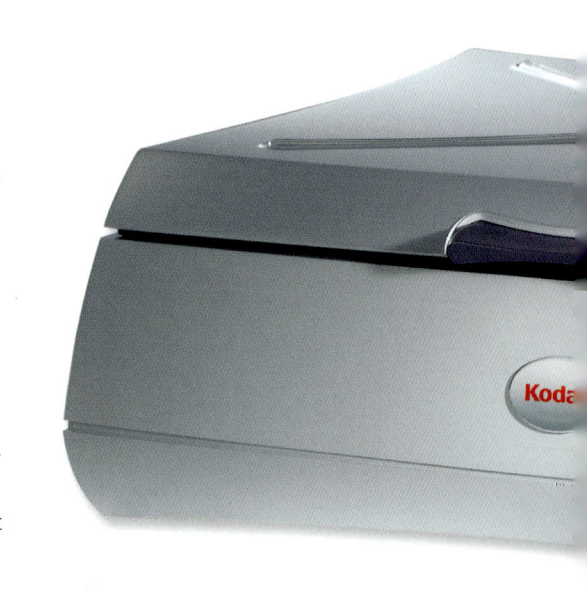

2.25 Drum scanner
Used for large-scale scans. Artwork needs to be wrapped around the drum, and therefore needs to be flexible to avoid damage.

2.26 A desktop scanner
This Kodak iQsmart[3] scanner can scan originals up to 11 x 18in (or European A3) and scans at a resolution of 5,500 dpi.

ORIGINATION AND PREPRESS

47

Typesetting

This ancient discipline was once performed by expert teams of people within the printers themselves, but is now to a large extent the domain of designers, editors, and other creative or production staff within the printer's clients. As such, there is a risk that typesetting skills are being lost, which is why many rules are now built in (and editable) within page layout applications, and presets can be adopted across all work.

Until the mid-1990s, typesetting was performed by specialist companies using dedicated (and usually expensive) filmsetting equipment. They supplied pages of film, rather than digital files. Typesetters were staffed by compositors, who had served a craft apprenticeship. The advent of desktop publishing marked the blurring of the boundaries between design and typesetting, and there are now far fewer typesetting companies. For simpler, smaller printing jobs, the "typesetting" is carried out by the designer, normally using page layout applications, such as InDesign or QuarkXPress. The typesetters that remain specialize in the larger, more complex jobs, such as legal and science or medical reference books, and, being labor intensive, much of this work is carried out in countries such as India. Some publishers supply authors with templates, however, and so for text books the authors essentially typeset the book as they write.

For most types of task the designer or typesetter will not have to key any text, as this will be supplied by the client in a wordprocessing application file. Typesetters often use InDesign or QuarkXPress, but some firms also offer more specialist typesetting applications, which can cope, at high speed, with complex page makeup (or typesetting complicated mathematics or foreign languages) and convert databases to typeset pages.

The effect of these innovations has brought down costs and reduced schedules dramatically, making much smaller quantities of printed items more economical than previously, particularly when in-house "typesetting" is combined with the short-run capability of digital printing.

Type measurement

Type is normally measured in points, picas, and units. These measurements can be confusing, in that the Anglo-American system is different from the European one, although both use the term "point" (pt.). The reason for these different systems lies in the fact that metal type foundries in Europe were casting type that was incompatible in size with that from other foundries. It was not until the early 18th century that an attempt was made to standardize a system of type measurement. This happened in France, when Pierre Fournier proposed a standard unit of measurement, which he called the "point." The innovations made by Fournier were developed by another Frenchman, Firmin Didot, to produce a European standard, but neither the UK nor the USA adopted this, although their system was based on points.

The Anglo-American system was based on a "point" measuring 0.013837 of an inch (0.35146mm). This has recently been altered to 0.01389in (0.3528mm) so that it is exactly 1/72 of an inch. This change, although slight, means that traditional typescales will not be quite accurate when measuring digital layouts. A pica (or pica em) is made up from 12 points and is 1/6 of an inch (4mm).

2.27 Point sizes

Characters in typeset copy are measured in units called "points." This system was first developed in France but the European, or Didot, point is slightly larger than the point used in the US and the UK. An inch contains approximately 67.5 European points and 72 Anglo-American points. Letters are measured from the top of the ascenders to the bottom of the descenders of the lower case letters. The point size is thus based on a "strip" holding all the letters in a sentence. In the metric system, type size is described by the height of the capital letters, or "cap height" (CH); the space between lines of type is called "line feed" (LF)—both are in millimeters.

The spaces between lines can also be measured in points. A line of, say, 12-point (12pt) type directly followed by another line of 12pt type said to be 12pt solid, or 12 "on" 12 point. Point spaces inserted between the lines make type more legible. Interlinear spacing is called "leading."

Line length is measured using a unit called a "pica em," which is 12 points long (approximately ⅙in or 4mm). The pica is an Anglo-American unit, in France and Germany the 12pt unit is called a cicero, in Italy a riga, in Holland, an aug.

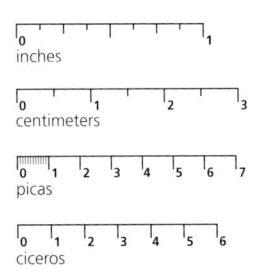

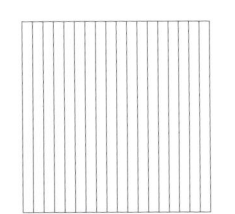

inches

centimeters

picas

ciceros

72pt em divided into 18 units

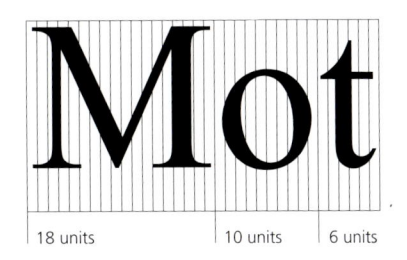

36pt em divided into 18 units

Mot

18 units | 10 units | 6 units

ORIGINATION AND PREPRESS

Graphic
72 points

Graphic
72 points

2.28 Body size

The point or body size of type is the distance from the top of the ascender to the bottom of the descender. This distance varies from typeface to typeface as well as from one point size to another. If there is no leading, type can be measured from base line to base line to establish the point size, as illustrated.

ORIGINATION AND PREPRESS

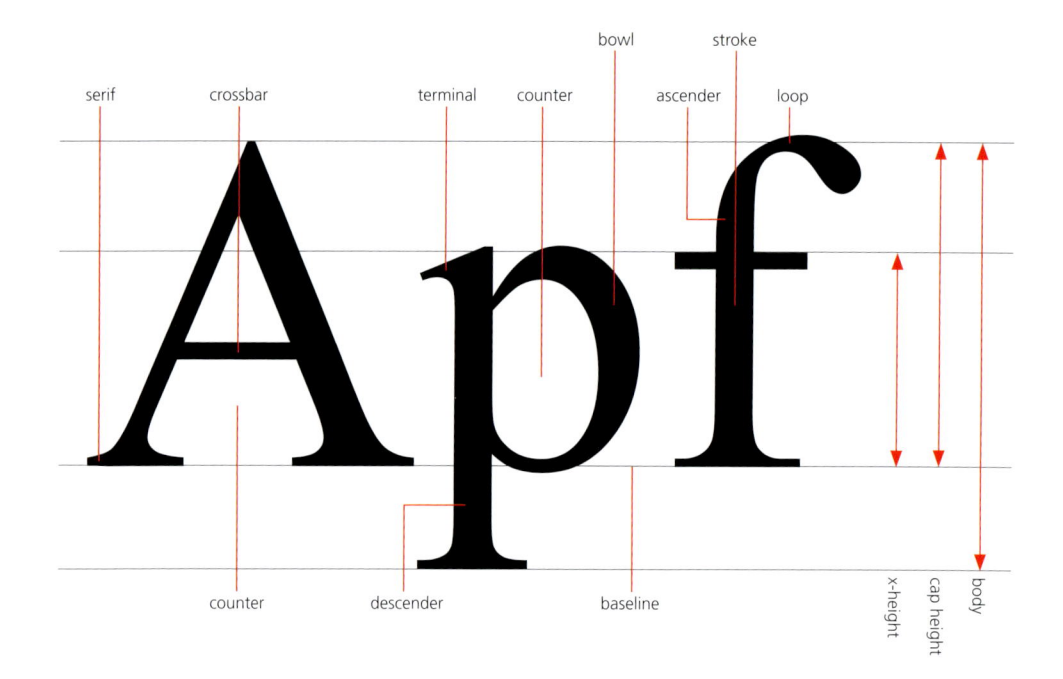

serif · crossbar · terminal · counter · bowl · ascender · stroke · loop

Apf

counter · descender · baseline · x-height · cap height · body

AT	AY	AV	AW	Ay	Av	Aw
FA	TO	TA	Ta	Te	To	Ti
Tr	Tu	Ty	Tw	Ts	Tc	LT
LY	LV	LW	Ly	PA	VA	Va
Ve	Vo	Vi	Vr	Vu	Vy	RT
RV	RW	RY	Ry	WA	Wa	We
Wo	Wi	Wr	Wu	Wy	YA	Ya
Ye	Yo	Yi	Yp	Yq	Yu	Yv

2.29 Type terminology
The characters in a line of type each have their own qualities. The terminology for the different parts of typeset characters forms a significant body of commonly used words. Some of these are illustrated (left).

2.30 Kerning
When the spacing between specified characters is deliberately reduced, leaving the rest of the setting the same, the result is called kerning. The technique is frequently used with certain letter combinations, such as Yo, Te, LY, and la. When these are set, there is often too much space between them, compared to the rest of the setting. Kerning solves this problem. If used properly, it can greatly improve letter-fit, legibility, and the evenness of a line of typesetting—it is particularly useful with large display type.

The European point measures 0.0148in (0.3759 mm), and 12 of these form a unit of 0.1776in (4.511mm). This 12-point unit is called a "cicero" in France and Germany, a riga tipografica (riga) in Italy, and an augustijn (aug) in Holland. There is no easy mathematical relationship between the Anglo-American point and the Didot point, and neither of them relates to the metric system. Thus in Europe, including the UK, typographic measurement in points coexists with metric measurements, which are used in virtually every other allied trade.

Other than for specifying text size or leading, many designers have abandoned the pica as a unit of type measurement and use millimeters (Europe) or inches (USA) to specify everything from page margins to line lengths.

Set width
Although many designers refer to a pica em simply as an "em," technically this is incorrect: a pica em is the square of the body of a 12-point piece of type; an em (so called because the letter M originally occupied the full unit width of a piece of type) is the square of any point size. A 36-point em, for instance, measures 36 points in width, whereas a pica em can measure only 12 points. The most important measurement in controlling line length is that of each character's width. This measurement is determined by dividing an em into vertical "slices." These are called set points or, more commonly in desktop publishing, units. The number of units in an em varies from one typesetting system to another, so, for example an em in a Postscript font is 1000 x 1000 units, whereas in TrueType it is 2048 x 2048 units; the more units there are in an em, the greater the possibility of refinement. Units not only control the widths of characters but also the spaces between them. Although the actual size of the unit varies according to the size of type, the proportions remain the same because there is always the same number of units to any one em regardless of size.

ORIGINATION AND PREPRESS

Typefaces and fonts

These often-confused words describe a simple set of concepts. Learning about different typefaces and fonts is time well spent, and it will help avoid the temptation to equate good design with the use of dozens of different, flashy, or incompatible fonts. In reality, good type design and type usage is usually a matter of making a few consistent choices, and obeying simple rules along the production chain.

Typefaces

Before the advent of phototypesetting and then desktop publishing, there was a relatively small number of typefaces, because of the labor involved in cutting punches in metal to the precise form required to cast type from them. The fact that typefaces could be designed in two dimensions has resulted in the massive proliferation of typefaces now available.

There is confusion about the difference between a typeface and a font, to the extent that the terms have become almost interchangeable. A typeface is the design of a set of characters and is often named after its original designer (e.g. Baskerville). It can have several different versions in addition to the basic roman font, e.g. italic, bold, condensed, or light. A font is the set of characters of a particular typeface stored in a file on the computer. Many popular typefaces (e.g. Garamond, Times, Palatino) are offered by more than one provider and have slightly different designs, so are not interchangeable. Font incompatibility problems, if different versions of the same basic typeface are substituted, can be a significant problem and cause text to reflow in a layout.

Fonts

Fonts for page layout applications can be PostScript, TrueType, or OpenType. PostScript Type 1 fonts for Macintosh have screen fonts for display on the monitor and printer fonts for printing and creating PDFs. Whereas the printer fonts are vector files, the screen fonts are bitmapped and larger sizes can appear jagged on screen. TrueType and the more recent OpenType fonts are vector files and both consist of fonts that are used both on screen and for printing. OpenType fonts, a cross-platform font file format developed jointly by Adobe and Microsoft will work on both Macs and Windows computers and offer enhanced typographic layout features as well as additional characters (glyphs). PostScript and TrueType fonts have different versions for the two platforms; consequently, switching a job using PostScript or TrueType fonts between platforms can cause problems, which do not occur when using OpenType.

Font copyright

Unless a font is supplied free, the user will have to purchase a license, which imposes certain conditions on its copying and usage. Typically, the license will not permit copying and distribution. This means that when you supply a job to a printer as an application file, your fonts should not be used, unless the printer already has a license for them. This problem has now been largely overcome by the use of PDFs, which have the fonts embedded in the document, meaning they cannot be used separately by the printer.

2.31 Typefaces
There are literally thousands of typefaces available and here are some of the more common faces along with bold and italic fonts

HELVETICA NEUE Capitals
Helvetica Neue Roman
Helvetica Neue Bold
Helvetica Neue Italic

ROCKWELL Capitals
Rockwell Regular
Rockwell Bold
Rockwell Italic

FUTURA Capitals
Futura Book
Futura Bold
Futura Book Oblique

TIMES NEW ROMAN Capitals
Times New Roman Regular
Times New Roman Bold
Times New Roman Italic

MYRIAD PRO Capitals
Myriad Pro Regular
Myriad Pro Bold
Myriad Pro Italic

BASKERVILLE Capitals
Baskerville Regular
Baskerville Bold
Baskerville Italic

DIN Capitals
Din Regular
Din Bold
Din Italic

Shelley Allegro
Shelley Andante
Shelley Volante

ORIGINATION AND PREPRESS

Page layout and design applications/suites

The heart of the in-house stages of print production are the commonly used page layout, publication design, and image-editing and manipulation software suites. The decisions made here can affect the entire print production cycle, so it is wise to get things right from the outset, rather than waste money at the proofing stage.

ORIGINATION AND PREPRESS

Page layout software

InDesign and QuarkXPress in their various versions are the applications that dominate page layout software on a global basis. Drawing applications such as Illustrator can also handle page layout work due to much improved typographic features, and FrameMaker (now available only on PCs) handles larger books and manuals, but without the versatility of InDesign and QuarkXPress. InDesign and Quark can import files of many different types and manipulate them to end up with a single digital document ready to be printed. Many types of files can be imported, including:

- Text from a wordprocessing document

- High-res scans of pictures (frequently having been manipulated or corrected by image-editing software, such as Photoshop) and digital images

- Files from drawing applications such as Illustrator

The applications enable the selection of typefaces (fonts) and the accurate positioning of the various elements within the page. They can create rule boxes, circles, and other shapes, and have a facility to lay percentage tints. Trapping in terms of overprint and knockout can be set. Proofs for internal use can be produced on an ink-jet or laser printer, and the job then sent to a repro house or printer in the form of a PDF file. If required, the printer, or repro/prepress house can then supply a high-quality digital proof, or a plotter proof, for final approval by the client.

InDesign and QuarkXPress have both expanded their feature sets in the last few releases. Web content can now be created within either, although specialist applications are advisable for dedicated Web site creation, and QuarkXPress supports the Job Definition Format (see p. 26) enabling electronic job tickets to be created at the design stage. Acrobat takes care of JDF tickets within the Adobe Creative Suite. An advantage of InDesign over QuarkXPress is the ease of integration with other applications included as part of the Creative Suite—in particular Acrobat—for creating the all-important PDF used for subsequent prepress and printing. It is also highly adept at handling transparency within images, and very complex layouts.

Plug-ins are third-party applications (e.g. XTensions for QuarkXPress) that add functionality to the basic page layout applications.

Illustration programs

Drawing applications such as Illustrator and CorelDRAW allow the user to create even the most complex illustrations for importation into page layout applications. These applications create vector-based files, which are not broken up into pixels but are defined by mathematical equations that calculate points of intersection and shape. They have to be edited in the program in which they were created, and are normally saved as either EPS (Encapsulated PostScript) files or in their native format (eg. .ai for Illustrator). They can be imported into page layout applications, positioned, scaled (without loss of quality), and cropped, providing a distinct advantage over pixel-based images.

Editing and retouching programs

Photoshop and other imaging software enables images to be retouched, resized, and edited. Images are either scanned from originals to produce high-resolution files, or are digital photos. The files are raster files, which consist of tiny pixels and are also described as bitmapped. Files are then saved out of Photoshop's native PSD format as EPS (Encapsulated Postscript files), TIFF (Tagged Image File Format), high-res JPEGs (Joint Photographic Experts Group), or GIF (Graphics Interchange Format) and PNG (Portable Network Graphic) if images are intended for online use.

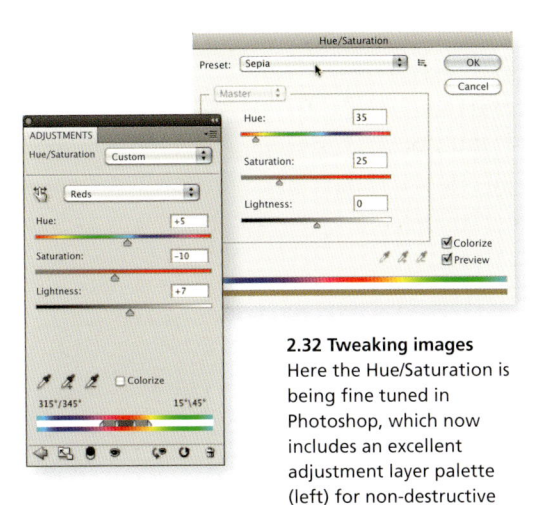

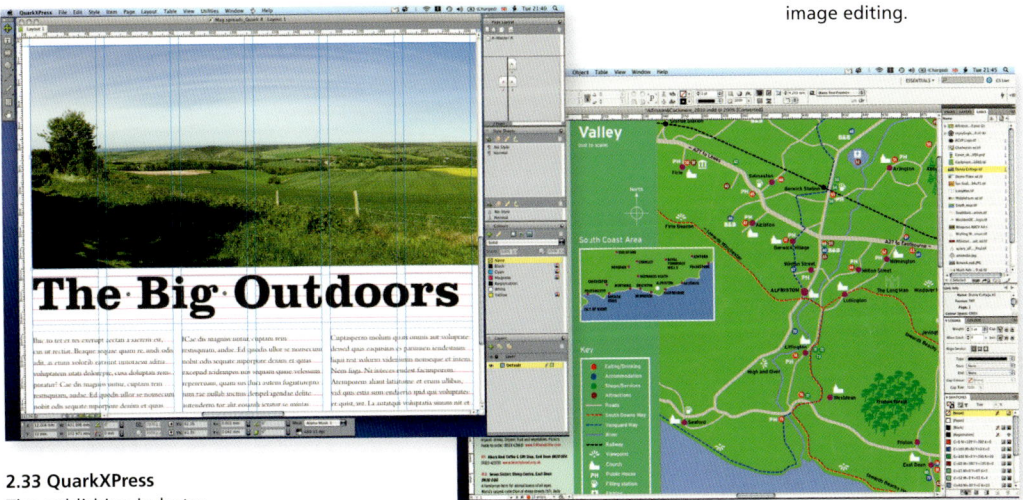

2.32 Tweaking images
Here the Hue/Saturation is being fine tuned in Photoshop, which now includes an excellent adjustment layer palette (left) for non-destructive image editing.

2.33 QuarkXPress
The publishing industry stalwart is still in wide use and is favored by many large design and production studios, but early 21st-century versions of the software lost some loyal customers.

2.34 Adobe InDesign
InDesign's advantages are its seamless integration with Adobe products such as Photoshop and Acrobat, and its ability to handle very complex layouts.

2.35 Adobe Illustrator
Illustrations and diagrams are prepared in drawing packages, such as Adobe's vector illustration suite, Illustrator. Images such as this may be imported into layouts as an EPS, or in its native Illustrator format.

ORIGINATION AND PREPRESS

55

Computers and peripherals

Although larger companies may have workstations dedicated to a particular application, most designers work on a desktop or laptop computer. This can either be a PC (such as Dell, Hewlett-Packard, IBM, or many others) or an Apple Macintosh (Mac).

The original distinction is made because both types of personal computer use a different operating system—PCs run on Windows and Macs use OS X. At one time software was not at all interchangeable between the two platforms (although the same applications were often available in different versions for each) but the platforms are now much more compatible since Apple began supplying machines with the Intel chip rather than the previously used PowerPC. The Intel chip is able to run either system natively, or can run a simulated version of Windows within OS X, allowing a Mac to launch Windows-based applications.

The Apple Macintosh has long been favored by graphic designers, not only because the operating system has been seen as more user friendly but also because, for many years, the main software used in desktop publishing was only available for Macintosh. Apple's adoption of the Intel chip, and Microsoft's development of its system through Vista to the current Windows 7, has facilitated greater interchangeability between the two operating systems. This has made it much simpler for creative professionals to exchange files amongst themselves, and with their clients.

Personal computers can be standalone or networked. In a network, all the personal computers and peripherals (scanner, printers, etc.) are linked to a server (a dedicated personal computer), which holds files centrally. All the devices on the network can communicate with each other and the server often acts as a daily backup for the individual computers in the event of crashes or other problems.

Peripherals available include separate hard drives, which are used to store files, particularly backups; printers which can be ink-jet or laser, printing color or black-and-white; scanners; and digitizing graphics tablets.

Printers

These can be simple inexpensive ink-jet devices through to sophisticated color laser printers with color-managed software. Large format, high-end ink-jet devices are now considered capable of producing digital proofs of a quality that is acceptable for use as a contract level proof for color matching on press. However, these devices need constant calibration and the operator must have a good knowledge of color management and reprographic systems. It is not reasonable to expect any device to act as an "out of the box" solution—accurate color proofing remains a highly skilled area of the overall workflow.

Scanners

There is a wide range of scanners available today and less scanning is being done on the high-end drum scanners owned by repro houses. Some of the larger publishers have bought high-end flatbed scanners and designers are doing much of the work previously done by prepress houses. There is still a noticeable quality difference between the inexpensive flatbed scanners and the more professional high-end ones.

Monitors and calibration

It is rare to encounter a CRT (cathode ray tube) monitor in a professional capacity as LCD (liquid crystal display) and LED (light-emitting diode) displays are now the standard. Machines such as the iMac with its integral LED-backlit screen heralded the end for the CRT monitor.

To display color accurately, monitors should be calibrated regularly, for which calibrating devices are available. This is particularly vital if the monitor is being used for remote proofing, where color accuracy is essential. Lighting conditions should also be carefully considered.

2.36 Wacom i3 AR digitizing tablet
The stylus is used to draw images, which are stored on the computer

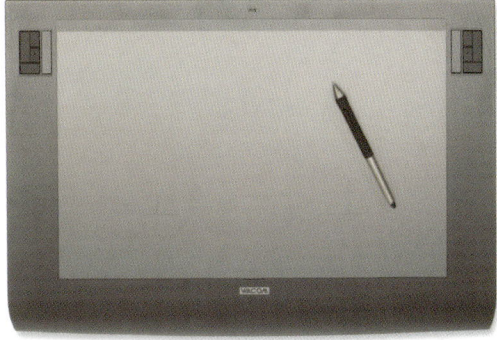

Courtesy of Apple.

2.37 Apple iMac
This personal computer is popular with graphic designers and is currently available with either a 21.5 or 27 inch screen.

2.38 Detachable hard drives
LaCie desktop hard drives provide flexible storage and are currently available in capacities up to a massive 3TB.

2.39 Dell Vostro
Dell computers are supplied direct from the manufacturer.

2.40 LaCie 324 Monitor
High-quality monitors such as this are required to judge color accurately on screen.

ORIGINATION AND PREPRESS

57

File formats and digital workflow

Even in these days of greater technology integration and understanding of all things digital, an incorrect or poor choice of file format can cause countless problems throughout the print production cycle, and therefore prove to be a costly decision. Here are some file format basics.

File formats

Types of files used in graphic design and printing include:

DCS (Desktop Color Separations) consist of five separate files. The first file indicates placement in a page layout application and the other four files are the CMYK separations.

EPS (Encapsulated PostScript) are object-orientated graphics files, but can also store bitmapped images, and are usually created within drawing applications. The resulting vector files can be output at any resolution or size; their printed quality is wholly determined by the resolution of the printing device. (However, they will generally not print accurately on non-PostScript printers).

GIF (Graphic Interchange File) is used for graphic images for the Web and is compressed. It is not really of sufficient quality for continuous-tone images and photos.

JPEG (Joint Photographics Expert Group) files are compressed to save storage space. They are used extensively for digital images including most images on the Web and those from the cheaper / consumer digital cameras. JPEGs are normally saved as TIFF files before being retouched or imported into page layouts. High-res JPEGs can be print quality, while 72dpi JPEGs are ideal for Web use.

PDF (Portable Document Format) files are created after application files have been exported to PostScript (see below). They are created with Adobe Acrobat Distiller and have become the de facto standard for viewing and printing files initially created in other applications. Fonts are embedded in PDFs, thus avoiding the need for the recipient to have font licenses. Low-res PDFs are small enough to be emailed and are fine for viewing on screen (but not print).

PDF/X is a standardized PDF file, which restricts the information in the file to that needed for platemaking and printing and as such is more reliable than an ordinary PDF.

PICT is an early Macintosh file format for images and is now little used.

PostScript is Adobe's proprietary page description language rather than a file format. It allows documents made with page layout or wordprocessing applications to be saved in a form that can be converted to PDF or used by RIPs (raster image processors—see opposite) to make printing film and plates.

PSD files are native Photoshop format files of edited or editable images.

TIFF (Tagged Image File format) are high-resolution raster files for bitmapped monochrome and color images—this format is widely used and generally preferred by the printing industry.

Digital workflow

This term describes the whole process of publishing and printing. It starts with digitizing images and text and ends with the final printed job. The workflow includes preflighting, color correction, proofing, imposition, raster image processing, platemaking, and color control on press. It can also include JDF (Job Definition Format)—the "electronic job ticket" discussed previously.

Preflighting

This is the process of ensuring that a PDF file, or original page layout document before PDF creation, is supplied to the prepress house or printer error-free. This prevents problems arising at a later stage that may cause a job to be delayed or cost more. Preflighting can be carried out using specialist software such as Enfocus Pitstop Professional (for PDFs), or by using Markzware's Flightcheck Professional which can scan a wide variety of file types, including those from InDesign, QuarkXPress, Acrobat, Illustrator, Photoshop, CorelDRAW, and more, for a multitude of different potential problems—the most frequently reported being missing fonts and low-res images. However, the preflight functionality now built-in to both InDesign and QuarkXPress is very powerful and is likely to fulfill all but the most demanding prepress requirements. It is best for the designer to preflight any files before sending them to the printer, but the printer (or prepress house) will usually also preflight, at an even higher level, before further processing.

Raster image processing (RIP)

A raster image processor converts Postscript language into a form that can be read by a high-resolution imagesetter or other output system including proofing devices, imagesetters, platesetters, and digital printing presses. It converts raster and vector data into a bitmap, creating the dots on the printing plate that make up the printed image. All output devices are RIPs, including proofing devices, imagesetters, platesetters, and digital printers. This has given rise to the term "ripping," often used to describe processing any type of file into a specific file format.

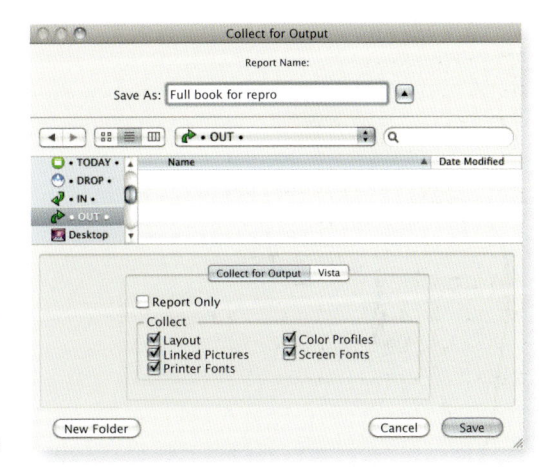

2.41 Collecting for output
Once a layout has been through the rigorous in-house process in InDesign or QuarkXPress to prepare it for the repro or prepress stages, it's vital to do a Collect for Output (Quark), or Package (InDesign). This means bringing together all of the component elements of the job, such as high-res images, the correct fonts, and so on.

ORIGINATION AND PREPRESS

59

Exchanging files electronically and on disk

Once files are ready to go to the printer, they can be sent as email attachments; via the Internet by various other means—such as by FTP sites or servers, or virtual private networks (VPNs) between trusted business partners—or on physical media.

There are several types of digital storage media, some of which, although in use until fairly recently, are largely obsolete—including floppy disks, SyQuest cartridges, Zip disks, and Jaz disks. Each of these required a special device to read and write to them. Now, where files are not being sent by email or Internet, they are burnt to CD (700MB capacity) or DVD (4.7GB capacity). Additionally, ultra-high capacity DVD-style Blu-Ray disks are now widely available, offering capacities as high as 25–50GB.

Where a job is not urgent, sending it on disk can be a good option, as it is small enough to send by mail, rather than courier. A printout should always accompany it, as a guide for the printer or repro house. Also, large files can take a long time to send via FTP, and thus create backlogs in uploading or downloading—although much faster broadband speeds are minimizing the problem. It is often advisable to "stuff" or "zip" a file or group of files (using StuffIt or WinZip). These widely available applications create a single, compressed, secure archive of the file or group of files, minimizing the file size, and protecting the data "envelope" from corruption in transit. It is decompressed at its destination and restored to its complete form.

Sending files as email attachments is quick and convenient, but limits on the size of attachments (either for the sender or recipient) often restrict them to 5–10MB, whereas many files for printed work are much bigger than this. Check the recipient's email security policy before sending, as some companies block attachments to prevent viruses entering their in-house systems. For bigger files, the method to use is FTP (file transfer protocol), using an FTP site or server. The client will often have an FTP site, and most larger printers and repro houses have them. Some require sender and recipient to have special software (e.g. Fetch or Transmit), but many are accessible via a Web browser, and files can be dragged to it from the desktop (and vice versa) to transfer them. There are also third-party websites (e.g. iDisk, Mailbigfile, Yousendit, and Dropsend) that are free or low cost and enable the transfer of large files. Most ISPs give users a small amount (15–50MB) of Web storage that can be used for this purpose. You may wish to ensure security either by password-protecting the files, or by requiring a password to access the FTP site. For very large file transfers, printers and publishers may use virtual networks or virtual private networks, with special software.

3.1 External DVD drives
For computers not fitted with DVD "burners" (writers), low-cost external drives are available.

3.2 mailbigfile.com
This is one of several online services that enable transmission of large files. The recipient receives an email with a link; clicking on it downloads the file to their desktop.

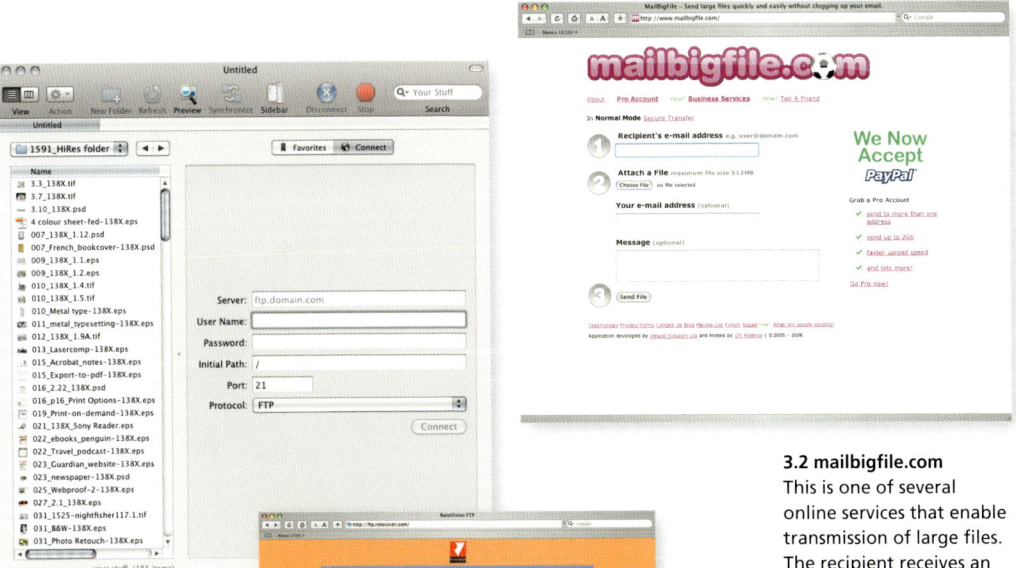

3.3 FTP clients
Transmit is one of several FTP Client software packages that enable files to be transferred to different virtual locations.

3.4 Browsing for files
Some FTP servers are accessible via a standard Web browser.

PROOFING AND PLATEMAKING

61

Types of proof

For color work, a high-quality proof is normally required, which is approved by the client and then given to the printer to match against on press. There are many types of proofs available, varying widely in cost and quality level.

Proofing from film
Although film has largely fallen into disuse, there may still be jobs that were previously printed from film and, when reprinting, may need to be proofed from film. This is normally done as a press proof (see below). There were photographic/electrostatic proofing methods of proofing from film, but these are no longer available from the majority of suppliers.

Press proofs (also known as wet proofs)
For offset lithography, these are produced on a special proofing press, or on the actual printing press that will be used for the job. A proofing press is in essence an offset printing machine that usually prints one or two colors at a time, with the paper fed in and taken off by hand. Before proofing, an offset plate is made from film or computer to plate in the normal way. This may be a plate specially made for proofing, or can be the same plate that will eventually be used for printing (a machine plate). Where a job is being produced by computer to plate and the proofing plate is also CTP, this will give an accurate proof, which will not be the case if the proofing plate of a CTP job is made from film, as the dot size, dot gain, and color balance will be different.

It is difficult or impossible to simulate on a proofing press all the printing conditions of the production machine, because the mechanics and speed are so different. Also, most color offset presses print ink wet on wet, whereas on a proofing press the previous color is usually dry before the next color is applied (wet on dry). However, if the same paper and inks are used as on the final job, a reasonably close result can be obtained.

The demise of film and increasing use of digital proofing (see below) has meant that the use of color proofing presses is in decline, so now when a press proof is required, it is more likely to be printed on a printing machine rather than a proofing press. This is an expensive option, as it means that the cost of making ready the printing press is incurred twice and plates will also have to be remade, if the press proofs are corrected. However, sometimes it is critical that the client sees a job in its final form on the material being used, before proceeding with production (e.g. a piece of promotional print with critical color and a long run). Cartons using spot colors often require press proofs, as photographic or digital proofs aren't close enough to the final result.

Digital proofs
Files (normally PDFs) can be proofed in-house on ink-jet or laser printers and for simple black and white work or straightforward jobs with spot color, it will not be necessary to have a further proof before printing. For four-color process work, a high-quality digital proof is required for the printer to match to on press, unless remote proofing is being used. The equipment needed to produce these proofs is a lot more expensive than an office printer, so digital proofs are normally obtained from outside suppliers, either a prepress or repro house, or the printer.

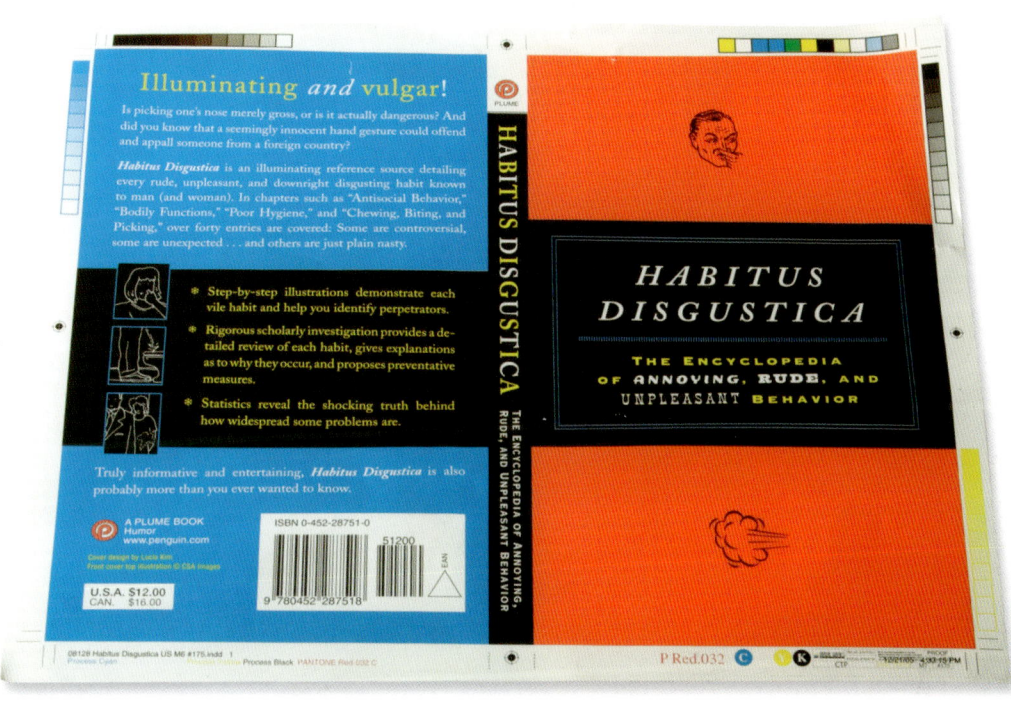

3.5 Proofs
Physical proofs in their many forms (see opposite) are vital tools for checking that text and images are going to be reproduced as desired at the printing stage, and for catching errors before they make it onto the page.

PROOFING AND PLATEMAKING

3.6 Dupont Digital Proofer
This Dupont Cromalin Blue device is a drop-on-demand ink-jet proofer that automatically calibrates itself.

3.7 Large-format Digital proofer
Can be used to proof large, high-quality, four-color works.

64

The proof should be made from the final PDF, so that if the client supplies application files (along with high-res picture files and fonts), these should be made into a PDF before proofing. This is important, as it's possible that the file may alter when converting to PDF rendering the proof of an application file unreliable. This may then not be discovered until the job is on press and will involve the delay and expense of remaking plates and going back to press again.

There are many types of digital proofs available, varying in cost according to the quality offered. Most digital proofs are produced on color-managed ink-jet printers, although other systems use thermal-transfer, dye-sublimation, laser, or electrostatic methods. Color-managed means that the proofing device is calibrated and uses an ICC (International Color Consortium) profile, so the proof gives an accurate representation of the colors that the press can reproduce. Most systems create the color with small pixels that are not the same as the CMYK halftone dots to be used for the final printing, but give a reasonable simulation of the printed result.

To achieve color management, the proofing device is fed with the ICC profile of the printing press being used for the final job, or with one of the international standard ICC profiles that the press falls within (such as SWOP or ISO coated). Most proofs carry a color bar (see p. 67) and are checked with a spectrophotometer (sometimes built into the proofing device). A label is then produced showing the variance from the standard and pass or fail. The label is attached to the proof as evidence that the required standard has been achieved.

The term "contract" proof describes a proof made to an agreed color standard and the need for such a proof emerged when newspapers and magazines were receiving display advertising files prepared to varying standards by different suppliers—many of which were difficult or impossible to match on press, and thus leading to disputes between advertiser, publisher, and printer. With a contract proof made to measurable industry standards, agreed to by all parties, the printer guarantees that the final printed result will be a reasonably accurate match to the proof, whereas this wasn't possible with earlier proofing methods. Agreed international standards include SWOP (Specifications for Web Offset Publications) in the US, FOGRA in Europe and Pass4Press in the UK. A contract proof will normally carry a color bar.

For some jobs, a "guide proof" may be adequate and is cheaper than a contract proof. A guide proof can be produced in house on a color laser or electrostatic printer and is used on the understanding that the color cannot be exactly matched, but will give the printer a reasonable guide.

Apart from Kodak Approval (see below), most digital proofs are on a special paper, rather than the paper being used for the job—however, some systems offer a range of papers, enabling the proof to be on something near to the final job paper. Earlier ink-jet proofing systems use continuous flow ink-jet (CIJ) technology and the more recent ones use drop on demand (D.O.D.) technology that is much cheaper in terms of both capital and running costs, while still offering good quality.

Current digital ink-jet proofing systems include dedicated devices such as Kodak Matchprint, Creo Veris, Dupont digital Cromalin Blue, but also software that can be used with much less expensive standard ink-jet printers—such software includes CGS Oris, EFI, ICG, and GMG. This category of software has now gained industry approval for use as contract proofs (see above). At the top end of digital proofing systems is Kodak Approval, which prints using CMYK halftone dots on the actual job paper, but its price puts it out of reach of all but the largest printers.

One important point concerns the use of a spot color as a fifth color, because this is normally simulated by the digital proof using CMYK, and, therefore, will not be accurate for color. Some digital proofing systems have special facilities for proofing special colors, or it may be necessary to have a press proof of either the whole job or just a sample to check the special color.

PROOFING AND PLATEMAKING

There is also a problem in the digital proofing of black-and- white photographs, as most digital proofing systems proof these as four-color blacks that will appear slightly differently when printed in black only. For top-quality, black-and-white photographic work, it may again be necessary to see press proofs, either of the whole job or some sample pages.

As all printing processes can now use PDFs as a starting point, it follows that a digital proof can be used for gravure, screen printing, or flexography, as well as offset lithography. Where a job is being printed digitally, the digital proof is usually produced on the digital press which will actually be used for the final job.

Color bars

These are usually on the proof and also on the printed sheet (but trimmed off before finishing). Color bars (see fig. 3.8) give the repro house and printer information about color, trapping, slurring, accuracy of platemaking, and dot gain. They can be read with a densitometer to check that the colors being printed are the same density as indicated by the color bar on the proof. The most recent advances in printing technology have enabled reading of this information to be achieved automatically by the computer controlling the inking on press, as it continually adjusts the ink flow to match the programmed standard required.

Remote proofing (also known as soft proofing)

This is already being used extensively by magazines and advertising agencies. Instead of checking a physical proof, the client checks a file sent electronically on a monitor that has been calibrated to match the monitor at the printer or repro house and both monitors mimic the color values that are achievable on the printing press. Corrections can be made using software (such as Kodak RealTimeProof) that is used to relay comments made on screen to the originator or by telephone in real time by using VOIP (voice over Internet protocol). The ambient viewing conditions (i.e. the lighting conditions in the room) will have an effect on the accuracy of the color, so strong colors and glare must be avoided.

Although, at the time of writing, remote proofing is a fairly recent development, we can expect it to very soon become the main method for proofing color for larger printers, repro houses, and clients, reducing time and cost in the prepress processes and making it more feasible to work with printers elsewhere in the country or anywhere abroad. However, smaller clients and suppliers will still depend on digital proofs, because of the costs and practical difficulties of installing high-quality monitors, calibrating them and ensuring the correct viewing conditions. Remote proofing of black text, such as in bookwork is common and obviously doesn't require special monitors or viewing conditions.

So, where a fast turnaround is required for quality, design-driven work (such as design magazines or advertising promotions featuring leading-edge design, illustration, or photography) remote proofing is an invaluable innovation allowing immediate on-site checking and quality approval. It is being adopted first by companies whose reputation lies in the quality of their print production and reproduction.

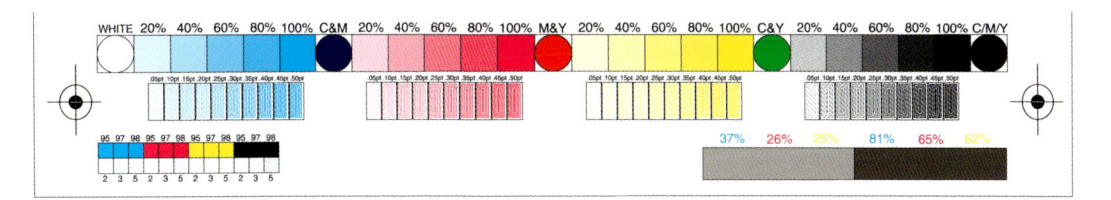

3.8 Color bar
A color bar is used on proofs and the printed sheet (outside the trim area) to check that color and other characteristics match the required profile.

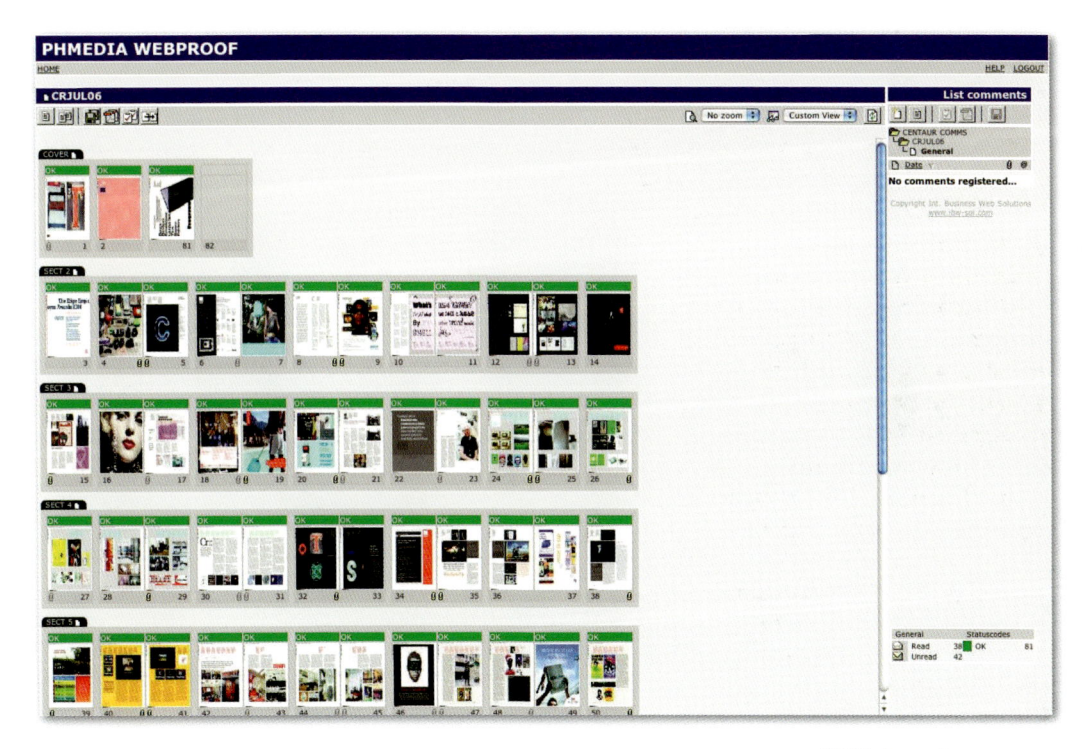

3.9 Web proofs
Example of remote proofing, as adopted by renowned design magazine, *Creative Review*.

PROOFING AND PLATEMAKING

Checking color proofs

Color proofs are your insurance policy against incorrect or poor color reproduction, blemishes on images, and the overall look and feel of the complete product as it will appear when printed (with allowances made for the paper type). Time spent with color proofs will be rewarded with the best possible printed article later.

When the client receives color proofs (i.e. high-quality proofs, not plotter proofs), they should be checked for sizing and color quality. As well as the actual color values, it is also important to check for blemishes, scratches, and process stains. On proofs made from film, register (the correct positioning of the films, so the dots are in the correct position relative to each other) must be checked: a subject that is out of register will look fuzzy and slightly out of focus, and the edge of the offending color will be seen to protrude slightly; this is easy to correct before printing at the imposition stage.

To check the actual color values on the proof, it is important to have correct viewing conditions. Ideally, the client will have a viewing booth (see fig. 3.11) with standardized lighting (usually Kelvin 5000) that matches that used for viewing at the reproduction house and the printer. This lighting simulates daylight so, if the client does not have a viewing booth, it is best to view the proof in daylight.

It is very important to view the color proofs under identical lighting conditions to those at the printer or repro house in order to avoid a condition known as metamerism, whereby the human eye perceives color differently on the same image under varying lighting conditions. That can mean a possible request for an unnecessary or undesired color correction.

To compare the proof with a transparency, the transparency should be viewed on a light box, again with standardized lighting. Any color correction required can either be done by the client or the repro house or printer, using Photoshop or similar software. Any but the most minor color correction will require a revised proof to match to on press.

Content should be double-checked, although any errors should have been picked up at an earlier stage in house. Bleeds (image that extends beyond the trim marks) and trim marks should also be checked. Check too that images are the right way round and not flopped left to right or top to bottom. Low-res or RGB images sometimes get through to this stage, so check that all images have been converted to high-res and CMYK.

3.10 Close analysis
Proofs of all kinds should be checked meticulously: they are your safeguard against repro errors and problems that might prove to be serious if not picked up in advance of printing. This type of magnifying glass, called a linen tester, is often used to check color on proofs at close range to pick up any problems that the naked eye cannot see.

3.11 Viewing Booth
A Verivide viewing booth with standard lighting for viewing and correcting proofs. The light box on the left is for viewing transparencies and comparing them with color proofs.

PROOFING AND PLATEMAKING

69

Checking color on press

The vast majority of printing jobs are produced without the client being present but, where there is a long run of a color book, promotional item, or packaging item, or where the color is critical, the client may wish to attend a press check, either for the first one or two workings (to set the standard), or for the complete run.

It is important to approach this job with the right attitude—which is not a question of telling the machine-minder how to do his or her job but more a question of interpretation: for example, does the client want a bright, sparkly result or a more subtle one? And which subjects are the most important?

When making ready, whether or not the client is present, the printer should have the approved color proofs to refer to, as well as the plotter proof or blueprint (ozalid). Before passing the color, the first sheet off the press should be checked against this to ensure that any corrections have been carried out and then the sheet should be checked for spots, which can sometimes occur in the platemaking process (if the spots are not in the original film or file, they can sometimes be deleted from the plate without removing it from the machine). It shouldn't be necessary to check for spelling or typos by this stage, as this will have been checked on the previous proofs. Any last-minute text corrections now will be expensive and affect the print schedule. Register and backup should be checked to ensure that all the color is positioned correctly.

Finally, the accuracy of the color values should be inspected. The color can be adjusted by regulating the amount of ink released onto the inking rollers and then on the plate. One major problem in adjusting color on machine is that it can be done only in "tracks" (that is, in strips parallel to the direction in which the sheets come off the machine); thus, if you increase the magenta in one picture, the magenta will be increased in all the other subjects in that track (see fig. 3.12).

You need also to be aware that the sheet you check on press will still be wet and will appear glossier than when dry, so you need to be aware of "dry back" and allow for this.

Another particular problem area is where the imposition dictates that the two halves of double page spreads are at opposite corners of the sheet; the two halves must match as nearly as possible, but without upsetting the color balance of other subjects in the two tracks. If using a special fifth color (e.g. a Pantone), this should be checked against a swatch book. Decisions about color adjustment need to be made very quickly, either because the press is already running or because it is making ready and productive time is being lost. Checking color on press can be an intimidating experience until the person doing it has gained experience. However, the printer will usually advise the novice on how to achieve the best result.

Most printers have standardized lighting, meaning that the printed sheet can be viewed in the same conditions as at the repro house; and the sheets will carry a color bar that can be compared with the color bar on the color proof to check that the color values match those on the proof.

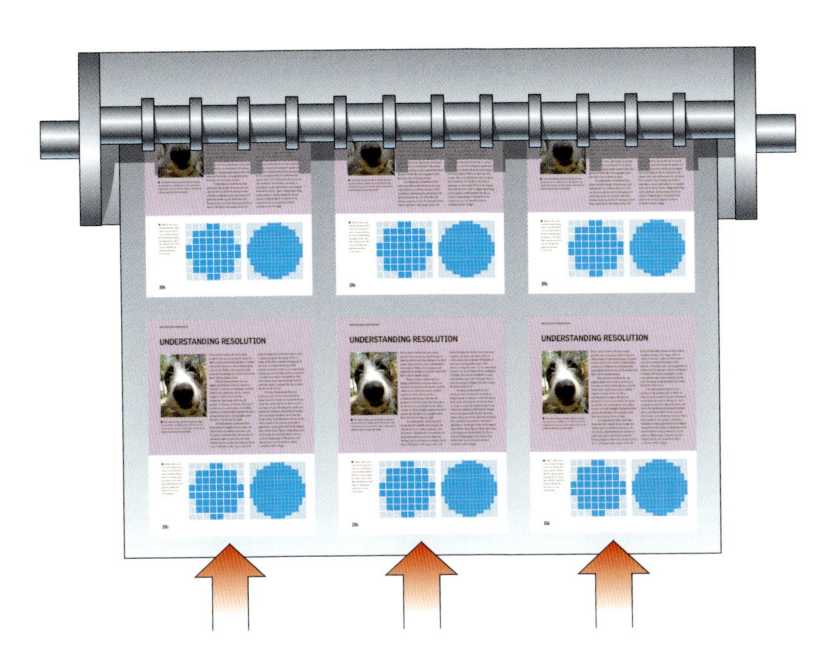

3.12 Tracking
The arrows show the direction in which the ink is laid on the paper. As the quantity of ink has to be the same for all subjects in the track, this can lead to problems. Where one subject needs a lot of a particular color, for instance, all subjects in that track have to have the same amount of that color. Often, compromises have to be made.

3.13 Checking the color
Expert eyes scan color reproduction and image quality at this printer based in China.

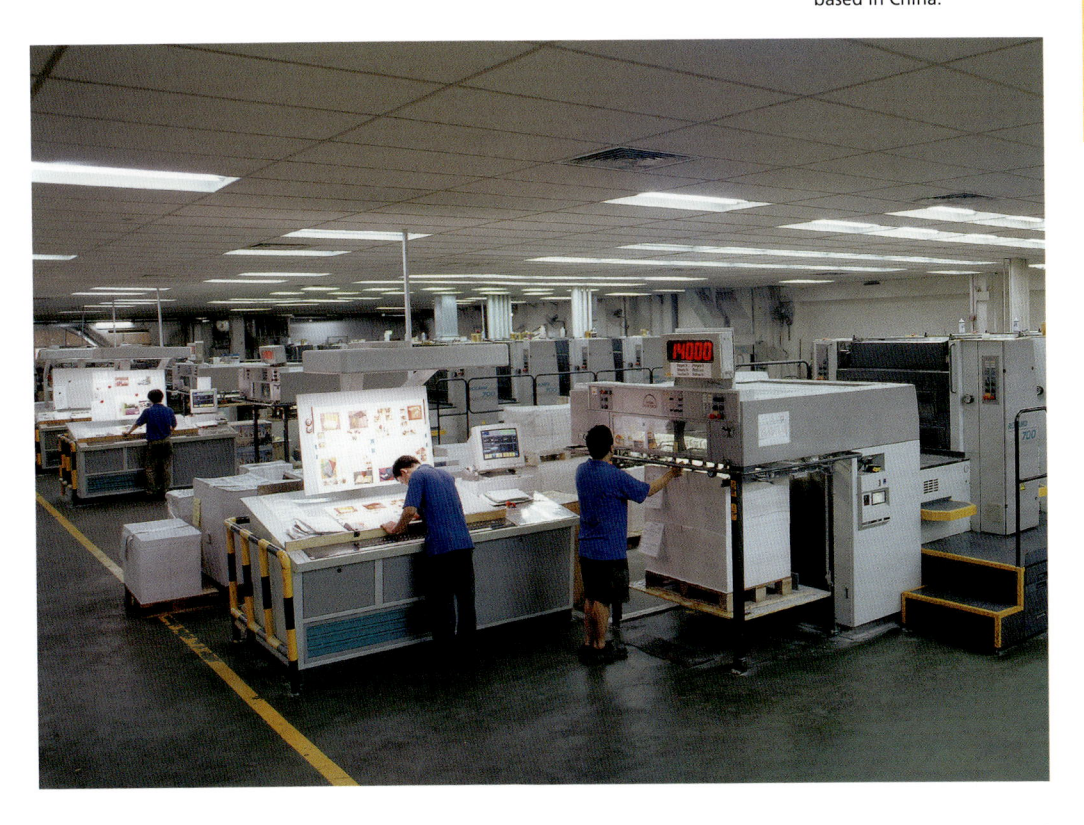

PROOFING AND PLATEMAKING

71

Imposition and platemaking

This section describes the processes used to make plates for offset lithography—for other processes see page 80. However, the principles of imposition are useful to learn in every case for all types of printing work that relate to multi-page publications.

Imposition

Imposition is the positioning of the pages in the right places on the plate, whereby when printed they reproduce in the required order and in the correct position, with the intended margins.

Most printing machines print 4, 8, 16, 32, or 48 pages (or multiples of these) at a time, and the printer will work out an imposition scheme that will print the required number of pages in the most economical way on the particular machine being used. The details of the imposition will not normally concern the client if the job is being printed in one, two, three, or four colors on every page; however, if the printing is to be planned so that, for example, half the pages are to be in four-color and half in two-color, the client must obtain the imposition scheme from the printer or binder. Illustrations and layout can then be planned according to which pages will print in four-color and which in two.

Normally, jobs are imposed as sheet work, but in sheet-fed printing they can be imposed as "work and turn" (half-sheet work). This means that all the pages in a job are printed on one side of the sheet, the sheet is then turned over to print the other side and then cut in two.

Imposition software

This is used with imagesetters (to produce imposed film) and platesetters (to produce plates). This software takes a PDF and positions it electronically in exactly the right page position. This is done by reading the page geometry in the PDF file and using it to position the pages accurately.

Prior to the development of imagesetters and platesetters, imposition used to be done with adhesive tape on clear plastic foils, positioned on a layout grid (accuracy being aided by using a punch register system)—this technique is known as stripping. Imposition software is fast and automatic and cuts out the many hours of labor (and the possibility of mistakes) incurred in painstakingly taping pages of film to large foils.

3.14 Imposition
This term is used to describe the organization of the pages on each side of a printed sheet so that they will be in the correct order when they are cut, folded, and trimmed. The illustrations (right) show the commonly used imposition schemes and the corresponding folding methods. Margins of about ⅛in to ¼in (3mm to 6mm) are left when printing and folding for trimming.

1 4-page work and turn

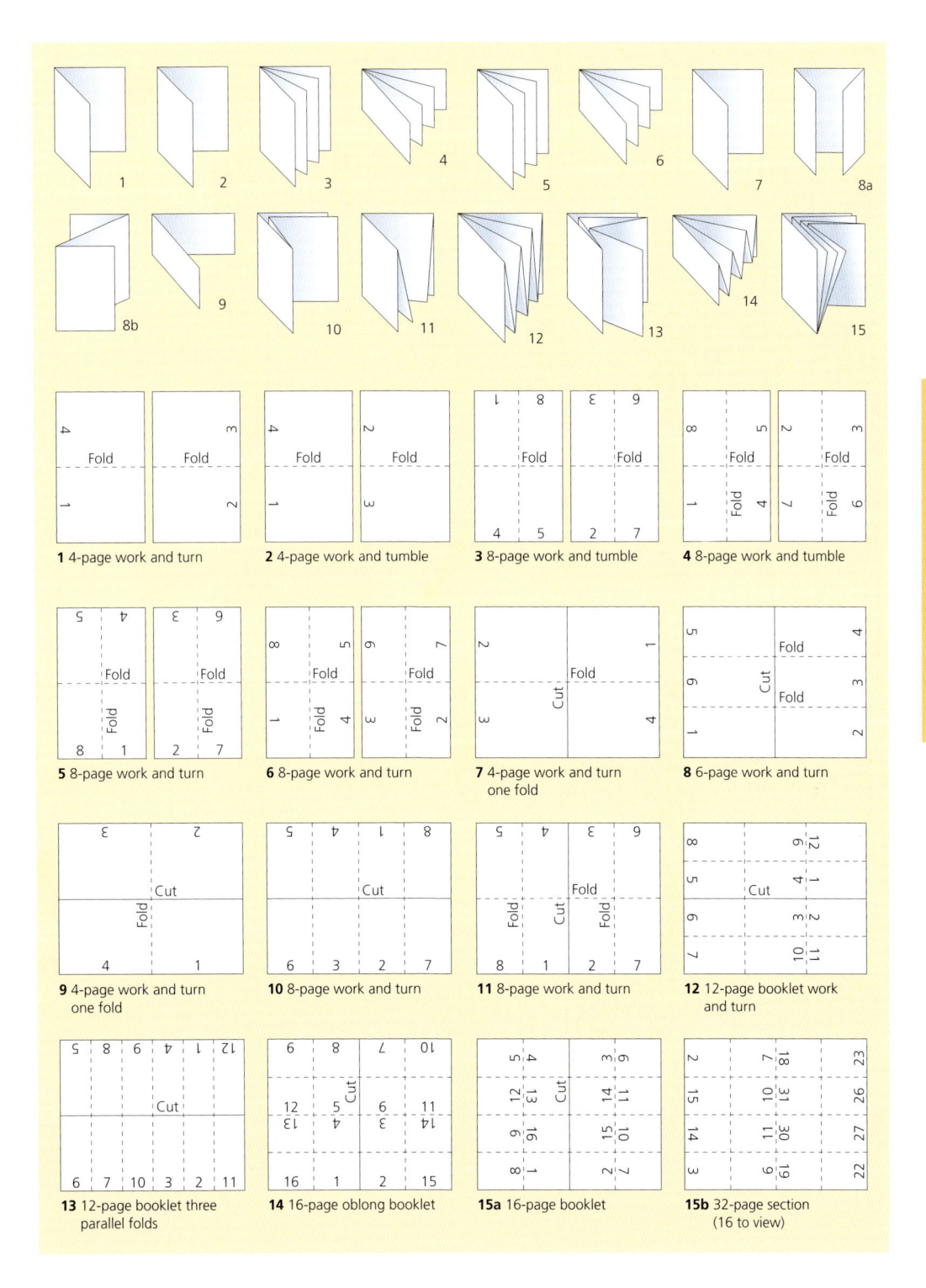

2 4-page work and tumble

3 8-page work and tumble

4 8-page work and tumble

5 8-page work and turn

6 8-page work and turn

7 4-page work and turn one fold

8 6-page work and turn

9 4-page work and turn one fold

10 8-page work and turn

11 8-page work and turn

12 12-page booklet work and turn

13 12-page booklet three parallel folds

14 16-page oblong booklet

15a 16-page booklet

15b 32-page section (16 to view)

PROOFING AND PLATEMAKING

73

PROOFING AND PLATEMAKING

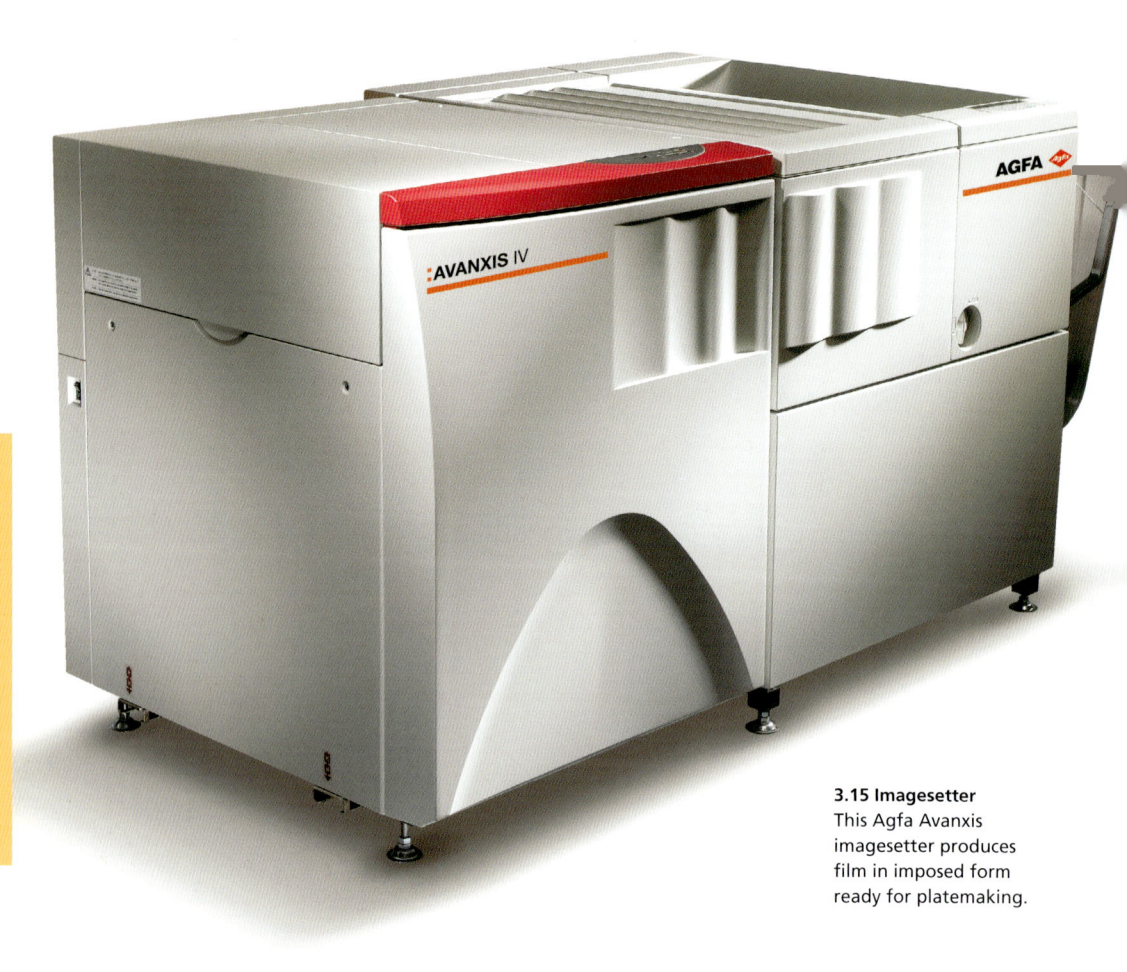

3.15 Imagesetter
This Agfa Avanxis imagesetter produces film in imposed form ready for platemaking.

3.16 Printing plates
The final result of the prepress process.

74

Where a job has been previously produced from film and the job is to be reprinted with revisions, the client can either supply PDFs of the altered pages, if the corrections only affect text, and the printer can prepare film from these. Or it may be better, if material is available in digital form, to resupply the whole job digitally, because today many printers will be working only computer-to-plate and no longer have facilities for making film or making plates from film. Where pictures only exist in the form of film separations, film can be sent to a prepress or repro house which has a copy-dot scanner. This scans four-color separated screened films and generates a file (e.g. jpeg) that can be used with page layout applications, in the same way as any other digital picture file, so it can be integrated, resized and retouched as required.

Imagesetter
This is the device used to produce film in imposed form. Some imagesetters (for example, those used for bookwork) are very large and produce a single piece of film containing up to 48 pages. Imagesetters and platesetters are raster devices and have a RIP (Raster Image Processor). Documents are normally a combination of raster (bitmapped) and vector (scalable line) information and this has to be converted to raster information, before making plates or film.

The resolution of an imagesetter is measured in dots per inch (dpi) and normally it outputs 1,200 or 2,400 dots per inch. This is so fine that even though the delicate serifs of a piece of small type are made up from dots, they look completely solid, even through a magnifying glass. The dots per inch of the imagesetter should not be confused with the lines per inch used on a halftone screen. In the imagesetter, the film is sensitive to laser light and the image area is exposed by the laser. The film is then developed in a film processor.

Most modern imagesetters are either internal-drum or external-drum. On an internal-drum imagesetter the film is positioned inside the drum and the laser moves to expose the image; with external-drum imagesetters, the film is on the outside of the drum and rotates, while the laser remains stationary. Imagesetters are being phased out and most printers now use platesetters to go direct to plate.

Platemaking from film
Once the blueprint (ozalid proof made from the film) has been checked by the client, the printer makes any necessary corrections and then produces plates from the film. The plate, which is usually presensitized (that is, coated it with a chemical that reacts to light), has the film placed over it. Light from an artificial source is shone through the clear parts of the film, and this has the effect of hardening the image area. Exposure is critical and can be checked with an exposure control step wedge. When the plate is developed and washed (normally in automatic machines), the image area will attract ink and repel water while the non-image (background) area will repel ink and attract water (see the lithography process, p. 88). There are many types of offset plate. They can be made of aluminum, polyester (with silver-based coatings), or photopolymer. Waterless plates for waterless offset (see p. 94) consist of aluminum for the image areas and rubber for the non-image areas. The printer will choose the type of plate needed, depending on factors such as the length of run and the sharpness of dot required.

Computer to plate (CTP)

Computer to plate (CTP) is now the standard technology in many professional print-based businesses, stripping away the need for film-making and making the print production process much simpler, more intuitive, and more efficient in terms of time and valuable resources.

In computer to plate (CTP or direct to plate) working, rather than an imagesetter producing film that is subsequently used to make a plate, a platesetter is used to image the file directly onto the plate, normally using a laser (either thermal or violet diode). Most plates for offset lithography are now produced by this method, which saves time and money while requiring fewer chemicals in the process. The platesetter can either be internal-drum or external-drum as for an imagesetter, or may be flatbed where large plates are being made for newspapers or books. Flatbed platesetters are faster and used by web printers for newspapers and magazines, but cannot achieve the quality of internal- or external-drum platesetters.

Processless plates are now available that can be used straight from the platesetter, with no chemical processing required—these use ablative technology, where a laser burns the image onto a coating over a metal or photopolymer base.

Printed images produced by computer to plate are more accurate than those on plates made from film, where the dot can distort slightly when the film is exposed to the plate.

Plotter proofs

Before platemaking, a proof is normally supplied for final sign-off and this will only be for position and content, not color quality, which will have been checked on a color proof at an earlier stage. Where film is being used, the proof could be a blueline (ozalid) that is just proofed in black or blue (like a dyeline), rather than color. For work that is going direct to plate, a plotter proof is produced digitally on a large-format ink-jet plotter. Plotter proofs show all four colors (but to indicate position and content and not color quality). Bluelines (ozalids) and plotter proofs can be proofed on both sides of the sheet and folded and trimmed to the final size for ease of checking. This is the last stage of checking before printing and any changes at this stage will be both costly and time-consuming, as the job may have to be color proofed again and re-imposed. When checking plotter proofs, the main aim is to check that the file has output correctly. Look particularly at the fonts and check that there are no symbols defaulting to letters due to font problems. If anything needs changing at plotter proof stage, rather than asking the printer to do it, it is safer for the client to make the correction into their application file and then make a new PDF. This means that if the application file is reused in the future, it will be correct. Also, it may be difficult or impossible for the printer to correct a PDF. If correcting a plotter proof, you will need to see a revised plotter proof (just of the correction–not the whole job) for final approval before printing.

3.17 Platesetter for CTP
The Agfa Avalon LF platesetter produces plates directly from files.

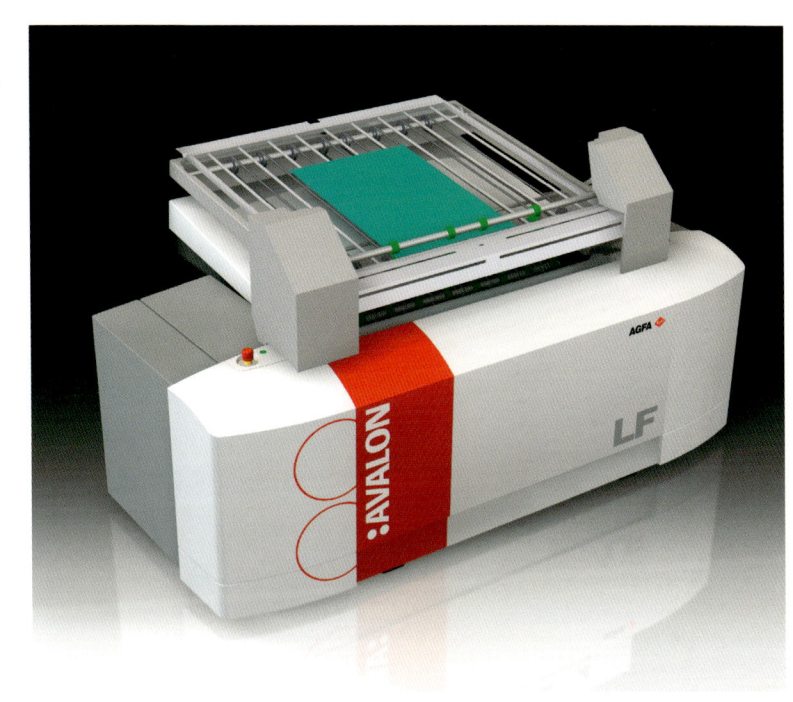

3.18 A large-format flatbed platesetter
This Agfa Xcalibur VLF platesetter is used for large plates for book printing.

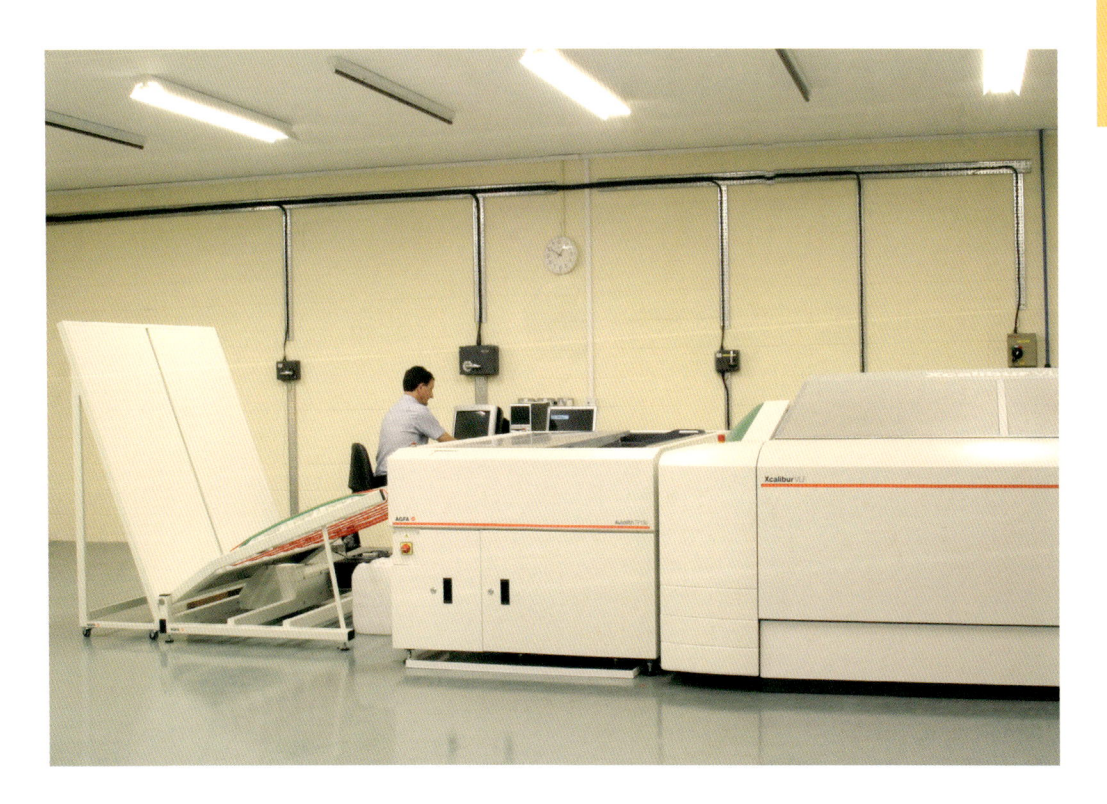

PROOFING AND PLATEMAKING

CTP and the PDF workflow

Integrating CTP with Adobe's PDF technology has benefits for both client and customer in terms of speed of service, quality, manageability, and a seamless digital workflow from layout to professionally printed finished article.

The integration of Adobe's PDF technology with CTP can enable printers to expedite jobs for the customer, especially if work is supplied to them from the outset as a prepress-ready PDF, with material from the layout files properly collected for output, and with all images and fonts embedded into a single PDF document. This can, says some anecdotal evidence, be as much as 50% quicker than the same work carried out by the printer or prepress house in PostScript.

Some printers recommend their clients use the plug-in EZ-PDF, because the user can simply go to the Print command and then select "Prepress" in the Print dialog box. This will launch Adobe Acrobat Distiller and handle the compiling process automatically. It is also possible to embed XML and job-ticket information in PDFs, as we have already explored in the section on JDF (see p. 26). It is advisable to divide long documents into manageable sections—perhaps corresponding to a signature, or group of signatures—during the layout stage and make separate PDFs of them.

If working direct from a supplied print-resolution PDF, the printer will then rip the file, trap it, and impose it for proofing and subsequent printing. Once the contract proof has been submitted and approved, the printer generates plastic or aluminum plates on a thermal platesetter, direct from the PDF file, using a laser to cut into the surface. If corrections need to be made at this stage on individual pages, then only that page needs to be put through the rip and a new plate made for press. It is advisable to have a plotter proof supplied so that a final check can be made of all the elements that will be committed to print. Plotters should not be used as color guides.

A further advantage of PDF technology, aside from expediting CTP and the digital workflow in general, is that it enables cross-platform publishing with relative ease, as low- or Web-resolution PDFs can be published straight to the Web. However, some people are against this practice as PDFs do not automatically scale to screen size within some browsers, and some people regard the idea as effectively publishing an image of a document (albeit one that allows interactivity) rather than being Web publishing in its purest form.

• Although PDF is an open format in that it can be read on any system with the free Acrobat reader, it is still a proprietary format owned by Adobe, albeit normally on a royalty-free licence. For users of software such as Adobe InDesign on either Macs or PCs, this is clearly not a problem, but there are uncertainties over Microsoft's ongoing position in all this, as it has developed a similarly capable system called XPS, and Adobe has had legal issues with Microsoft offering PDF-making as a Save As option within its Office suite. For most professional printing applications, however, such wranglings are not a significant consideration.

3.19 Plotter proofs
The final stage in the CTP proofing process, plotters should be used by the client as a final positional check for every element of the print job.

3.20 Creating a PDF
A press-ready PDF can easily be generated directly from your page layout software package using a variety of appropriate settings.

PROOFING AND PLATEMAKING

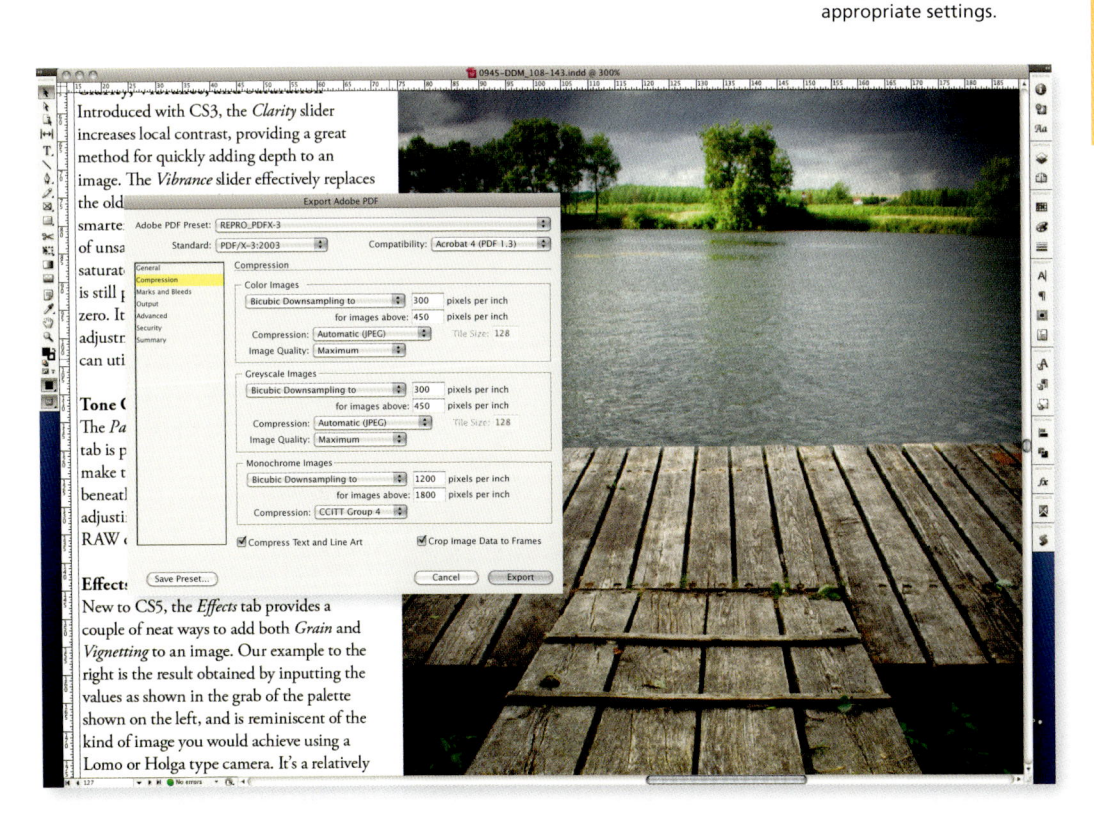

79

Platemaking for other processes

Many other printing processes are used to make different products and printed materials; some are old technologies that have found a new home in limited-edition work, while others are necessary to print onto different types of surface. Some of the platemaking techniques for these are now digitized, but others remain unchanged.

Digital Printing
(See p. 96.) There is no plate required for digital printing as the printing surface is automatically created on the press from a PDF.

Letterpress
In letterpress (see p. 108), the printing surface is made up of individual pieces of type for each character, and pictures are cuts (blocks) produced by making a negative of the original, exposing it to a metal plate and etching away the background resulting in the non-image area being below the surface; the thin plate is mounted on a base of wood or metal to bring it up to the height of the type. The blocks and type when assembled in a chase are called a "forme" (see fig. 3.21). Pictures can also be original wood engravings, where the wood is cut, leaving the image raised above the background.

Letterpress also had duplicate plates (stereos or electros) made by making a mold from the original relief surface, which could be in the form of type, blocks or a mixture of both, following which, molten lead was poured into the mold. Similarly, a version of letterpress also used plastic or rubber plates made from molds and the process was used extensively for printing paperbacks in the latter half of the last century. Neither method is now in common use.

Flexography
(Also see p. 110.) This is primarily used for printing packaging and some newspapers. This method now uses a fully digital workflow, and the prepress stages are the same as for offset lithography, and flexographic printers are producing their plates in-house rather than at outside specialist platemakers, as previously. This is improving the economics and lead times of the process, resulting in flexography taking a bigger share of the overall market for print.

Flexography uses flexible photopolymer plates with a raised surface and these used to be mounted on the plate cylinder manually, using double-sided adhesive tape. Now, as in offset, the latest computer to plate (CTP) techniques image directly onto pre-mounted photosensitive plates or onto sleeves, avoiding the time and cost of manually mounting individual plates. Another technique is laser engraving, where the non-image area is cut away by a laser. Specialist software is used to deal with the special colors often required in the printing of packaging and the requirements of the flexography process. In book production, photopolymer plates are used on belt presses (see p. 108).

3.21 Letterpress forme
The type is held in position in a chase (frame). Furniture fills the non-printing space and pressure is exerted by quoins to hold the contents firm.

3.22 Photopolymer plate
Used for flexography, a printing process that is now largely digital and used to print packaging and even some newspapers. The flexible plate can be made direct from a digital file.

PROOFING AND PLATEMAKING

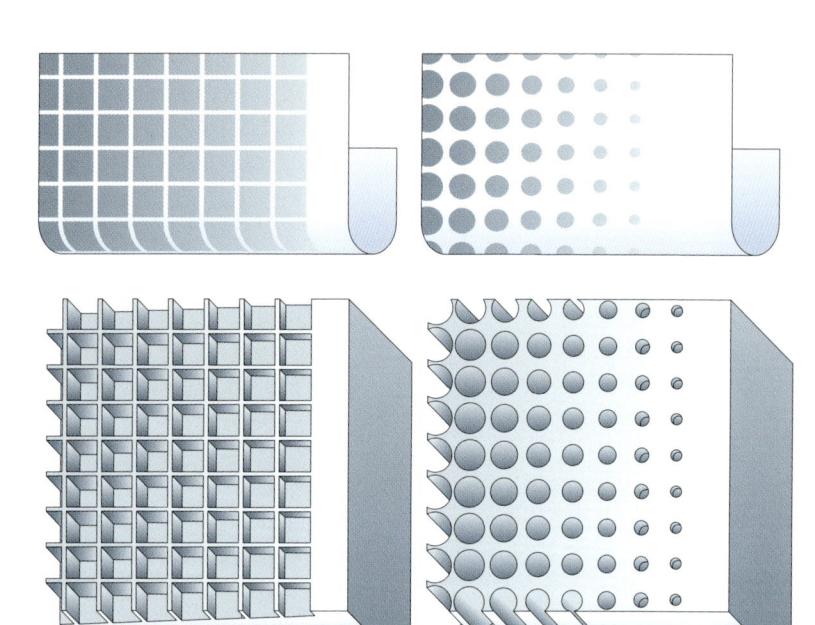

3.23 Gravure printing
A conventional gravure cylinder (right) has cells that vary in depth but which have equal surface areas. A variable surface variable depth gravure cylinder (far right) has cells that vary in size as well as depth. The enlarged details above the illustrations of the surfaces of the plates show the printed results.

3.24 Gravure laser cylinder engraving machine
The image, which is in digital form, activates the laser, which evaporates the plastic surface of the cylinder. This is a Hell K6 HelioKlischograph.

Gravure

(see p. 100) The image in gravure is "intaglio" (recessed). Most gravure printing surfaces are cylinders made of solid steel electroplated with a thin, highly polished metal skin that forms the printing surface.

In conventional gravure, the printing surface is made up of cells that are all the same area but vary in depth, with the deepest ones representing the darker areas of the subject and carrying the most ink, and the shallower ones corresponding to the lighter areas of the subject. This enables the process to give different shades of gray without using the halftone process. To make the cylinder, the copper surface is given a light-sensitive coating that is exposed to light through a film positive. The non-image area is hardened and the cylinder is then etched, leaving the image area recessed below the surface.

Most gravure cylinders, however, are now engraved using electromechanical engraving, equipped with a diamond stylus that cuts cells into the cylinder, making deeper cells for the darker areas of the image. Unlike conventional gravure, the cells vary in depth and area. Often gravure cylinders are chromium-plated to prevent wear on long runs. Gravure (like offset and flexography) now uses a digital workflow and this, combined with electromechanical engraving has brought down the start-up costs of gravure and enabled it to compete with web-offset at lower runs than previously.

Screen printing

In screen printing the image is achieved by use of a stencil that can be produced either by hand, photographically, or more directly from a digital file. The screen on which the stencil is placed is a fine mesh made from nylon, polyester, or stainless steel, which is a lot more expensive, but more durable for long runs. Its use also enables finer image detail. Different grades of mesh are used, depending on the thickness of the ink deposit required and the amount of fine details needed in the image.

Hand-cut stencils are made using film that has two layers. The stencil is cut on the top layer, following a layout; those areas representing the image areas are cut out with a sharp knife, leaving the backing film behind. The same process can also be done by a computer-driven pen plotter, using a knife. The film is then transferred to the screen and the backing film peeled away to leave the film blocking the openings of the mesh in the non-printing areas.

Obviously, handcut stencils cannot be used for small type, photographs, or fine drawings, and so for these a photographic process is used. Photostencils can be produced either by the "indirect" or by the "direct" method. In the indirect method, a photographic positive is produced (using the halftone and four-color processes where necessary), and this is placed in contact with the stencil film and exposed to light. Light passes through the clearer areas of the film, hardening the light-sensitive coating, while the darker areas of the film leave the coating soft, so it can be washed away chemically. The stencil is then transferred to the screen and the backing film is removed. This leaves the mesh blocked by the light-hardened areas of coating on the non-image areas.

In the direct method, light-sensitive solution is applied directly to the screen. A film positive is exposed to the coated screen and, after exposure, the soft (image) areas of the coating are washed away with chemical solution.

The latest techniques for making screens make the stencils from digital files, using an ink-jet printer to print a positive image directly onto the photosensitive emulsion and then exposing that to light. We can expect that these techniques will soon replace the photomechanical methods of making stencils for screen printing.

An introduction to the processes

The choice of print process is related to the choice of print materials, and there are many other terms and techniques that cover most forms of printing and are useful to know. Here we explore the main print processes and their associated terminologies.

The main printing processes can be defined according to the physical characteristics of the printing surfaces used. Letterpress is a "relief" process, where the image to be printed is raised above the background; this raised surface is inked by rollers and then pressed against the paper to make the impression. Lithography is "planographic," meaning it uses a flat printing surface: the image area is chemically treated so that it accepts ink and rejects water, while the non-image area is treated to accept water and reject ink. Gravure is a modern version of the "intaglio" process, meaning that the printing image is recessed into the cylinder with tiny cells that become filled with liquid ink; the non-image area is wiped free of ink with a doctor blade, whereby ink is deposited on the paper from the recessed cells.

There are certain principles in printing that apply regardless of the particular process that is being used. It is important, for instance, to use the right size of press for the job: it would be uncommercial to use a large book press for a short run of headed notepaper, and equally uncommercial to use a small offset press for 100,000 copies of a magazine. Equally, the size of the job should in general be selected to match the profile of the machine being used for printing. For example, a machine might be designed to fit four pages of 8½ x 11in (approx. A4) size to view (i.e. on one side of the sheet) so, should the page size be increased even a little in either direction, it would mean that only two pages to view could be printed at once, thus doubling the amount of platemaking and printing and the time taken to do the job.

Make-ready
An operation that applies to all printing processes is "make-ready"—that is, all the operations that take place on a press prior to the first good copies being produced. These operations can include setting up the press to accept the size and thickness of paper being used, putting the printing plates on, putting the correct sort and color of ink on the press, adjusting the folder (on a web-fed press), or ensuring that the color is of the right strength and that the image is in the right position. Make-ready is a crucial area in printing, as the eventual cost of the job and the quality of the result depend on this part of the process. Most modern printing techniques aim to reduce the downtime and expense involved in make-ready.

Sheet-fed and web-fed
Most printing processes require the paper to be either sheet-fed or web-fed. For sheet-fed printing, the paper must first be cut into sheets of a suitable size. The "feeder" section of the press picks up the sheets, usually by a combination of metal fingers and vacuum suckers, and feeds them through the printing cylinders, where they are printed. The sheets then pass onto the delivery end of the press, still as flat sheets—folding or other finishing processes are a separate operation requiring other machinery. For web-fed (also known as roll-fed) printing, the paper is supplied to the machine in the form of rolls (reels). The front end of the press has a reelstand that holds the paper as it is unwound and fed through the press. The actual method of printing is the same as with a sheet-fed press,

Letterpress    Lithography 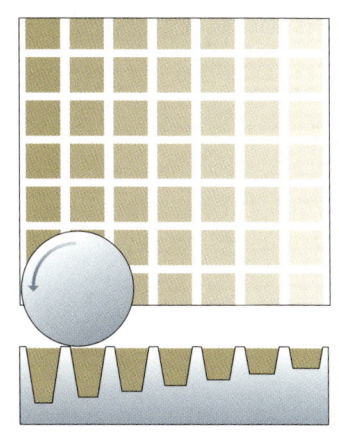   Gravure

4.1 Processes
Letterpress (top left) is a relief process. The printing surface is raised above the non-printing surface. Halftone dots vary in size.

Lithography (top center) has a planographic (flat) printing surface. The image area accepts ink and repels water. The non-image area attracts water and repels ink.

Gravure (top right) is an intaglio process. The printing image is recessed into the cylinder and filled with ink. The cells vary in depth, but not in size.

4.2 The make-ready
Here a printer goes through the all-important preparatory stages prior to printing the first good copies of a job.

PRINTING PROCESSES

PRINTING PROCESSES

| Cyan | Magenta | Yellow | Black |

| Cyan | Magenta | Yellow | Black |

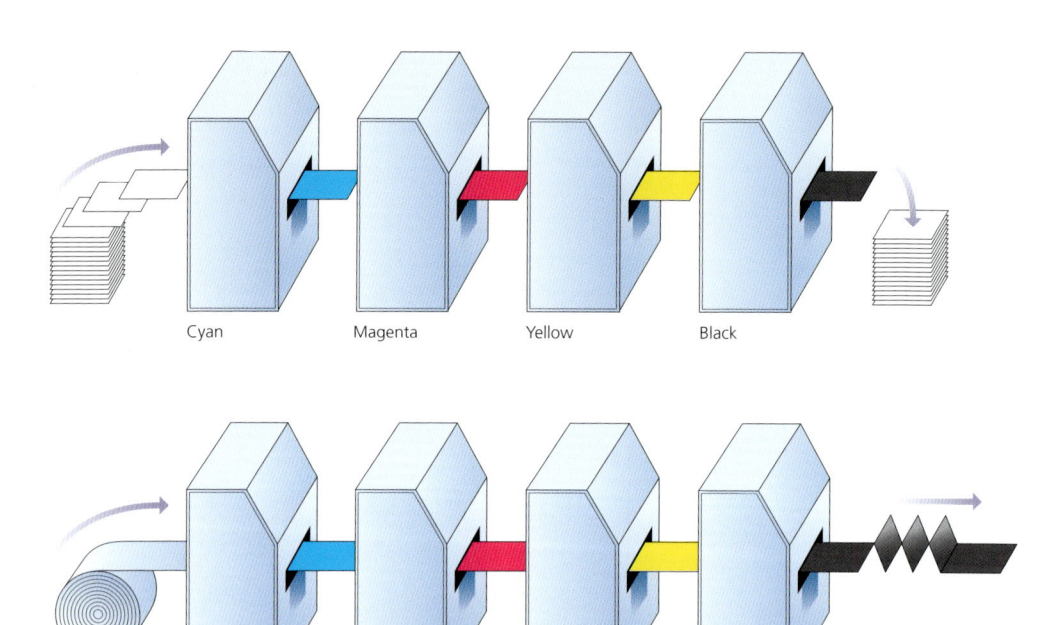

4.3 Sheet- and web-fed
Printing presses require paper to be either in sheets or rolls. In sheet-fed printing (top) the paper is cut into sheets of the required size before being printed. In web-fed printing (above), a large roll of paper is unwound as it passes through the press and is folded at the other end—the web is cut after it has been printed.

86

but printing can take place at much higher speeds because the machine is not slowed down by having to pick up and put down each sheet before printing the next. Most web presses also incorporate some form of finishing facility after printing. Usually this is confined to folding, but it can also include various types of gluing, stitching and perforating to deliver special products for direct-mail and other purposes.

The advantages of web-fed printing are speed, the fact that folding can be done at the same time, and that paper on rolls is cheaper than paper in sheets. The disadvantages are that web-fed presses involve a very high initial outlay, need more make-ready time, and mostly produce only items of a fixed length. Web-fed presses therefore usually lend themselves to long runs and standard formats.

The length limitation arises from the fact that each length of paper going through the press to be brought into contact with the printing surface (an impression) must be the same length as that printing surface. This length is known as the "cut-off." If the press were to be used to print a shorter printing image, it would require the same length of paper per impression, and the printed sheets would then have to be cut down to size, with consequent wastage. (This does not apply in gravure, where the cutoff can vary). In the past, web-fed presses used to waste more paper than sheet-fed paper in the make-ready process, as their high speed meant that more paper was spoiled before acceptable copies were produced. Today, the latest developments in web-fed technology have significantly reduced both the make-ready time and the amount of paper wastage required to achieve an acceptable quality of printing throughout.

4.4 Paper feeding through a web-fed press
The "web" of paper is the continuous roll of paper that spins through the rollers of the press.

Offset lithography

This is the predominant process used in printing today, being used for a wide range of items from letterheads to packaging, books, and magazines. However, the use of digital printing is increasing rapidly and this process is likely to gain shorter run work from offset lithography.

The basic process of lithography was invented by Senefelder in Bavaria in 1798, but it was only when the "offset" principle was applied early in the 20th century that lithography started to be used for commercial printing. Since the 1960s it has gradually taken over as the major printing process.

The lithography process
Lithography (or "litho") is a planographic process, as the printing surface is flat rather than raised as in letterpress, or recessed as in gravure. The area to be printed is treated chemically so that it accepts grease (ink) and rejects water, while the non-image, or background, area is treated to accept water and reject grease. The whole surface has both ink and water (with the addition of alcohol to aid dispersion) applied to it. When the plate is pressed against the surface of the paper, only the image area is printed. When lithography was first employed, smooth stone slabs were used to make the printing surface, and this method is still used for limited editions of fine-art prints, using flat-bed presses. The next development in lithographic printing came with the introduction of grained metal plates. These can be curved around a cylinder to allow the use of a rotary press. Finally, the "offset" principle was developed.

The offset lithography principle
Where lithography is used, it is nearly always as offset lithography. This means that the inked image on the metal plate is "offset" (printed) onto a rubber blanket wrapped around a rotating metal cylinder and the image is then transferred from that blanket onto the paper. One reason for using a blanket is to prevent the delicate lithographic plate from coming into contact with the more abrasive paper surface, which would cause significant wear and tear on the plate during the run. Another advantage of the offset principle is that less water comes into contact with the paper than in direct lithography. Moreover, the rubber blanket responds to irregularities of surface so that it is possible to print on to a wide variety of surfaces, including metal for cans and boxes: special inks are used for this, and the printed metal is heat-treated after printing to give a rub- and scratch-resistant surface.

The offset press
As with letterpress, all offset presses have to perform the operations of feeding, inking, printing, and delivering the paper but, in addition, water (with alcohol) has to be applied to the plate by a dampening unit.

Almost all offset presses use the rotary principle, which means that the press acts rather like a mangle—the cylinders roll against each other. The printing section of the press consists of three cylinders: a blanket cylinder around which the sheet of rubber is wrapped; a plate cylinder, with the metal plate wrapped around it; and the impression cylinder that carries the paper and presses it against the blanket cylinder to create the impression. Offset litho requires minimal make-ready and the rubber blanket compensates for differences in the surfaces being printed by adapting itself to the profile of the material.

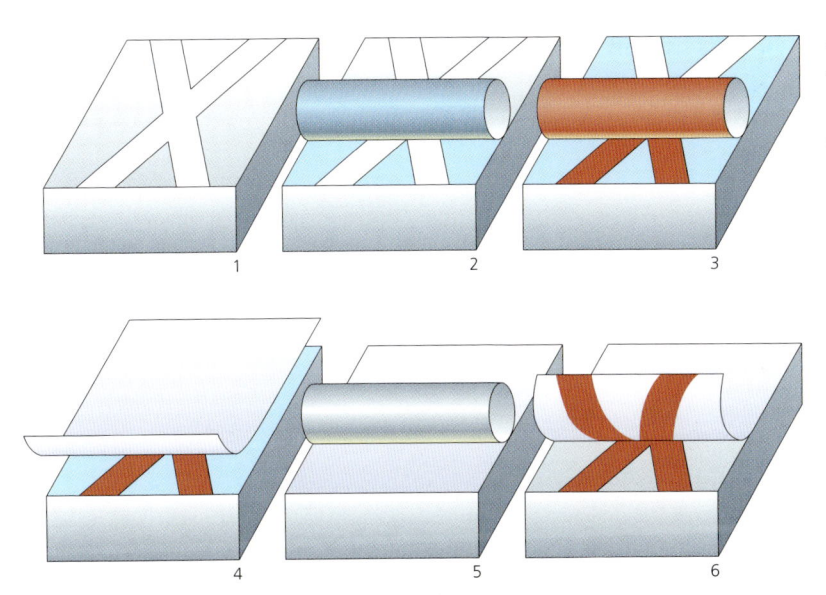

4.5 Lithography
A planographic printing process, this utilizes the principle that grease and water do not mix. The image area of the plate is treated with a greasy medium (**1**) and the plate is first dampened by rollers (**2**), then inked (**3**). The ink adheres to the greasy image but not to the dampened areas. The paper is moved into position over the plate (**4**) and then plate and paper are run through the press (**5**), producing the printed page (**6**).

4.6 Offset lithography uses the principle of planographic printing. It is called "offset" because the image is printed first on a rubber blanket and the rubber blanket then prints (offsets) it on to the paper.

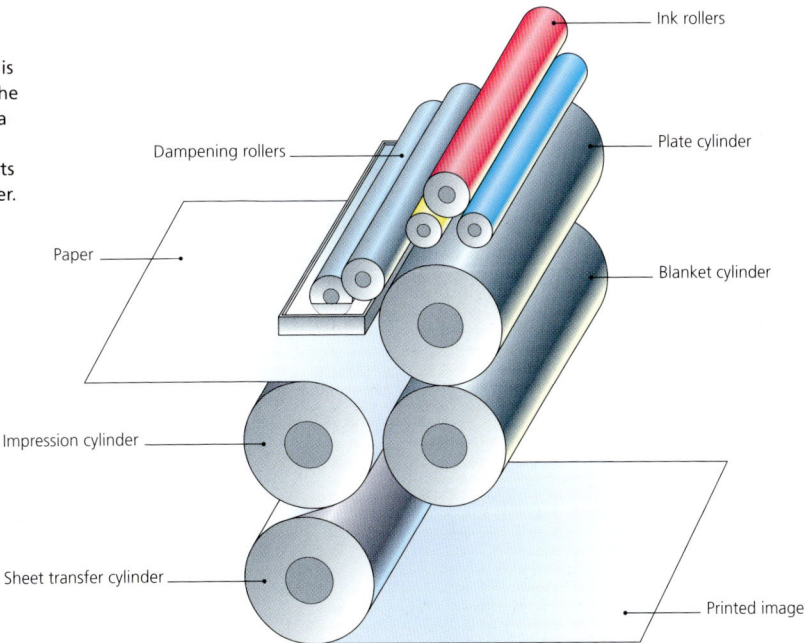

PRINTING PROCESSES

89

4.7 Small offset press
This Heidelberg Printmaster QM 46 press is sheet-fed and prints one color, on one side, on a sheet size of 11 x 17in (or European A3). It is typically used by "instant" print shops for items such as stationery, or low-cost promotional fliers.

4.8 Medium offset press
This Heidelberg CD 102 sheet-fed press prints six colors on a sheet size of 30 x 40in (or European B1) and is used for commercial work.

Sheet-fed offset

Sheet-fed offset presses range in size from small offset presses, which can print on paper up to 8½ x 11in (or European A4) size, to huge machines that can print on sheets 40 x 60in (approx. twice European A0 size) or bigger. Sheet-fed offset machines may print a single color on only one side of the sheet, or have multiple units enabling them to print up to six colors on both sides of the sheet in one pass through the press—printing both sides of the sheet is known as "perfecting."

Commercial printers will often use six-color presses to print the four process colors (cyan, magenta, yellow, and black), using the other two printing units for a fifth color (typically a Pantone color, which may be difficult to match in process) and a seal or varnish to add gloss or matt effect to the image and protect it from rubbing during finishing. Alternatively, the six printing units can be used for Hexachrome (six-color printing—also known as Hi-Fi), or to print two blacks (one for illustrations and one for text) when printing co-editions of books in more than one language (so the text can be easily replaced). Often, the presses are designed in such a way that a six-color press can, for example, either be used to print six colors on one side of the sheet, or print four colors on one side and two colors on the reverse side.

Sheet-fed presses can print from 4,000 to 15,000 sheets per hour. The range of work that can be printed using sheet-fed offset is enormous and covers most items printed with the exception of specialized work such as certain types of packaging and long runs (50,000 plus) of publications.

Presses can be categorized by grouping them into three size ranges. The first of these includes those that print on paper up to 11 x 17in (or European A3) size. Described as "small offset," these are the machines used by "instant" printers and small local printers. Work produced using small offset presses consists of business cards, stationery, short runs of business forms, leaflets, price lists, and so on. These machines are also used by "in-house" (in-plant) printers, where a large company has an internal facility for its smaller printing and photocopying requirements.

The middle category includes machines that print on paper up to 30 x 40in (or European A0) size. Most print two or more colors. They are used by medium to large commercial printers for publicity brochures, annual reports, and medium runs (5,000 to 30,000) of general color work.

The largest sheet-fed presses can print on up to 40 x 60in (approx. twice European A0 size) paper, or even larger, and are used for long runs (up to 100,000) of color work.

Some sheet-fed presses are fitted with a sheeter at the feeder end that cuts reels of paper into sheets that are then fed directly into the press. This combines the economies of buying paper in reels, with the flexibility of sheet-fed printing.

Web-fed offset presses

These offset machines, which print onto rolls (reels) rather than sheets of paper, have taken over from sheet-fed machines for many types of work. Their advantages compared with sheet-fed machines, as discussed earlier (see p. 84), account for their growing use.

Most web-offset presses are "blanket-to-blanket"—that is, the web of paper runs between two blanket cylinders, so that both sides are printed simultaneously; each blanket cylinder thereby acts as an impression cylinder for the other (see diagram, page 93). Speeds range from 15,000 to 50,000 or more impressions per hour and most print four colors on both sides of the paper. A commonly used size of web-offset press will print 16 pages of 8½ x 11in (or European A4) size at once.

Web-offset machines include the specialized bookwork presses that print 32, 48, 64, or 96 pages in black only—in fact, most straightforward black-and-white books, such as novels, are now printed using this type of machine. Unlike most color web-offset machines, they have short make-ready times and can be economical for short (e.g. 500) runs.

Web-offset machines fold the paper as they print, and color work will usually require drying to prevent smudging. This is achieved by passing the web through a heated tunnel after printing and before folding. Methods of drying include gas-flame, hot air, ultraviolet, and infrared radiation.

Although web-offset printing is carried out at high speeds, the quality can be as good as that of sheet-fed, because of the sophisticated controls on the presses. In fact, where a thick film of ink is used, color web-offset machines can produce better results than sheet-fed ones because they normally include a drying facility. The percentage moisture content of the paper is important for drying, to prevent subsequent "growth," or warping of the finished job. Also, the paper mill must ensure that the paper is reeled with correct tension to avoid it breaking on the press, which is both time-consuming and expensive.

Web-offset machines are used to print magazines, vacation brochures, mail-order catalogs, books, and long-run promotional items. Most newspapers are produced on web-offset presses, enabling the use of color on every page, rather than on just a few pages. However, flexography (see p. 110) is gaining an increasing share of newspaper work.

Press controls

Modern sheet- and web-offset machines have sophisticated electronic controls to adjust and maintain color and register and reduce make-ready times, as well as automatic plate loading. Although the capital cost of the machines is thereby increased, the outlay is soon recovered, as the press will spend more of its time printing and less being made ready. These controls also allow better and more consistent quality. ICC (International Color Consortium) color management is an international standard for measuring color at all stages in the prepress and printing processes. It works by having an ICC profile for all the devices in the workflow, enabling optimum color reproduction to be achieved by the prepress devices that have been calibrated to the press being used. This should mean that the colors seen on a monitor or digital proof are matched at the printing stage. On the printing press, CIP4 is a standard used to ensure that the colors printed match the original files. The software does this by scanning the printing plate and automatically setting the ink keys on the press to give the correct color. Once the job is running, it continuously checks the ink levels and makes adjustments as required to maintain consistency of color throughout the run. Electronic controls also check the register (the correct positioning of all the colors being printed).

The result is a "closed loop" system, meaning that once set up, the electronic controls monitor color and register and ensure there is no variation from first sheet to last. The settings are recorded and can be loaded quickly for reprints.

4.9 Timson T48 web-offset press for book printing
It produces 96 pages at a time, folds, and runs at about 18,000 impressions an hour.

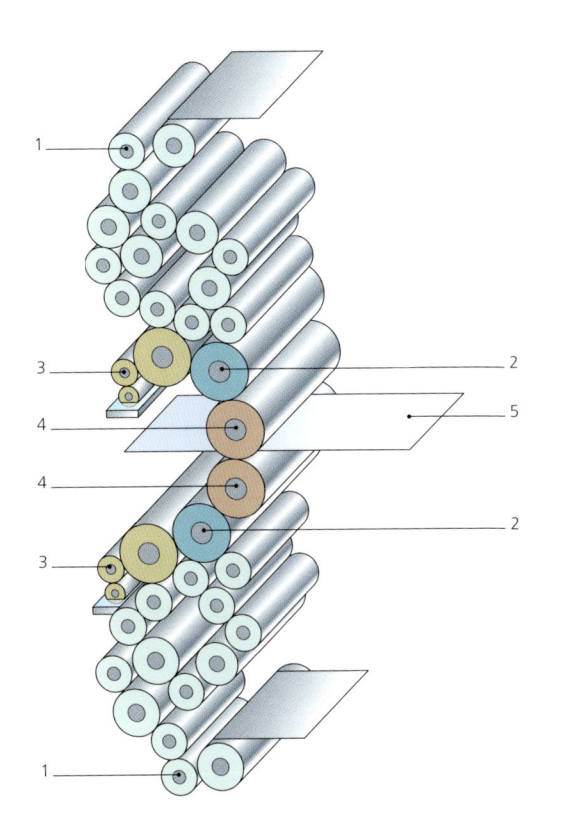

4.10 Blanket-to-blanket printing
The sheet or web of paper is printed on both sides simultaneously–blanket cylinders act as impression cylinders to each other. The ink is transferred by a bank of inking rollers (**1**) on to the plate cylinder (**2**). The plate cylinder is kept damp by dampening rollers (**3**). The image area is printed on to the blanket cylinder (**4**), which in turn transfers (offsets) the image on to the paper (**5**). The same sequence takes place on the underside of the paper so that both sides of the paper are printed in one pass through the machine.

4.11 Web-offset press
This KBA Compacta 215 web-fed press prints four colors at high speed and folds on press. It is used for magazines and long-run promotional printing.

PRINTING PROCESSES

93

Waterless offset printing

This is a version of the offset process in which no damping is required. The non-image area of the plate consists of silicone rubber and repels ink, without requiring the use of water. The advantages are that there is less waste on start-up as much of this in the offset process is caused by the need to get the ink/water balance correct. There is low dot gain, and the process is more environmentally friendly as it doesn't require the use and disposal of the chemicals in the damping solution. However, in the absence of water, the ink rollers have to be temperature controlled to keep the ink cool enough, so the press has to be adapted and special inks are required. It is expected that the use of waterless offset will grow as the technique is developed and its environmental advantages become appreciated.

Direct imaging

This is a hybrid process with elements of both offset printing and digital printing. Here, blank waterless plate material is stored on the press and each color is directly imaged onto the plate material from the

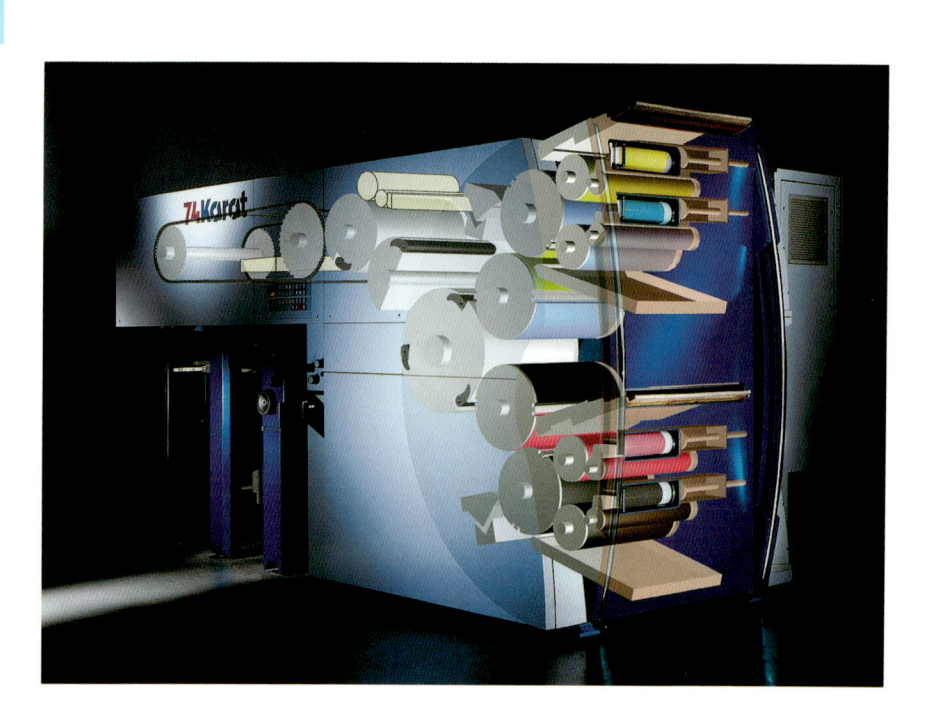

4.12 Direct imaging offset press
On this KBA Karat 46 press, the waterless plates are imaged on the press itself. This press is designed for quick make-readies and short runs.

digital file. Unlike digital printing, the process does not allow the printing of variable data, as once the plate is imaged on press, it is used for the whole run. This system is economical for longer runs than digital printing and shorter runs than conventional offset, so finds a niche for runs of 500—1,000. It therefore lends itself to use in "instant print" shops and in-house printing. Heidelberg, previously the leading manufacturer of direct imaging presses has discontinued making them, but other DI presses such as the KBA Karat continue to be made.

Offset characteristics

As the image is laid on the paper rather than pressed into it by a raised surface, there is little "squash," or a thickening spread of the type or of the image. Even on soft, fibrous papers, fine detail can be maintained as the rubber blanket responds to the surface better than non-offset processes. In the past, offset blacks tended toward an appearance of grayness because of being diluted by the water, but modern inks have largely overcome this problem.

SUMMARY OF OFFSET LITHOGRAPHY

Advantages
- Good reproduction of detail and photographs
- Cheap printing surface
- Fast make-ready
- Rubber blanket enables the use of a wide range of papers

Disadvantages
- Color variation due to problems with ink/water balance
- Dampening can cause paper-stretch or warping after binding
- Dense ink coverage difficult to achieve
- Fixed cut-off of web-offset restricts available sizes.

Advantages and disadvantages

Most of the disadvantages of the offset process originate from the use of water for dampening. This factor makes it difficult to maintain the color balance throughout the run, although modern press controls are coping with this more and more efficiently. Moreover, some water from the dampening system comes into contact with the paper and can make it stretch, causing register problems. Offset inks are tacky and can cause a problem known as "picking," where the fibers are lifted off the surface of the paper, leaving holes in the image. It is important when printing high-quality color to monitor the atmospheric conditions of the press-room and, in many print companies, press-rooms are air-conditioned and humidity controlled; this is desirable to maintain the correct moisture content of the paper and helps to ensure good register. The advantages of the process include the faithful reproduction of detail and the ability to print fine-screen halftones. The rubber blanket accommodates most paper surfaces.

The predominance this process has enjoyed in recent years is under threat at shorter runs from digital printing, where developments will make digital competitive at runs of thousands rather than hundreds and allow customized variable data printing, and also at long runs from web-fed gravure, where economical runs for magazines and catalogs are coming down from 300,000 to 150,000.

PRINTING PROCESSES

Digital printing

This method of printing is ideal for shorter runs of color and black-and-white work. Unlike most of the other printing processes, it does not require film or a plate to be made. Instead, it takes a file (PDF, PostScript, or other suitable file) and transfers the image digitally to the printing device.

Dispensing with the printing plate reduces the start-up cost, although the cost per copy is higher as paper and the special ink/toners generally cost more than for offset litho—a few digital presses are now starting to use ink rather than toners. As there is no printing plate, data (such as the recipient's name and address) can be changed from one impression to the next. This can be done in color rather than just in black and means that the recipient can receive a truly "personalized" product with type and pictures different from all the others in the run. Sophisticated software enables digital presses to run from databases of customer details and preferences, which could result, conceivably, in a magazine containing adverts for products known to be of interest to the recipient.

Digital printing has also enabled both ultra-short run reprinting and "print on demand" (P.O.D.). An example is found in book publishing: printing by offset litho needs a minimum run of around 500 in order to be economical, but this could result in the additional cost of the stock being held in the publisher's inventory for many years or the book becoming out of date. Digital printing means that publishers can print as few as one copy economically and—as it can be done quickly—the books can be printed when there are customer orders, rather than being printed beforehand and held in stock.

Digital printing quality can be slightly inferior to offset, particularly when the job has large areas of flat tints or solid colors. However, digital printing is still a developing technology and we can expect that quality standards will soon match those of offset litho for both black and four-color work. The widespread use of digital printing will continue to grow dramatically as presses and consumables become cheaper and quality improves. Digital press manufacturers believe that the break-even point with offset will eventually increase from 500 to 3,000. As we will see, there are two main methods of digital printing.

4.14 Digital press
An example of a digital press, which prints four colors on one side of the sheet direct from file.

PRINTING PROCESSES

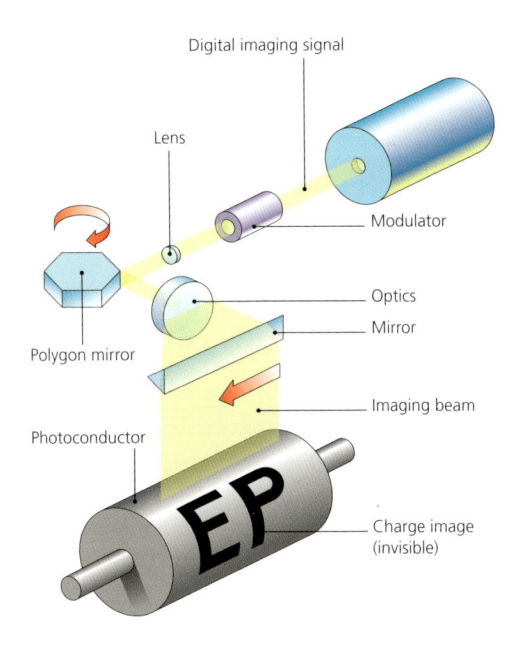

Laser printing

Under this heading, there are several methods of transferring the image from the digital file to the printing surface. The most common is electrophotography or xerography, most closely associated with Xerox, the photocopier and digital technology company manufacturer who developed the process commercially. It works by using the physics of electrostatics: particles of matter that are charged negatively and positively are attracted to their opposites. A photoconductive surface (e.g. a drum or belt) is given a positive charge of static electricity; in photocopying, a lens projects the image to be printed on to the surface; the positive charge remains where no light falls (i.e. in the image areas), but is removed from the non-printing areas by means of the light reflected from them. In working from a digital file, the same principles apply, but the image is created by a laser exposing the photoconductive surface point by point.

The surface is then dusted with negatively charged toner, which sticks only to the positively charged areas. This toner is then fused by heat to the paper. Although a laser is the most common method, the surface can also be imaged with an LED (light-emitting diode), LCD (liquid crystal), EBI (electronic beam imaging), or other device. Some systems (e.g. Indigo) use liquid ink rather than toner.

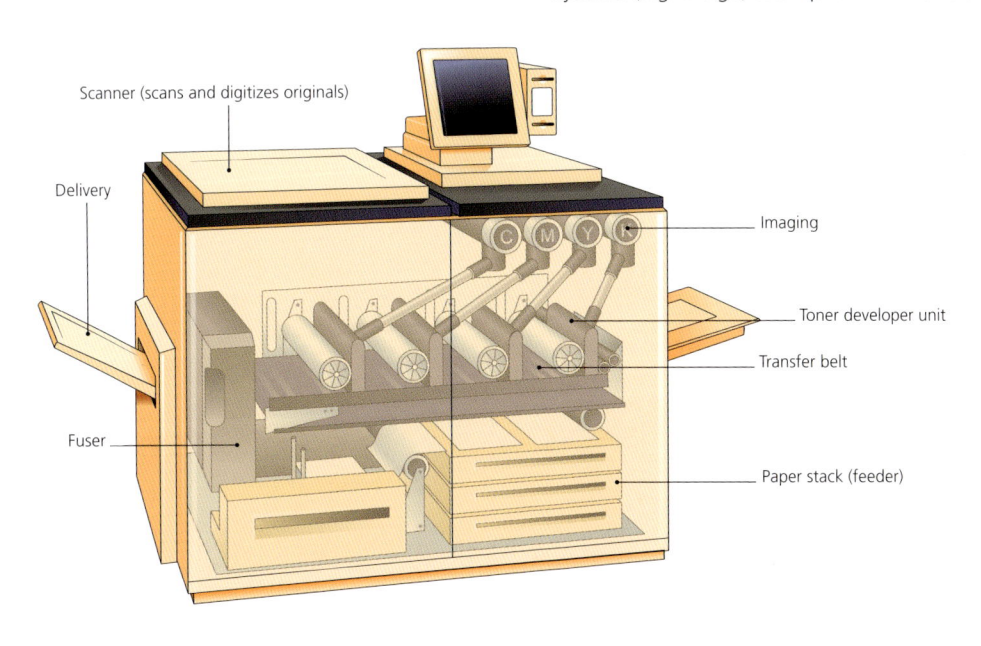

4.13 Laser imaging system for electrophotography
A photoconductive drum is given a positive charge of static electricity; the digital image is projected onto the drum's surface; the positive charge remains in the image areas, but is removed from the non-printing areas by means of the light reflected from them.

PRINTING PROCESSES

Magnetography

This is another process used for digital printing (e.g. as on the Nipson press). Here, the printing drum has a magnetic coating. The image is created on the drum by energizing tiny electromagnets and is then developed by exposure to magnetic toner particles before being transferred to the paper.

Some systems print one color on one side of the paper per printing unit, requiring four printing units to print in color on one side of the sheets, whereas other systems create a four-color image on a blanket by reimaging the drum and applying each color in turn. Many systems are equipped with on-line finishing equipment to collate and staple.

Makes of digital presses include Xerox's Docutech, Docucolor, iGen, and Nuvera presses; Xeikon, Canon, Kodak Nexpress, Konica Minolta, Océ, Delphax, HP Indigo, Nipson, and IBM.

Ink-jet printing

Ink-jet heads deposit droplets of ink on paper, in response to instructions from the digital file for the job. The image is produced by means of a dot matrix that creates the letter or graphic image. Ink-jet printing presses can produce large or very large format jobs such as posters; where paper is on a roll (reel) the job can be printed to any length. Larger flatbed ink-jet presses can print on rigid plastic, metal, or wood for large display pieces. It is a rapidly growing process and its growth is coming at the expense of screen printing, because of the lower start-up cost of ink-jet, due to its ability to print direct from a digital file.

4.15 Kodak NexPress 2500 digital press
Prints four colors to a high-quality standard.

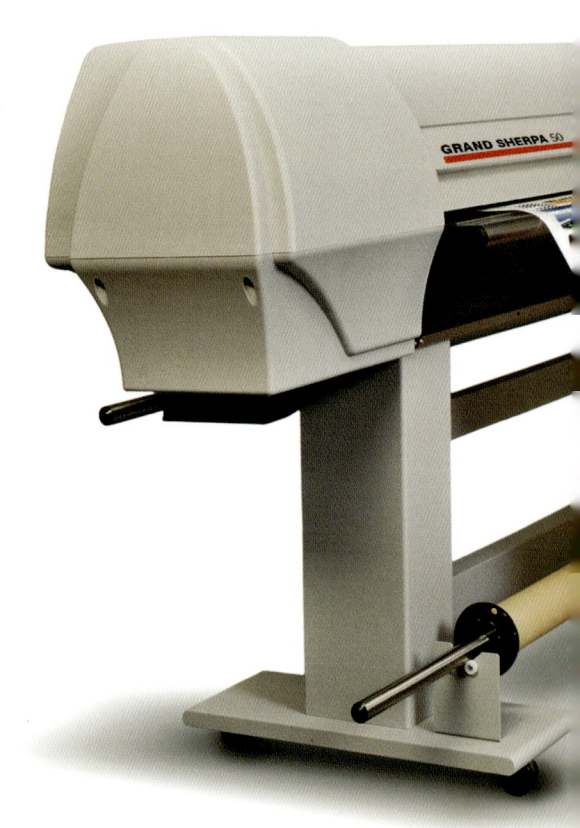

SUMMARY OF DIGITAL PRINTING

Advantages
- Economical for short runs (500 or less)
- Enables personalization of data
- No film or plate cost
- Shorter lead time
- Large formats possible with ink-jet printing

Disadvantages
- Quality on earlier machines was inferior to offset, but the latest presses can match offset quality
- Consumables (toner/paper) more costly than offset
- Slower press speed
- Currently only available for smaller sheet and reel sizes (although large format ink-jet presses can print posters and display material)
- Most presses won't print special colors

PRINTING PROCESSES

4.16 Large format ink-jet press
This Agfa Grand Sherpa 50 prints on a continuous reel of paper or plastic for large posters, signs and point-of-sale material

Gravure

Before the modern version of gravure was invented, the basic principles had long been applied: pictures were engraved on plates and printed on flat-bed presses. The introduction of photographic, and now digital, methods of preparing the plates and cylinders has enabled the development of the modern gravure process—photogravure or rotogravure—where the printing surface is produced from film or directly from a digital file, rather than engraved by hand.

The process

Gravure is an "intaglio" process; that is, the printing image is recessed into the plate or cylinder, rather than being flat, as in lithography, or raised, as in letterpress. The image consists of cells engraved into a copper-plated plate or cylinder (for a description of how these are made, see p. 82). On the gravure press these cells are filled with liquid ink. The cells vary in depth, so that they will leave the required amount of ink on the various parts of the printed image. A blade called a "doctor blade" is scraped across the surface of the plate or cylinder to remove any excess ink. The paper is fed through the press on a rubber-covered cylinder that presses the paper into the recessed cells to pick up the drops of ink that form the image.

The ink is very thin and, being spirit-based, dries through evaporation in a heated drying tunnel immediately after printing. The process, therefore, unlike web-offset, does not need elaborate drying arrangements (although gravure presses do need equipment to extract the solvent fumes). This problem is now being addressed by the use of water-based inks.

The gravure press

Most gravure printing is done with web-fed machines, which, as in other web-fed processes, use reels of paper and fold the printed paper. The machines are usually very large, printing up to 128 pages of 8½ x 11in (or European A4) size and running at speeds of 50,000 impressions or more per hour. As printing is from a cylinder rather than a plate (with a gap where the plate is clamped, as in web-offset), it means that the cut-off length is not fixed, enabling different sizes to be produced on the same press. As with web-offset, the machines have sophisticated electronic controls for register and color. There are now very few sheet-fed gravure presses and these are mainly used for security work.

Uses of gravure

Web-fed gravure predominates where runs are very long (300,000 copies or more), such as weekly magazines, mail-order catalogs, and color supplements. However, it is predicted that economic runs will soon come down to 150,000 copies, opening up the possibility of gravure being used in place of web-offset on an increased number of magazine titles. Gravure is also used for some kinds of packaging, printing on cellophane, decorative laminates and wallpaper (where these are not printed by flexography).

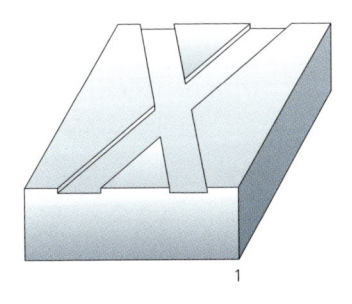

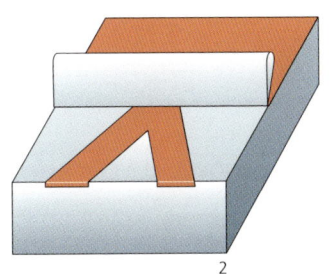

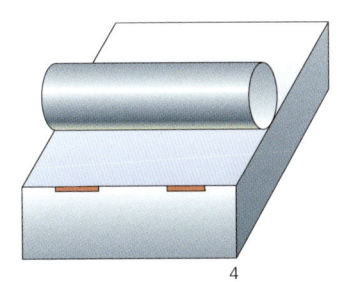

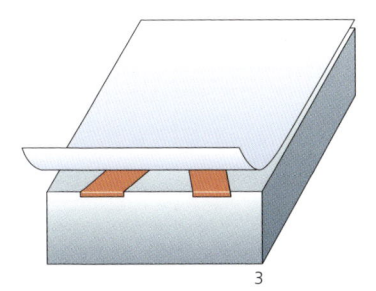

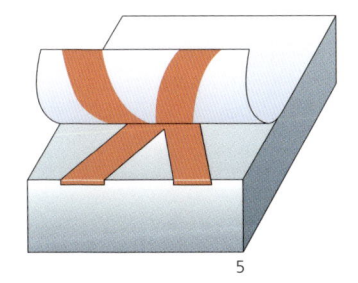

4.17 Gravure
This is an intaglio process. This means that the image to be printed has to be etched or incised into the printing cylinder (**1**). Ink is applied by a roller and a thin, flexible steel blade (a doctor blade) is drawn across the cylinder, removing excess ink from the non-printing areas (**2**). The paper is then positioned over the cylinder (**3**) and pressed against it by a rubber-coated roller (**4**). The pressure forces the paper into the recesses of the cylinder so that it picks up the ink, thus forming the image. The finished print is then removed (**5**).

4.18 Web-fed gravure press
used for long runs, printing at high speeds. They are often used for the printing of packaging and magazines. Four or five units can be used together to print in color.

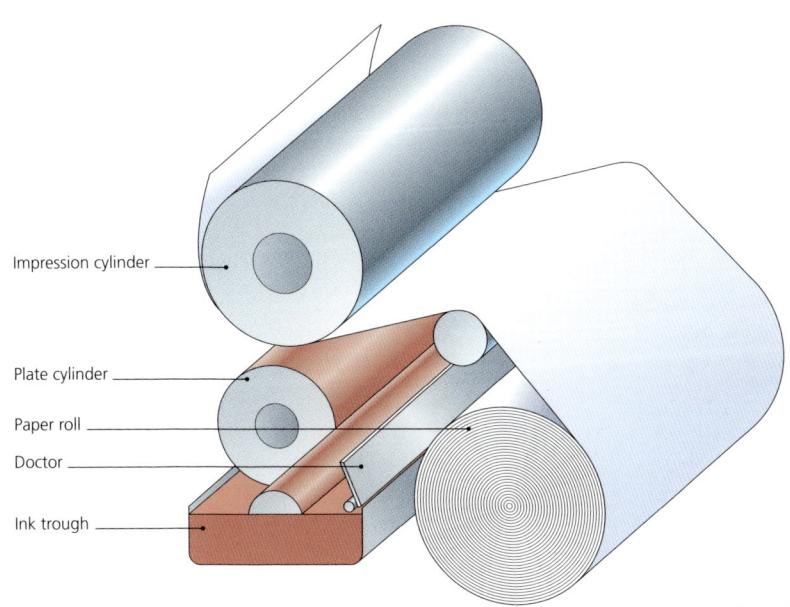

Impression cylinder
Plate cylinder
Paper roll
Doctor
Ink trough

PRINTING PROCESSES

101

PRINTING PROCESSES

4.19 Gravure press
This KBA TR 10B press is used for multi-color printing of magazines and mail-order catalogs.

Characteristics of gravure

Because of gravure's cell structure, type can look fuzzy close up, as the cell walls break up the fine detail. The reason for this is that every item on a gravure plate or cylinder is screened, including the type. However, gravure printing of photographs is often superior to that produced by other processes, as gravure gives a "true" halftone effect: the darker areas of the photograph actually carry more ink as they are printed from the deeper cells. Also, photographs printed by gravure have greater contrast between light and dark areas, as a heavy layer of ink is carried. They have good detail (unlike the type) as finer screens are used than with other processes. These qualities are evident even on cheaper papers.

Advantages and disadvantages

The main disadvantage of gravure printing is the very high prepress cost of plates and cylinders. Modern digital engraving techniques are bringing this cost down through automation of the process, but the cylinders are still many times the cost of offset plates. This is why gravure is used only for long runs; the high cost of start-up has to be recovered over a large number of copies.

One of the advantages of the process is its relative simplicity – compared to offset lithography, for example—after the printing surface has been made. There is no problem of ink/water balance, so maintenance of consistent color throughout the run is not as difficult. Presses can run at very high speeds (50,000 impressions or more per hour), and drying is straightforward.

Gravure permits fine-screen work on papers for which offset lithography would need a coarser screen. Nowadays, with paper costs accounting for an increasing proportion of the total cost of any print job, gravure's ability to print on lower-quality, lightweight paper is probably its biggest single advantage—and this also reduces mailing costs.

SUMMARY OF GRAVURE

Advantages
- Simple printing method and press mechanism
- Can maintain consistent color
- High speed
- Straightforward drying by evaporation
- Good results obtainable on cheaper paper
- No fixed cut-off (as with web-offset)

Disadvantages
- High cost of cylinders
- Viable only for long runs (150,000 +)
- Longer lead times than offset
- High cost of proofs, if press proofs needed
- High cost of corrections for reprints, as cylinder must be replaced

PRINTING PROCESSES

Screen printing

The use of stencils to apply an image goes back many centuries, but it was only at the beginning of the 20th century that this was allied to the use of a screen, giving the process its name. It is perhaps the most versatile of the printing processes.

The process
A stencil, cut by hand or made digitally or photographically (see p. 83), is supported on a screen of synthetic fibre (such as nylon or polyester), or metal. Originally, this screen was made of silk–hence the earlier name "silkscreen printing." The screen is stretched tightly over a frame of wood or metal, and ink is spread across the screen by means of a rubber squeegee that squeezes the ink through the screen in the image areas. The stencil prevents ink going through in the non-image areas.

The screen printing press
Many screen printing presses are manually operated and consist of a simple frame hinged to a flat surface. The equipment can be very cheap and, as such, it is often used by people printing at home. There are also semi-automatic presses in which, while the screen is raised and lowered and the squeegee is pulled across the screen automatically, the material to be printed has to be inserted and removed by hand.

Automatic and hand-operated machines may have vacuum bases to help them separate the paper from the screen after printing. These consist of a flat piece of plastic laminate with regularly spaced holes connected to a vacuum pump; the vacuum suction holds the paper firmly to the base. Fully automatic presses also feed and deliver the paper (or other material) automatically, and some have an impression cylinder that holds the paper while the screen moves in unison and the squeegee remains stationary. These presses can attain speeds of up to 6,000 copies per hour.

For hand-operated presses used on short runs (a few hundred or less) of items such as posters (and even t-shirts), the sheets are laid out to dry on racks. The semi-automatic and automatic machines often have drying tunnels and sometimes ultraviolet drying units.

Uses of screen printing
The fact that the process can apply a very thick film of ink onto a large sheet makes it ideal for posters. Also, virtually any type of material can be printed on, including wood, fabric, glass, plastic, and metal. Screen printing is therefore used for plastic and metal signs, t-shirts, CDs and DVDs, simulated-wood car dashboards and door trims, bottles, transfers and electronic circuits. It can also print on very light papers and is therefore used for printing dressmaking patterns. Ink-jet printing (see p. 98) is gaining display and point-of-sale work from screen printing, however, because of its lower start-up costs.

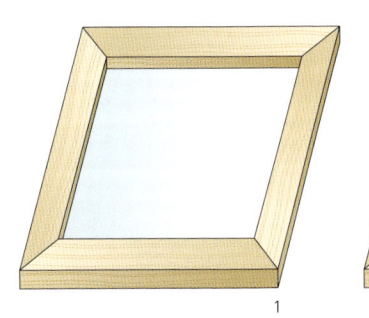

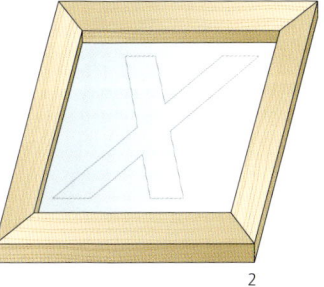

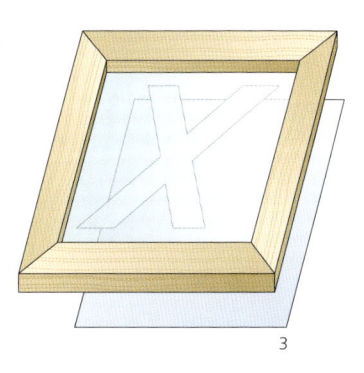

4.20 Silk screen printing in its simplest form uses a stencil. The image is cut into the screen and the printing area is peeled off. A fine gauze, stretched over a wooden border, forms the frame (**1**). The stencil is then transferred to the underside of the frame by heat and the stencil's protective backing is peeled away, masking off the non-image areas so they do not print (**2**). The paper is placed beneath the screen (**3**). Ink is applied to the top of it and spread by a squeegee (**4**). The ink passes through the screen in the areas where the stencil is cut away to produce the image (**5**). In commercial silkscreen printing, digitally produced photostencils are used.

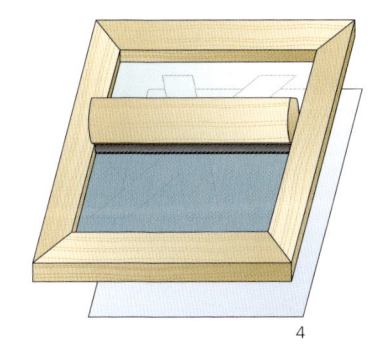

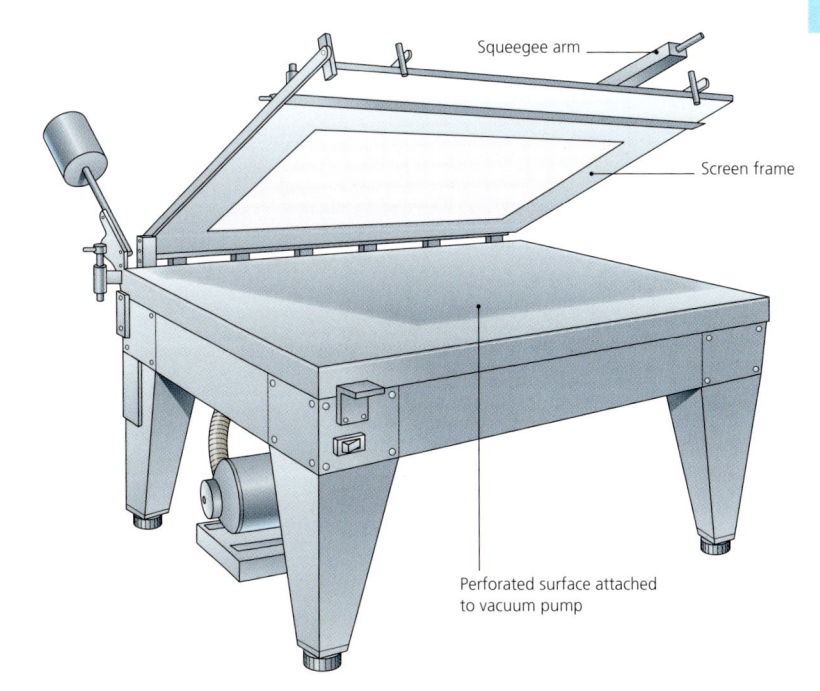

4.21 Screen printing press The paper is laid on the flat surface, which is perforated, and a vacuum holds the paper flat. The screen frame is then pulled down onto the paper and the squeegee pulled across to force ink through the mesh in the image areas of the screen onto the paper.

Squeegee arm

Screen frame

Perforated surface attached to vacuum pump

PRINTING PROCESSES

105

Advantages and disadvantages

Screen printing usually has a distinct appearance because of the thick film of ink. Although this is an advantage for most screen-printed products, it does mean that small type does not always reproduce very sharply and the fine details of photographs are difficult to reproduce to the same standard as can be achieved using other processes. The nature of the coarse screen means that halftone screens of 50 are usually the limit. Large billboards are often printed in sections by screen printing but are viewed from a distance, so that the coarse screen is not evident to the naked eye.

Because of the thick layer of ink, screen printing can even print white on black, as well as printing metallic and fluorescent colors to much better effect than other processes. Also, the stencils are cheap to produce and short runs are more economical than with other processes, with the exception of ink-jet printing. Another obvious advantage is the wide range of materials on which printing can be done.

4.22 A CD being screen printed
Some CDs, DVDs, and other similar disks can be printed onto directly by screen printing. A variety of ink-jet kits are available for labeling in the home, from low–cost, low-tech label kits, to dedicated machines that can be connected to the desktop computer like any peripheral device and print onto the disk itself.

PRINTING PROCESSES

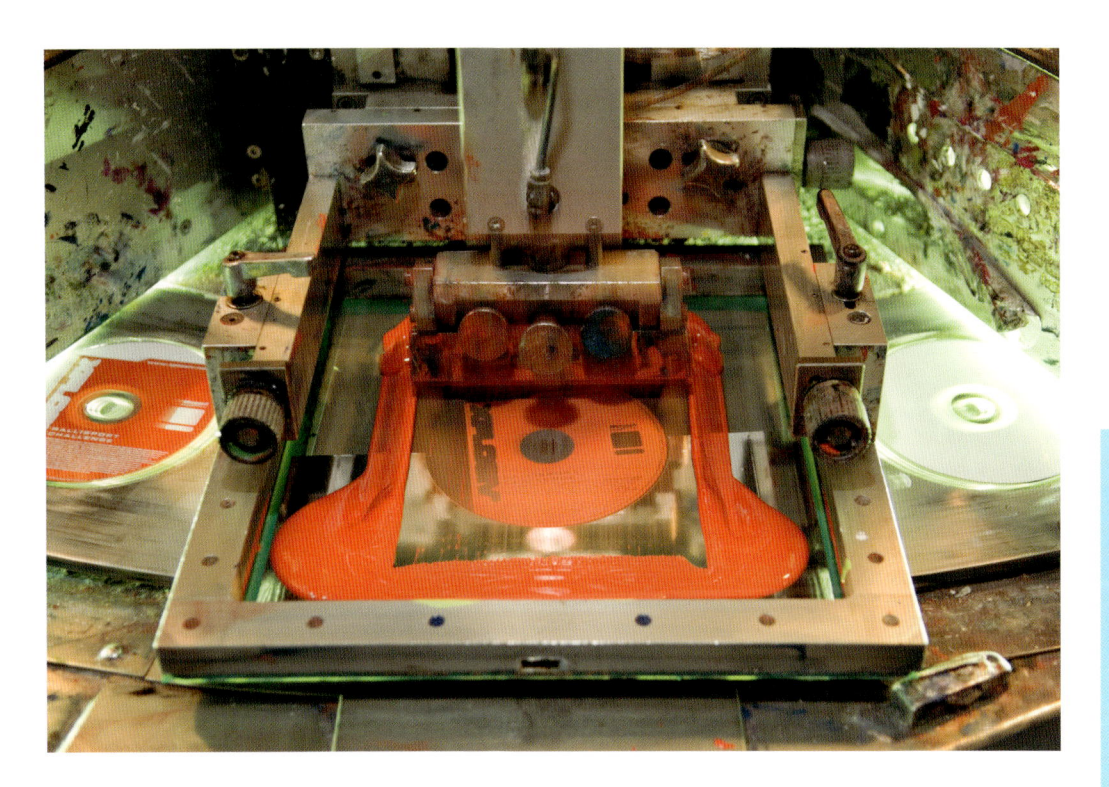

4.23 Screen-printed clothing
A lot of people are familiar with the principle of screen printing from school art classes, and from the iconic screen-printed t-shirt.

SUMMARY OF SCREEN PRINTING

Advantages
- Can print a heavy film of ink
- Economical for short runs (even below 100 copies)
- Can print on virtually any material

Disadvantages
- Difficult to achieve fine detail
- Very low screen halftones
- Low output qualities
- Drying requirements

107

Letterpress

Letterpress was the main printing process until the 1970s when it was overtaken by offset lithography and is essentially now a redundant process. It was the printing partner of hot metal typesetting, which has also disappeared from commercial use.

This is a "relief" process—that is, the printing surface holding the image to be printed is raised above the non-printing background. This raised surface is inked by rollers and then pressed against the paper to make the impression. Because the background is lower than the printing area, it comes into contact with neither the inking rollers nor the paper, and therefore does not print.

In traditional letterpress, all the text is printed from metal type and the illustrations (whether line or halftone) from letterpress cuts (blocks). These elements are assembled together to create a "forme" inside a rigid frame (chase) that is placed in the press. The printing surface, therefore, may be made up of hundreds or thousands of different pieces of type, blocks, and spacing. The various types of letterpress machines used are described in the history section of this book. Letterpress is however, still used in a very specialized way for private press limited-edition books, and short-run work such as invitations and duplicate books that can be numbered and perforated at the same time as printing. Converted letterpress machines are also used for foil stamping (blocking), embossing, die cutting, and creasing.

The Cameron belt press

Letterpress survives in book printing, although it too is being phased out in favor of web-offset presses, such as the Timson. However, there are still several installations of this press worldwide. The Cameron belt press is a version of the rotary press where flexible relief plates are mounted on two continuous belts that revolve against a web of paper. The belts vary in length depending on the number of pages in the book. The printed pages are cut and folded into four-page units, collated in order, and fed directly into a binding machine, so the process can turn reels of paper into bound paperback books, or book blocks for subsequent casing in, in one operation. However, the belt press can print in only one color, and the binding has to be unsewn. Also, it cannot print fine screen halftones.

The great advantages of belt presses are that they can produce virtually any size of book and lend themselves to short runs, down to two or three thousand copies, enabling runs to be geared closely to the demands of the market.

Letterpress characteristics

Letterpress ink is dense and gives a strong black image. When type is printed on to a soft paper the "squash" or "bite" can be seen around each character, and this adds distinction to private-press work when the right typeface is used: typefaces made up from fine lines print better on paper with a smooth surface using a lighter impression, as otherwise their fine detail is either buried in the soft paper, or flattened into a distortion of the type designer's intended look and feel for the face.

4.24 Letterpress
The image areas of the letterpress type or cuts (blocks) are raised while the non-image areas are recessed so that they do not pick up ink. The plate is (1) inked by a roller (2). Paper is placed over the inked image (3) and pressed on to the image (4) in the press by an impression cylinder, resulting in the image being printed on the paper (5).

Advantages and disadvantages

Except in the specialized areas mentioned above, letterpress has largely given way to offset lithography. The disadvantages of letterpress are the fact that modern methods of origination are mainly digital or photographic and do not lend themselves to the creation of a raised surface; the high cost of the metal type and blocks; dwindling availability; the fact that more expensive papers are required to achieve the kind of quality offset can achieve using cheaper ones; and the relatively slow speed of most letterpress machines.

The advantages of the process are the denseness of the ink (not diluted by water or spirit, as in offset or gravure) and the quality of the impression—excellent characteristics for high-quality private-press work.

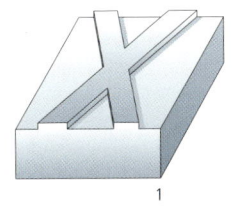

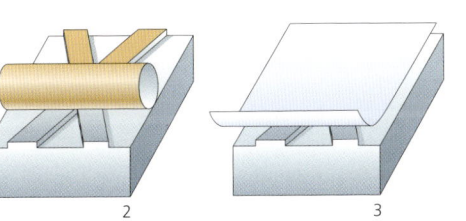

4.25, 4.26, 4.27
Letterpress printing from metal type and blocks or woodcuts is still in use at private presses. On the left is a forme of type being locked up prior to printing (Rampant Lions Press, UK) in the center is an impression being made on a Hopkinson & Cope hand press (Fleece Press, UK). The press room (right) at I.M.Imprimit, UK, showing on the left the typecases and "stone" on which the type is imposed in chases. A Harrild iron hand press is on the right in the foreground and two further Harrild presses on the left.

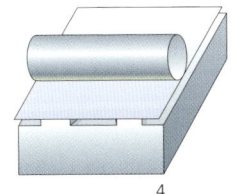

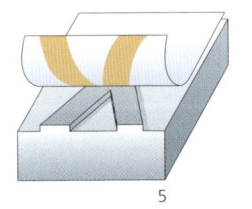

PRINTING PROCESSES

109

Other processes

Paper is not the only material onto which print is applied, and many materials and products require the use of less common and sometimes highly specialist printing processes. Here is a rundown of the main contenders.

Flexography

This process is a derivative of letterpress, using flexible photopolymer plates and thin, fluid inks (often now water- rather than spirit-based) that dry by evaporation (sometimes assisted by heat). The image is raised as in the conventional form of letterpress printing.

The flexographic press

Most flexographic printing presses are web-fed because of the nature of the products they are usually employed to print. Ink is applied to the plate by a metal roller; this roller, known as an "anilox" roller, has cells etched into it that hold the ink and transfer it onto the flexible plate for printing. Many machines are multicolor presses, for four-color work.

Uses of flexography

Flexography is used mainly for packaging—printing on cellophane, plastics, and metallic foils; in fact, it can be used to print on virtually any material that will physically pass through the press. It is used also to produce some of the cheaper magazines and comics as well as local and national newspapers. In fact a good proportion of national newspapers worldwide are printed by flexography, with its advantage of not suffering the problems of ink and water balance. As drying is by evaporation, the ink dries instantly and doesn't come off on the hands of the newspaper reader as happens with offset printing.

Advantages and disadvantages

Flexography is relatively inexpensive as the plates are cheap to make and make-ready times are short. Also, the drying part of the process is rapid and the rotary principle enables high-speed presses to be used. It can print on different materials. The disadvantages include difficulty in reproducing fine detail and a tendency to color variation.

Flexography used to be the poor relation of the other processes, but improvements in inks, presses and techniques have ensured that it can more than hold its own in areas such as packaging and newspaper printing.

Collotype

This process (also known as "photogelatin") is, like lithography, a planographic process. It has curiosity status as only a handful of printers in the world can still print by collotype. However, this process is the only one that can produce high-quality black-and-white or color continuous-tone prints without the use of a screen.

The image is carried by a film of gelatin that has been made light-sensitive by being treated with potassium or ammonium bichromate (called, confusingly, "dichromate"). The gelatin that lies in a film on a thick sheet of plate glass or a metal plate, is placed in contact with a photographic negative and exposed to light. The gelatin then hardens according to the amount of light reaching it—the harder the gelatin, the more capable it is of accepting ink.

4.28 Flexographic printing press
This inexpensive, swift process has a downside for some kinds of work in its difficulty in reproducing very fine detail.

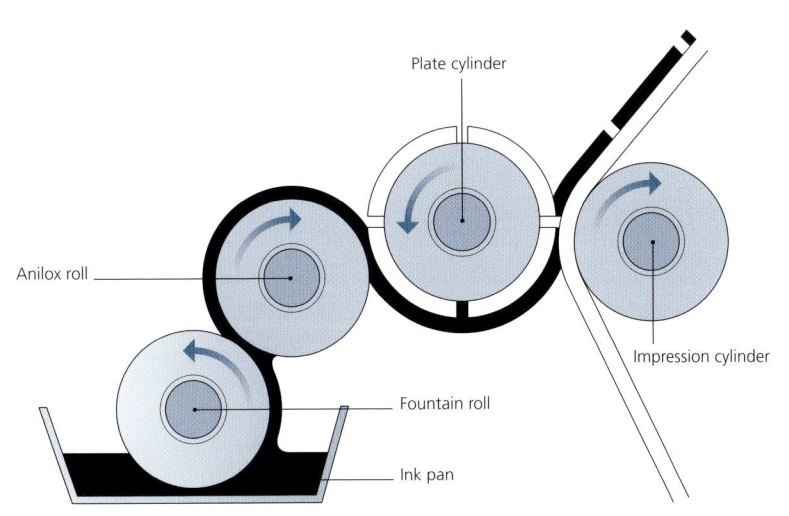

4.29 Flexography
The liquid ink is transferred to the flexible relief plates by a metal anilox roller engraved with cells, which hold the ink.

Plate cylinder
Anilox roll
Impression cylinder
Fountain roll
Ink pan

PRINTING PROCESSES

111

4.30 Engraving process
This skilled, sometimes handmade approach is often used on business cards, letterheads, and invitations where a personal touch is required.

4.31 Lenticular method
The "3-D" style effect popular in the 1970s is experiencing a strong renaissance in promotional items, retro designs, and on special-edition magazine covers—such as this issue of design magazine *Creative Review*.

As with lithography, the process depends on the principle of grease repelling water: the unexposed parts of the gelatin are kept moist with water and glycerine so that they repel the ink, while the exposed parts accept ink to a greater or lesser degree. This gives a result rather like a photograph as it can print gradations from the deepest black to the lightest tones of gray. The tone is not broken into dots, as it is with a screen.

Collotype presses are similar to direct (as opposed to offset) litho machines but run at particularly slow speeds; it may take two days to produce 2,000 sheets—the maximum that can be taken from any one plate. Nevertheless, this process can produce extremely high-quality results and is consequently sometimes used for printing small runs of fine-art reproductions. Earlier works often portrayed botanical specimens, flora, and fauna in stunning detail on very large page sizes and are now collector's items.

Duplicating

This process is used mainly in offices and schools, rather than by commercial printers, to produce circulars, forms, price lists and other items with runs of perhaps a few hundred where quality is not a paramount consideration. The process is "stencil duplicating"—in the past a waxed stencil was cut by a typewriter, but this is now imaged direct from a digital file or scanned from printed copy. This makes the paper stencil allow ink to pass through in the image areas. This process has been developed by companies such as Riso and Duplo. Quality is limited but no real skill is required to operate the equipment. As the cost of digital presses comes down, it is likely that duplicated work will increasingly go digital in the future.

Die stamping and copper engraving

These processes, like gravure, are intaglio processes. A steel or copper plate is engraved by hand or etched using digital or photographic techniques to create a recessed image. Ink is deposited in the recesses of this "female" die and a "male" die of card or plastic (previously made from the "female" die by pressure) presses the paper onto it to depositing the ink and simultaneously producing a bas-relief effect. The paper or card is raised in the image area and indented on its back.

Copper is cheaper to prepare than steel and is therefore used for shorter runs. Most of this work is done on hand presses but power-driven presses, known as die stampers, are used for runs of 1,000 or more. This technique can also be used for "blind-embossing," where a raised image is produced but no ink is used.

The process is used for high-quality business cards, letterheads, and invitations, where the glossy bas-relief effect adds distinction. Rotary versions are used also in banknote and security printing.

Thermography

In this process the image is first printed in the normal way by letterpress or offset using an adhesive ink. The ink image is then coated with a resinous (thermoplastic) powder and the surplus is shaken off (from the non-image areas). The printed sheets or card stock, are subjected to heat that fuses the thermoplastic resin with the ink to give a hard, raised image. The result is glossy and simulates the results of copper engraving, but is coarser and much cheaper. It is commonly used for invitations, business cards, and letterheads.

Lenticular printing

Optical grade plastic lenses are laminated over two printed images and give the impression of movement, or a three-dimensional or doubling effect as either the hand or eye move. These are also known as auto-stereo images. This process is enjoying an increasing use, particularly in promotional printing.

PRINTING PROCESSES

113

History of paper

Paper and ink are the two main raw materials used in the printing process. Both have been continually refined and improved by succeeding generations. So many combinations of ink, paper, and process are now available that it is increasingly important for the printer and client to make the right choices.

Paper

Nearly all printing is done on paper. It forms a major part of the cost of most printed items—sometimes more than half of the total cost. The making of paper has important impacts on the environment: the sustainability of the wood and other raw materials used; the heavy energy and land resource demands made by the paper-making process; the disposal, or neutralizing, of pollutants, and the disposal and recycling of paper after use.

History of paper

The ancient Egyptians wrote on papyrus, woven from plants of the same name and the word paper is derived from this. Papyrus started being used around 3,000 BCE. In Europe, writing was done on vellum or parchment made from processed calfskin or sheepskin (as papyrus doesn't grow in colder northern climates). China used bamboo or silk. All these materials were expensive and this restricted the growth of written communication.

A method of papermaking, using cotton rags as the raw material, was developed in China and was first described (by a Chinese official Tsai Lun) in 105 CE, although it is thought that it had been in use for 200 years or so before that. The process was slow to spread to other countries, not reaching Spain, for example, until the 12th century and Italy until the 13th century. England's first paper mill was established in 1490 and America's in 1690. Even though paper was much cheaper than the writing materials that preceded it, the fact that it was made by hand rather than machine still made it a costly product and this only changed in the 19th century with the invention of paper making machines driven by steam, using fibers derived from wood pulp. In France, Nicholas Louis Robert patented the first paper making machine in 1798 and the Fourdrinier brothers then developed this in England. Modern paper-making machines use the same basic technology as the Fourdrinier machine.

The introduction of paper made from a cheap and available raw material (wood) on mass production machinery had a real impact and resulted in an explosion of written and printed communication, enabling books, newspapers, and stationery to be available to the many, not just the few. The 19th century also saw developments in printing, such as the rotary printing press and machine-based typesetting that helped enable this dramatic increase in the availability of printed items.

5.1 Papyrus
A sheet of richly textured, handmade Egyptian papyrus paper.

PAPER AND INK

How paper is made

Papermaking is one of the oldest techniques known to mankind, but today it is approached with a commitment to sustainability and environmental protection and renewal. The ways in which this material is made have a significant impact on the end result of all your hard work.

Pulp

Paper basically consists of vegetable (cellulose) fibers with various additives to control the physical characteristics, printability and esthetics of the finished product. The choice of fiber is important. High-quality papers—some still being made by hand—might utilize cotton, linen, or hemp fibers—all of which are high strength yielding and very durable materials. These raw materials give strength and stiffness. Straw, bamboo, and esparto grass are other materials used to produce fibers, some of which, due to their shape and lack of flexibility, yield a weaker paper but one with even texture, softness, elasticity, good opacity, and bulk. Quality book papers were usually made from esparto, but this has now been replaced by the bulky hardwood, eucalyptus. Most paper (more than 90%) is now made from wood pulp, largely from softwood coniferous trees such as spruce or pine.

Chemical pulping

The object of all chemical pulping is to dissolve the sticky, resinous lignin and other glutinous materials so that the fiber within the wood can be extracted. After the initial debarking, wood is cut into small chips (⅝ x ½in [16 x 3mm]) and these are then cooked at a high temperature and pressure using a variety of pulping liquors depending on the source of the wood and the process available. Caustic soda and sodium sulfide have formed the basis of the "kraft" pulping process since the late 1800s whereas sulfite pulping technology relies principally on the use of sodium, calcium, or magnesium sulfite, and sulfurous acid for pulping, and is often used for woods with a low resin content. The extracted fibers are washed and bleached before being further processed.

Mechanical pulping

Mechanical or groundwood pulps are different from chemical pulps. Chemical pulps are essentially separated, whole cellulose wood fibers from which the lignin and other bonding material has been removed. The fiber length of these pulps is the full fiber length of the source from which the pulp is made. In the mechanical pulping process, bundles of fibers are torn from the debarked pulping log and therefore contain a mixture of whole fibers, broken fibers, lignin, and various other wood gums. The groundwood pulp, made into paper is soft, bulky, absorbent, and opaque, but it is weak and will deteriorate, become brittle, and discolor over time—especially if it is exposed to sunlight, as the lignin gradually decays.

Papers for different uses need to have different properties and the properties of groundwood are desirable in many grades where permanence is not essential. Among these grades are newsprint, tissue, toweling, wallpaper, and some printing paper, both coated and uncoated.

Other processes exist that combine both mechanical and chemical pulping technology. These processes are covered by the general terms, semi-chemical or chemi-wood.

5.2 A Swedish pine forest
For every tree felled for paper making, three new trees will be planted.

5.3 The Arctic Paper Munkedals mill, Sweden

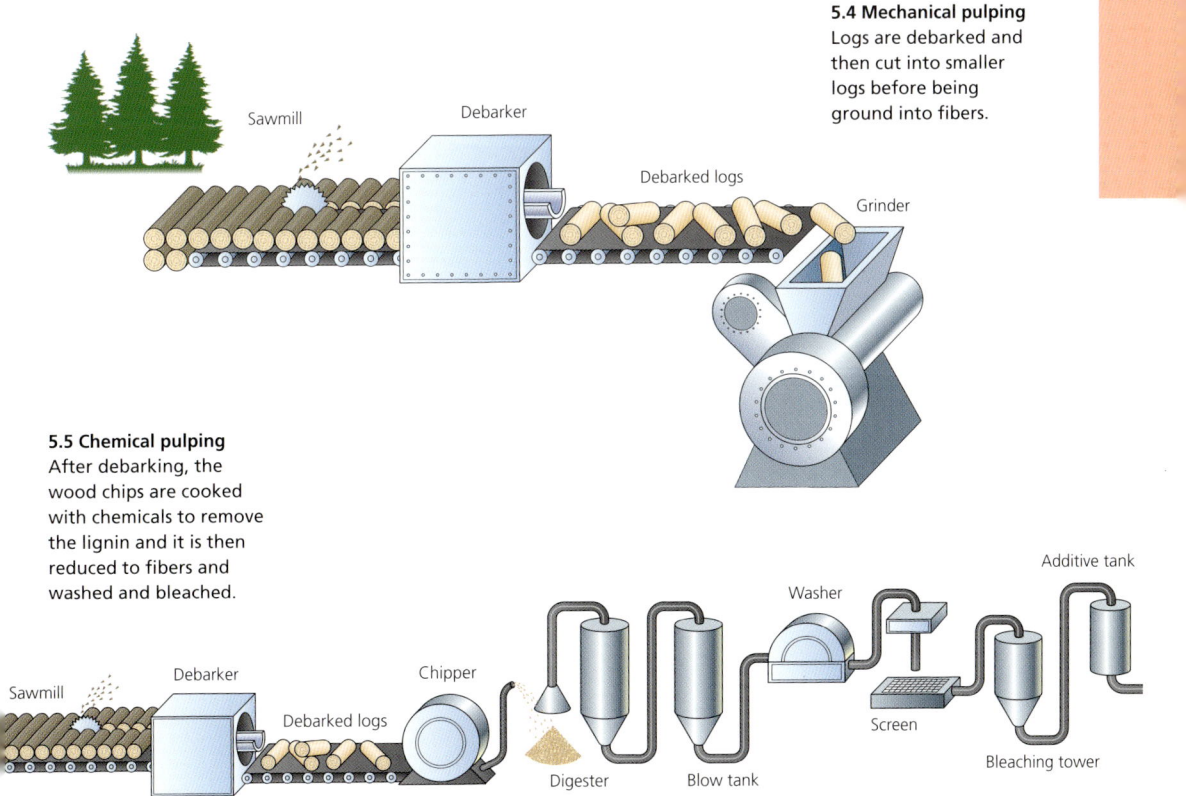

PAPER AND INK

5.4 Mechanical pulping
Logs are debarked and then cut into smaller logs before being ground into fibers.

Sawmill Debarker Debarked logs Grinder

5.5 Chemical pulping
After debarking, the wood chips are cooked with chemicals to remove the lignin and it is then reduced to fibers and washed and bleached.

Sawmill Debarker Debarked logs Chipper Digester Blow tank Washer Screen Additive tank Bleaching tower

117

5.6 Wastepaper being sorted prior to recycling
Recycling is a simple procedure, but relies on people's commitment to ensuring that paper is put back into the production chain rather than simply thrown away.

Recycled paper

Recycled paper contains a percentage of fibers made from either post-consumer waste (wastepaper) or pre-consumer waste (cleaner paper waste, known as "broke," from printers or the paper mill itself). Environmental and economic pressures have resulted in a big increase in the amount of recycled paper produced in recent years, and we can expect recycled to take an increasing share of paper made in future. The environmental advantages are that wastepaper is reused, rather than disposed of in landfill sites or incinerators; using wastepaper obviously reduces the number of trees used in papermaking, and also uses less energy and far less water than when pulping trees.

Both the USA and the UK now obtain a large proportion of their fibers from pre-consumer and post-consumer wastepaper. In the USA, a third of all fibers used comes from wastepaper and nearly half of all wastepaper is recycled. In the UK, two thirds of all fibers used in papermaking come from wastepaper. Traditional paper manufacturing countries, such as those in Scandinavia, recycle far less paper, as their smaller populations create less waste and they have sustainable forests.

To make pulp from wastepaper, it is dissolved in water and then cleaned and de-inked. It can then be bleached to yield a whiter-resulting paper. The fibers can then be mixed with fibers from trees or used on their own for 100% recycled paper. When virgin pulp is added, this is done to add both strength and whiteness—the fibers from wastepaper are shorter than virgin fibers and untreated paper with a high percentage of recycled content can appear both limp and gray, due to the ink from previous use.

Newsprint, as used for newspapers, is often 100% recycled—paper with less than 100% recycled content can be used for most printed products, but paper with a high percentage of recycled content will not be bright white and uncoated paper can be more absorbent than paper made from virgin fiber. Care is thus needed in printing to allow for these differences, but recycled papers are improving all the time and demand for them is helped by companies and organizations specifying them, in order to meet environmental targets and legislation. Often, the printed product will carry wording stating that it is printed on recycled paper.

Handmade paper

Small amounts of paper are still made by hand for prestigious applications such as letterheads, limited-edition books, and artists' paper, where completely random orientation of fibers is important, particularly for watercolor paintings.

The process is very slow and expensive, as each sheet has to be hand-produced. Pulp (normally made from cotton rag) is fed into a small vat fitted with an agitator. A mold of fine mesh wire surrounded by a frame (deckle) is dipped into the vat. The paper maker withdraws the mold gently shaking the frame as water drains away leaving the fibrous mat to be extracted and dried on felt sheets by pressure and hanging in a warm atmosphere.

Usually, the deckle edges are left uncut and the paper has a watermark. This is created by raised areas on the wire mesh screen that create a translucent area in the paper. Similarly raised horizontal and vertical lines create the effect for "laid" paper.

Mold-made paper

This is a high quality grade of paper usually made from cotton rag pulp on a cylinder mold machine, rather than a Fourdrinier machine.

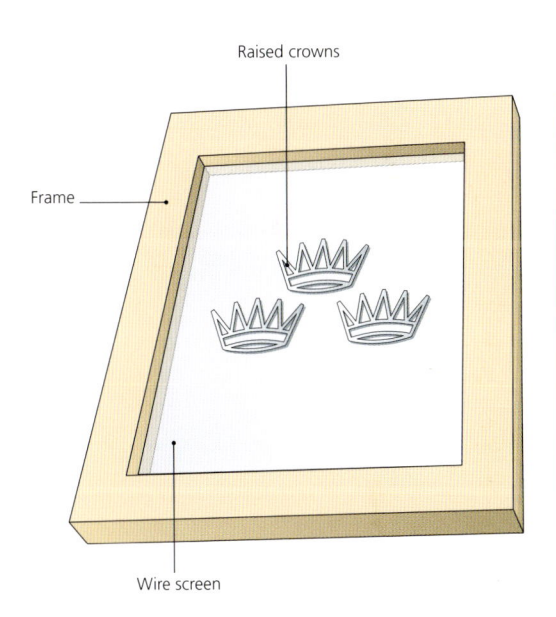

5.7 A mold used for making paper by hand
The mold is dipped into a vat containing the pulp. The frame is then shaken to drain off the water, leaving the fibers in the mold. The watermark is raised and creates a translucent area in the paper.

PAPER AND INK

119

Pulp processing

The characteristics of a paper can vary greatly, not only as a result of the choice of pulp, but also in the way in which the fiber is processed to make the paper. An average fiber is 0.1378in (3.5mm) in length and around 1.4 thousandths of an inch (30/40 microns) in diameter. Each fiber has smooth sides and is fairly rigid.

Where the paper mill makes the pulp and paper on the same site (an integrated mill), the pulp is kept in liquid form and fed to the stock preparation area of the paper mill. Where the pulp and paper are made at separate mills, the pulp is dried and supplied as sheets in bales to the paper mill. In this case, on arrival at the paper mill, the breaking process uses a hydrapulper or slusher to convert the pulp back to liquid form. The slusher is a large circular metal tank where the pulp sheets are dispersed in water using blades to break them up.

The pulp must then be rendered in such a form that it can be manufactured into paper that exhibits desired properties. To achieve this, the absorbency, strength, or plasticity characteristics of the individual fiber may have to be increased. This is achieved by a process referred to as "beating" or "refining." A refiner consists of a bladed cone rotating in an outer shell between which the fibrous suspension is passed. By controlling the consistency of the fiber suspension, the speed with which it passes through the refiner and the pressure of the cone within that shell, it is possible by a process of fiber rubbing, bruising, crushing, cutting, plasticizing, and fibrillation to render the fibers suitable for the manufacture of a wide variety of papers. This is a key process in the paper-making cycle. It can control strength characteristics, sheet density, tensile strength, tear resistance, folding characteristics, sheet formation, opacity, dimensional stability, porosity, and oil resistance.

Prior to refining, or immediately afterward, certain additives may be mixed into the fiber furnish. These might include titanium dioxide, clay, or calcium carbonate to control opacity, whiteness, smoothness, and other characteristics; bleaching agents to develop brightness; sizing to control oil and water absorbency; anti-foaming agents, and sheet-formation aids. The pulp is normally refined at a consistency of about 2–3% before being further diluted and fed to the machine chests, to which coloring pigments or dyes may be added.

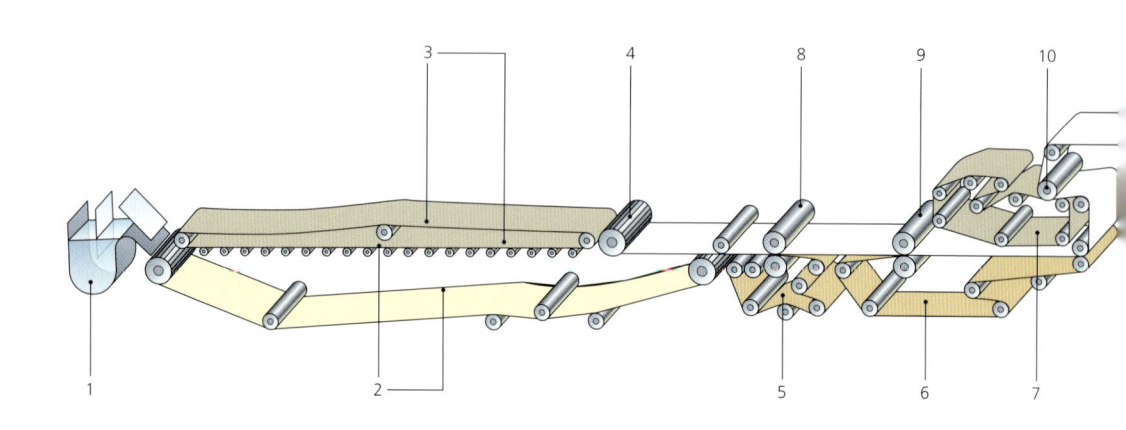

5.8 Baled sheets of pulp from a pulp mill

PAPER AND INK

5.9 Papermaking
In the Fourdrinier part of the machine the paper pulp is fed out of the flow or head box (**1**) on to the Fourdrinier wire screen belt (**2**). Deckle straps (**3**) ensure that the paper pulp does not slide off the wirescreen belt. In the press part of the machine, the dandy roll (**4**) forms the web of paper. The paper, conveyed by belts (**5**, **6**, and **7**), is pressed between sets of rollers (**8**, **9**, and **10**) that extract excess moisture. The paper is then conveyed to the dryer where it is passed between the upper and lower felts (belts covered with felt) (**11** and **12**): The felts themselves are dried by passing over a number of felt driers (**13**). In the calender part of the machine the now dry paper is fed through a calender stack (**14**), which polishes the paper to give it a good finish, then on to a winding reel (**15**). When this reel is full, the machine feeds the paper onto another reel (**16**). The paper from the full reel is then unwound and fed by rollers on to a further winding reel.

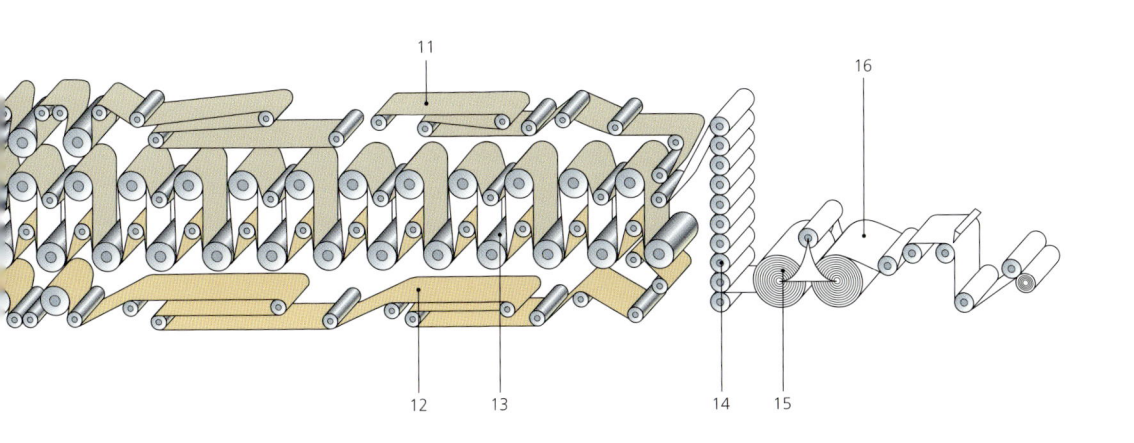

121

PAPER AND INK

5.10 Paper machine
The drying section of a paper machine at Arctic Paper, Munkedals in Sweden. The web of still damp paper is passed around the large metal drying cylinders heated by super-heated steam

5.11 Gloss finishing
Calendering roll makes a gloss surface on the paper.

The paper machine

A paper machine has to produce from this very dilute, aqueous, fibrous suspension a "mat" of fibers that exhibits uniform dimensional, physical, and visual characteristics—a sheet of paper. The magnitude of this task can be illustrated by considering a fiber 0.787–0.1181in (2–3mm) in length, and 1.6 thousandths of an inch (40 microns) wide, in a 0.3% aqueous suspension being presented to a machine of up to 20ft (approx. 6m) in width and weighing perhaps thousands of tons, and producing paper at a speed of up to 3,000 ft (approx. 1,000 meters) or more every minute.

The pulp is fed from a "head box" through a slice aperture on to a continuous moving wire (a wire mesh), at what is called the "wet end" of the paper making machine. Slice setting, consistency of stock, and the rate of flow of the furnish on to the wire, controls the basis weight (substance) and bulk of the paper. The wire may vibrate from side to side in order to help maintain random fiber orientation. Water drains through the mesh, aided by foils and vacuum boxes beneath the wire. Consolidation and watermarking may be achieved by the use of a "dandy roll"—a mesh-covered roll that rotates on the partially formed paper sheet. It carries wire marks called "electros" and/or "embossings" that compress the sheet and produce areas of light and shade due to changes in sheet density. These watermarks can be used to identify branded papers or be used as security features.

During the Fourdrinier manufacturing process, one side of the sheet is in contact with the wire. As a result, a very fine impression of it may be detectable on the "wire side" of the sheet and its characteristics may be slightly different to those of the top side. Twin-wire papers overcome this characteristic by effectively laminating two sheets together immediately after sheet formation to leave the smoother top sides (the "felt") for printing.

At the end of the wire section, the fibrous web is still 92–93% water, but it has matted together sufficiently for it to "jump" into the press section where it is transported by felt through a series of granite and rubber composition presses.

The press section removes more water by virtue of its "mangle" action and also imparts a polished surface to the wet sheet.

The remaining water is removed by passing the paper around a succession of large, metal drying cylinders heated by steam. These slowly reduce the moisture content in the paper until it arrives at the dry end of the paper-making machine, when most grades of paper will now hold approximately 4–5% moisture. Before the paper-making process is complete, however, the web may pass through a size press and/or coating station in order to further control or alter the final characteristics of the sheet. Size, in the form of starch solution, gelatin, or other surface sealants may be applied, usually by roll-coating, to both sides of the sheet—the added weight being only fractions of an ounce per ten square feet (a few grams per square meter). This application, also known as surface treatment, supplements any earlier "internal sizing" and helps to seal off loose fibers in the surface, controls ink receptivity, any tendency to feather at the touch of pen and ink, or adds a specific characteristic to the sheet, such as color, slip, release properties, moisture/vapor permeability, or security features.

After further drying by a second group of cylinders the paper may be "calendered" on the machine (see fig. 5.11). Calendering imparts a variety of finishes depending on the number of cylinders used. These finishes are known as Antique or Wove, English finish, and Smooth, the latter being the most calendered as the fibers have been flattened and polished the furthest. Finally, the paper is wound to form a very large "jumbo" reel that may weigh up to 50 tons (45 tonnes) or more.

PAPER AND INK

Off-machine processes

The conversion of paper into functional, decorative, or protective products is normally achieved by different basic operations: mechanical processing, application of coatings or by impregnation. Although some of these operations may be accomplished on the paper machine, the great majority are performed by "off-machine" secondary techniques.

Off-machine processes can be used to improve and enhance the characteristics of a printing paper or produce a completely new product, such as carbonless, release, or gummed papers, photographic, pressure-sensitive, or thermal reactive products.

The most common form of "after processing" involves coating with a pigment dispersed within an adhesive system. This is applied uniformly, usually from an aqueous mix, to the paper web by a roll-application system. A flexible blade is then used to spread and monitor the thickness of the applied layer by adjusting its pressure and angle of application.

For the production of coated art papers, a single coating is applied, and clay is often the primary ingredient. For higher-quality papers, a higher coat weight is normally necessary and this may be achieved by a double coating operation. After coating, a surface finish can be applied to the paper by a process of supercalendering that produces the very high gloss effect characteristic of art papers.

If the paper is to be web printed, the jumbo reel is slit into smaller reels of the specified size of the press otherwise it is "sheeted" (made into sheets) and precision trimmed before being bulk-packed or ream-wrapped for mill or merchant stock, or dispatched directly to a customer's premises.

5.12 Fresh from the maker
Jumbo reels from the paper-making machine, prior to being slit down into narrower reels and then sheeted, if required.

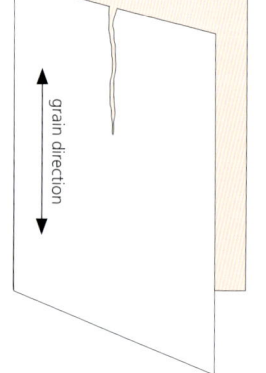

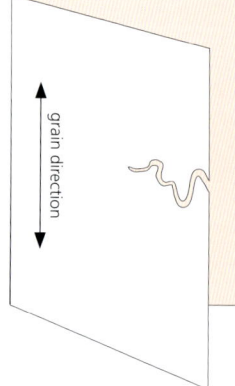

5.13 Grain direction
Grain direction is the direction in which the paper is made. In publications, ideally it should run parallel with the fold to avoid curling. You can test for grain by tearing a sheet of newspaper—it will tear more cleanly in the direction of the grain.

PAPER AND INK

5.14 Reels after slitting
Reels that have been slit down from the jumbo reel and are now ready for use on web presses or may be sheeted for sheet-fed presses

125

Types of paper

Most people have the concept of different paper types from perhaps buying writing paper, or paper for their laser or ink-jet printers. However, what are the main different types of paper, and what do their different classifications actually mean?

Acid-free paper
Acid-free is paper with a pH rating of 7 or higher rating of alkalinity. It has a much longer life expectancy than paper with a higher acid content and is used for books and other publications that are intended to last in good condition. It is treated to neutralize the acids that occur naturally in wood pulp. Where paper is not acid-free, it can yellow and deteriorate over time.

Bulky mechanical (newsprint)
This is a machine-finished paper, made mostly from groundwood pulp or recycled fiber and used for printing newspapers and cheap handbills. It soon discolors and becomes brittle when it is exposed to light, due to the impurities (lignin) contained in and around the fiber, that were not removed in the pulping process. Bulky news is used in mass-market paperback books, for example.

Mechanical papers
Described as mechanical, these contain a large proportion of mechanical wood pulp, but also some chemical pulp to increase strength. The mechanical element may be bleached. Paper can be produced with a smooth surface by super calendering (SC), machine finishing (calendering on machine, [MF], or machine glazing [MG].) A grade called WSOP (web sized offset printing) has size applied at the paper-making stage to give an improved printing surface for offset printing. These papers are used for cheaper leaflets and magazines—halftones up to 120 lines per inch screen, or more, can be printed satisfactorily.

Freesheet (woodfree)
This description is a misnomer because the paper is still made from wood pulp, but it is produced by the chemical, rather than the mechanical process. (To be described as woodfree, the chemical wood pulp content should be at least 90%.) Strong sheets with good whiteness are produced for use as general printing and writing papers, continuous stationery, copying papers, and magazine papers. These grades will take color, but with not such good results as coated qualities. This category includes "bond" paper with a fine formation (used for stationery), and "bank" that is a lighter weight version of bond.

Cartridge papers
These are tough, hard, sized papers that were originally used in the production of cartridges. The term has been extended to most rough-surfaced heavy papers, such as papers used for drawing and painting.

Board
Board is normally used for covers to catalogs and paperback books, and for the production of cartons. It may be uncoated or supplied coated on one or two sides. Board weights normally start at 50lbs. (150gsm). The thicker boards may be made by laminating two or more plys of material together. Paperback book covers are specified in point thickness ranging from 10 point (200gsm) up to 15 or 17 point (300gsm) for larger and heavier books. Even thicker board is used for packaging, children's board books, or binding cased books (see p. 147).

Antique

This normally relates to a bulky paper with a naturally rough finish (antique wove), similar to that of an uncalendered handmade paper. It is mainly used in the production of books.

Antique laid

This has a different surface characteristic as it shows the laid lines and chain marks of the dandy roll within its surface. This paper is not suitable for halftones or line work with large solid areas of color or fine detail.

English and smooth finishes

Although uncoated, these are often used for publications that contain black-and-white halftones or color work. The smoothness of these finishes provides a receptive surface for the reproduction of fine line illustrations and photographs.

5.15 Paper types
Choosing and using paper is one of the pleasures of design, publishing, and printing work.

PAPER AND INK

Coated papers

Gloss art paper is coated on both sides with china clay or chalk and calendered to give a very high smoothness and gloss. It is used for the printing of halftones and color, and high-quality magazines and promotional material. The base paper of cheaper coated papers can contain groundwood or recycled fiber.

Matt art, or silk-finish coated paper, is produced in a similar way to art paper by coating with china clay or chalk, but the calendering process is only used to consolidate the surface rather than to produce a high gloss. As a result, the surface has a matt appearance but still gives excellent reproduction of black-and-white halftones and four-color images without the glare effect from gloss interfering with the ease of reading the text portions of the publication. One way of producing a similar effect is to calender in the conventional manner but with a micro-embossed roll.

Blade-coated cartridge paper is midway between being an uncoated and a matt art paper. It has a lighter coating than art or matt art, but reproduces halftones well. It is used for some magazine work and illustrated books, like this one.

Chromo paper is coated on only one side and is used for posters, proofing work, and the printing of book jackets and labels.

Cast-coated papers are characterized by exceptionally high gloss. Cast-coated papers are used in the production of prestigious cartons or covers for presentation material, and corporate annual reports, and so on.

Plastic papers

These are made completely from plastic or with a plastic, or latex, coating over a base paper. Although expensive, these products are ideal for the production of some waterproof maps, workshop manuals, and books for young children. They are very tough and washable. They require special printing techniques and inks.

5.16 Newsprint
One of the most familiar papers: absorbent, low cost, and easy to recycle.

Carbonless copying papers

Carbonless copying papers are produced by employing a coating of microcapsules that rupture under the pressure of a stylus or printer key, releasing a solution of colorless dye. This transfers to the reactive surface on the sheet below where the dye is converted to its colored form.

Papers for digital printing

Developments in digital presses will eventually lead to digital printing being able to print on the whole range of papers that can be printed by offset lithography, but until then many digital presses require the use of paper specially made to meet the requirements of the process. Many digital presses use toners instead of conventional offset inks, and these react with heat as the image is fused onto the paper. Coated stocks can cause problems in electrographic printing, as the coating acts as an insulator. Also, the moisture levels are more critical in digital printing. Special papers (often supplied by the press manufacturers) are plastic-based and have the look of coated stock, without the problems caused by coating. These papers are usually more expensive than their equivalents used in the offset process.

Technical papers

Many types of highly specialized papers are manufactured either through modification to the basic paper-making process, blend of pulps, use of additives, or after-processing. These include papers for currency, photography, filters, electrical cable winding, decorative laminates, security applications, self-adhesive, and postage stamps.

5.17 Glossy magazines
Quality magazines are often described in terms of the paper—glossy, or more accurately, coated stock.

5.18 Shiny plastic papers
These can be expensive but are ideal for products that face "difficult" conditions—like children's books and maps!

PAPER AND INK

Specifying papers

When purchasing paper, great care must be exercised in specifying the quality and quantity required. Obviously, when the client supplies the paper, the printer must be consulted well in advance to ensure that it will be suitable for the equipment planned for use in the printing and finishing processes. The following are a few of the most important considerations.

Basis weight (substance)
This refers to the weight of the paper and in the USA, basis weight (substance) is described as the weight of a ream (500 sheets) of paper in one of several standard sizes. For example, a book paper might be described in the USA as having a substance of 60 pounds. This means that a ream (500 sheets) of the basic size of 25 x 38in weighs 60 pounds. In most other countries the metric system is used where paper substance is described in grams per square meter (gsm)—the weight in grams of a sheet of the paper having an area of one square meter. The conversion table on page 218 enables substances of both systems to be compared.

Sizes
In the USA, sizes are given in inches. For large jobs, such as long runs of books or magazines, the paper may be made especially for each job, and (depending on the width of the paper making machine) can be made to virtually any size. In the metric system, sheet sizes are given in millimeters, as are reel widths. Smaller jobs have to be printed using standard sheet sizes (see p. 218 for US and metric standard paper sizes). Most books are produced in standard sizes that fit standard paper sizes and printing machines. (Also see Appendix, p. 214 onward, and Glossary.)

Grain direction (for sheet-fed paper)
Grain direction is the direction in which the web of paper runs through the paper making machine with the result that the fibers tend to lie in this direction. When specifying paper it is important to state the grain direction for two reasons. In binding, pages open more easily and the book handles better if the grain direction of the paper runs parallel to the spine (right grain), also there is less strain on the binding edge. In printing, the printer normally prefers the grain to run across the printing direction as this helps to prevent stretching through pressure or change in moisture content, thus helping to maintain registration.

Specifying grain
Sometimes these two requirements conflict with each other and usually the printing requirement takes precedence. To specify grain, state whether the sheet is long grain (LG) or short grain (SG), depending on whether the longer or shorter dimension of the sheet runs with the grain. When filling out a paper order form, the machine or grain direction should be the second dimension and be underlined. Obviously, in web-fed printing, the grain always runs round rather than across the reel.

Bulk
This is used to describe the thickness (caliper) of the paper and is mainly used in book production (for example, volume controlled papers). To achieve bulk, it is not always necessary to increase the basis weight (substance) of a paper. Certain papers such as antique wove can be made bulkier (called hi-bulk grades) by being manufactured with more "air" and fillers in the paper without necessarily increasing the weight. It is therefore possible to have paper of a common weight but with several

different bulks. In the USA, bulk is expressed as a "bulk factor" that is the number of pages that make a thickness of one inch. The trade term for this reference is PPI (pages per inch). The metric system used elsewhere describes bulk with a volume figure that gives the bulk in millimeters of 200 pages of a 100gsm paper. Therefore the thickness of the sheet in microns is the weight multiplied by its volume divided by 10, so 80gsm vol. 18 gives a sheet with a thickness of 80 x 18 ÷ 10 = 144 microns.

Shade

Shade or tint must be specified. Paper manufacturers will offer their standard shades, with their own codes or names (the range goes from natural to blue white), but when a special shade is required, it is advisable to submit large samples for color matching. Note that some papers are "metameric"—that is, they exhibit different shades under different lighting conditions. Partly for this reason, white is, in fact, the most difficult shade to specify and match.

Opacity

On thinner papers, there is show-through, where the print on the other side of the sheet is visible. This matters less on books where the area of type on one side of the sheet backs up that on the other, but low opacity will be a problem on jobs with irregular type areas and illustrations. Opacity can be measured (with an opacimeter) and specified. Most papers have an opacity in the range of 90% to 95%.

Special instructions

All special instructions relating to packet and bulk packing on pallets, maximum acceptable weight, reel wrapping, truck loading, and delivery times and dates must be given concisely and clearly.

Paper testing

Tests are carried out during the manufacture of paper, covering most of the paper's characteristics. These include bulk, brightness, basis weight (substance), gloss, moisture content, opacity, and many other properties.

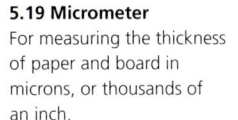

PAPER AND INK

5.19 Micrometer
For measuring the thickness of paper and board in microns, or thousands of an inch.

Potential problems with paper

Paper is not inert, it reacts to its environment and this may cause printing and processing problems. The manufacturing process itself can result in minor defects, leading to production problems. Some of these are outlined below.

Curl stability
Paper is affected dramatically by temperature and changes in humidity. Perhaps the one most important factor is RH (relative humidity), since this alone will determine whether or not the sheet will lie flat or expand/contract and even curl. This will have a considerable effect on the end result, particularly if the printing involved requires a high degree of color registration accuracy.

In an ideal situation, the print room should be both temperature and RH controlled to match that of the paper conditioning environment. This will ensure that the moisture content within the paper remains constant and so the sheet will not change its initial characteristics.

Linting/picking
A common problem with both coated and uncoated paper is that of linting, or "pick." Usually, this is a problem of debris that is either loose on the surface (bad paper to begin with or cutter dust) or that lifts as a result of the printing process (ink tack pulling tiny particles away from the surface). The overall effect would be white spots (known as "hickies") appearing on the printed surface. Modern paper-making technology has minimized this problem.

Squareness
Obviously, to achieve a good print result the sheet must be square. Modern precision-cutting technology can produce very accurately cut sheets and "out of squareness" is rare.

Long edge
This is usually a problem associated with lighter-weight papers of 35lbs, (60gsm) or below, and manifests itself as a slackness on one edge of the reel, caused by differing profiles across the paper web during manufacture. This may prove a particular problem if different webs are to be matched as in multi-part continuous stationery.

Bulk after printing
Paper is specified prior to printing and the characteristics may change during the print process. This is particularly true with high-bulking book papers where the pressures encountered during printing tend to flatten the sheet and cause a 3–5% reduction in bulk.

Ink rub
This can occur when illustrated work is printed on matt art paper. It is caused when the matt coated surface of the paper rubs against the ink on the opposite page. It can take place either during printing or the later finishing and binding processes (particularly folding). Remedies include using specially formulated inks, allowing more time for drying, and printing a sealer, particularly over illustrations. Stacking of printed sheets in smaller piles also helps to reduce the pressure and tendency to incur rub.

Binding problems

As previously mentioned, the printer and binder often require opposing grain directions with paper stock. It is worth remembering that with certain types of format, grain direction can cause serious binding problems. Probably the best example of this is using a heavy, coated paper on a large, landscape format. The wrong grain direction (across paper) will cause tremendous strain in the spine and no matter how well the book is bound it will eventually begin to break the binding. The pages may start to have a "wave" effect and curl after binding.

5.20 Showing its age
Some papers with a higher acid content than others can yellow with age—a problem for publishers storing as-yet-unsold books in warehouses for significant periods.

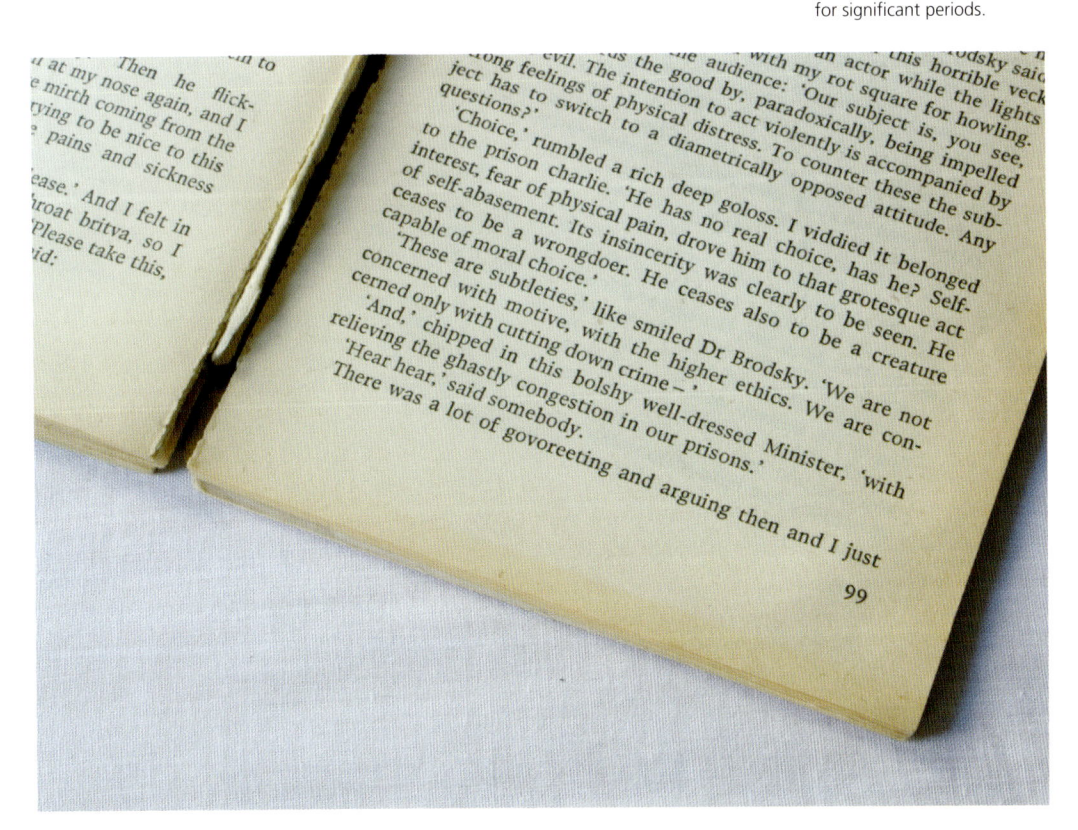

Paper and the environment

Papermaking is a process that involves major environmental considerations and, on the whole, increasing segments of the industry are seeking to better meet their obligations with respect to both the appropriate legal requirements and to follow good environmental practices.

Sustainable forests

It is in the interests both of the environment and the paper mills to replace the trees used for paper. In fact, in many forests grown for the paper industry, two or three trees are planted for every tree cut down. We should not confuse the chopping down of trees for use in papermaking with the destruction of the tropical rainforest, where the trees are not replaced; or the devastation caused from clear cutting, where all vegetation is removed, leading to destruction of wildlife habitat, soil erosion, and silting of streams and rivers. The trees used in papermaking are more like a crop, such as corn that is replanted after harvesting. Also, much timber used in papermaking is from the parts of a tree left over from the timber used in furniture and construction.

In recent years, two organizations have been set up to promote responsible management of the world's forests. They are the Forest Stewardship Council (FSC), and the Programme for Endorsement of Forest Certification schemes (PEFC). Both organizations accredit third parties who can certify that the products they use are the result of responsible and sustainable forest management. This also means that no "old-growth" trees were cut down in the logging stage. This is done by recognizing a "chain of custody," where there is accreditation of all the parties involved in making a printed product—forest owner/manager, pulp mill, paper mill, printer, and publisher. Thus the end-user knows that all the parties involved can prove that the source of the wood they use originates from a sustainable and well-managed forest.

The FSC criteria are more stringent than those for PEFC, and therefore fewer forests are FSC certified than PEFC certified, although FSC accreditations are on the increase. It is therefore considered "best practice" to use FSC papers, but for any given job, there may not yet be an FSC paper available that meets the job's quality or price requirements, in which case there will usually be a PEFC paper available. The use of FSC papers is promoted by organizations such as Friends of the Earth, the Green Press Initiative in the USA and Canada, the Rainforest Alliance, the Sierra Club, Greenpeace, and the World Wildlife Fund. Printed products can carry the FSC or PEFC logos. Increasingly, large companies and governments are specifying the use of paper from sustainable forests.

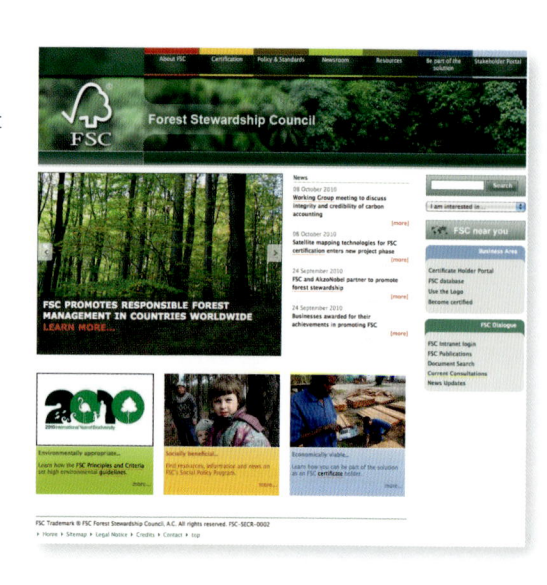

Recycling
Recycling has dramatically reduced the amount of virgin wood pulp used and also made good use of wastepaper that would otherwise be disposed of in landfill sites or incinerated.

Energy conservation
Paper mills use enormous amounts of energy and are making concerted efforts to reduce energy use, both to help the environment and to reduce one of their major cost areas. Alternative energy generation methods in use today include biogas and wind power.

Water conservation
Similarly, the papermaking process depends on the use of very large quantities of water. Many paper mills now recycle their water in a closed system.

Pollution
In the past, the paper-making process could result in toxic by-products, such as those resulting from the use of certain bleaching chemicals; one of the most harmful to both humans and the environment is dioxin. Whether released into the air or ground water, a tiny amount of dioxin can cause environmental and health damage, including cancers. Most pulp is now made using chlorine-free or partial chlorine bleaching processes. Alternatives now include bleaching with hydrogen peroxide or ozone, instead of chlorine. The two main processes are referred to as TCF (Totally Chlorine Free) for virgin pulp, or ECF (Elementally Chlorine Free) when a combination of virgin and recycled fibers is used.

PAPER AND INK

5.22 Harvesting timber in Sweden (left)

5.23 Planting eucalyptus in Brazil (right)

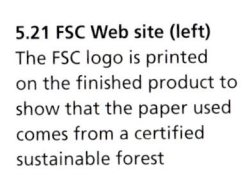

5.21 FSC Web site (left)
The FSC logo is printed on the finished product to show that the paper used comes from a certified sustainable forest

Ink and toner

Although paper is the major cost element in most printed jobs, the cost of ink is also significant. The different printing processes each require inks specially formulated for that process. Even within each process, there will be differences in the ink formulation to allow for the particular press or paper, or substrate used, drying requirements, light fastness (for posters exposed to sunlight), and toxicity issues (when printing food packaging). Some inks are liquid (for gravure or flexography) and some are a paste (e.g. for offset lithography).

In the 15th century, when Gutenberg first printed from movable type, the ink he used was made of boiled linseed oil with resin, soap, and lampblack. Modern inks are made of the following ingredients:

- **Pigment** (in powder form) or dye (in liquid form)—this gives the ink its color

- **Resins**—form the binder for the pigment

- **Liquids**—to make the ink fluid so it can be transferred to and from the ink rollers, and blanket, on the press. These combine with the resins to form the vehicle in which the color is carried to the paper (or other printing surface)

- **Additives**—to give good press performance and drying

Most inks are made by mixing the above ingredients and then grinding them in a three-roll mill that breaks down the ingredients until they have a smooth consistency.

Drying ink

There are five main methods of drying ink: evaporation, chemical curing, heat setting, penetration, and oxidation.

Evaporation is used when inks contain liquid solvents or water. Evaporation is a very fast and effective method of drying, and is used in gravure and flexography.

Chemical curing "dries" ink by linking the pigment molecules in the ink, thereby solidifying it. This is done by adding a catalyst immediately before printing to start the solidification process. A similar method uses ultraviolet light or infrared to "cure" the ink. The UV or infrared drier is an extra unit on the press. Work dried by this method can proceed for finishing immediately, whereas most offset printed work using other drying methods has to be left for several hours before it can be finished.

Heat setting web offset presses have gas or electric drying ovens that dry off the solvents in the ink.

Penetration is used with paper and board, where the ink dries by being soaked down into the paper, rather like blotting paper. It obviously cannot be used on plastic or foil that are non-absorbent.

Oxidation is a method of drying where the ingredients absorb oxygen from the air. This causes the ink molecules to join together, so that the ink film slowly solidifies. It is a slow process and, when the printing is on paper or board, is used in conjunction with penetration.

5.24 Ink mill (right)
An ink mill breaks down the ingredients until they are of a smooth consistency.

5.25 Ink on rollers (left)
There are many different types of ink; some are effectively "grease," which repels water—one of the principles of offset lithographic printing.

PAPER AND INK

5.26 Pantone inks ready-mixed
The Pantone color-matching system is an industry standard.

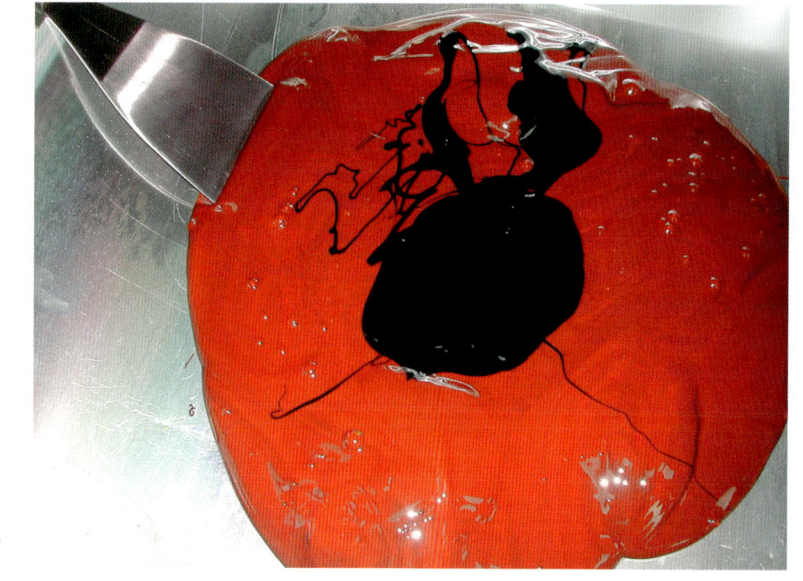

5.27 Mixing ink
Special colors can be handmixed by some printers to match swatches supplied by the client.

Specifying ink

Unlike paper, the type of ink is not normally specified by the client, but is chosen by the printer after consideration of the process being used, the machine, the paper, and whether any special finishing operations, such as varnishing or laminating, are involved.

Four-color process inks are normally made to a standard within a particular country, although increasingly to an international standard, so that a four-color set will give the same result, regardless of the printing location. When using process colors, all the prepress operations depend on the use of standard process colors.

Special colors used to be mixed by hand by the printer to match a swatch supplied by the client and, although this is still possible, most special colors are specified using the Pantone Matching System (PMS), a proprietary system consisting of a book of color swatches with reference numbers for both uncoated and coated paper use that relate to inks that the printer buys ready-made or can mix to exact instructions. This has made the matching of colors a much more exact process.

Metallic inks contain fine metallic powders such as aluminum, copper, or bronze to give a gold or silver effect, or produce metallic blues, reds, greens, and so on.

Digital printing

This uses toner instead of ink or prints by ink-jet. Toners can be dry or liquid and contain the pigments and particles that can be electrically or magnetically charged. Developments in digital printing are leading to ink being used rather than toners and this will reduce the cost of consumables in digital printing. The ink used in ink-jet printing is solvent (sometimes water) based.

Inks and the environment

Ink is now being made with regard to its environmental impacts. This includes using renewable sources such as vegetable oils or soy rather than mineral oils and using water (aqueous inks), rather than solvent based inks in flexography or gravure, to reduce emissions. Correctly formulated inks are also needed to enable alcohol-free damping in offset lithography, or waterless offset. Leftover ink (ink sludge) is hazardous waste and was normally incinerated, but is now starting to be recovered and used to make recycled ink.

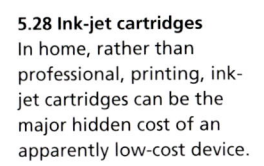

5.28 Ink-jet cartridges
In home, rather than professional, printing, ink-jet cartridges can be the major hidden cost of an apparently low-cost device.

PAPER AND INK

Finishing processes

The finishing and binding processes can either ensure that a printed product serves its purpose, or produce a product that is difficult to handle and doesn't last as long as intended. A good understanding between client, printer, and finisher/binder must be established if the end result is to fulfill its function. Although most printers will have some finishing and binding capability, specialist processes will go to a separate finishing house or bookbinder. Most book manufacturers perform all the main functions under one roof.

Dummies
Unless you are producing a fairly standard product, it's advisable to have a dummy prepared by the printer/finisher using the actual job paper. The dummy can be shown to the client for approval of bulk, paper type, and binding style. Where the product has a spine (e.g. a book or magazine), the dummy will also show the designer the spine width to allow for the jacket or paperback cover.

Cutting
Most printed items have to be cut at some stage, either before printing to cut the paper down to the size of the press, or in the finishing process—before folding or after binding, stitching or sewing—to give a clean edge. Cutting is done on a paper-cutter (guillotine) that consists of a large steel bed; a movable piece of steel at the back (back-gauge) used to position the paper correctly; a clamp to hold the paper firmly at the point of cutting; and a very sharp, electrically driven blade. Although cutters are essentially very simple pieces of equipment, they can have sophisticated extras such as photoelectric or laser beam guards to prevent the blade coming down if the operator's hands are in the cutting area. Also, most cutters today have facilities to make them programmable by computer. In this case, the program automatically moves the back-gauge to the required position for the next cut and this facility can save a great deal of time where there is a complex sequence of cuts to be done. The programs are then stored for use on repeat jobs. The bed can have compressed air fed to it to enable the stack of printed work to "float" into position, thus avoiding manual handling of heavy piles of paper, speeding up the cutting process, and making it easier and safer for the operator.

Scoring and perforating
Scoring is done on board or thicker grades of paper to facilitate folding. In offset litho printing, perforating rules can be affixed around or across the cylinder; scoring wheels can be brought into the operation between the printing unit and delivery of the sheets; or it can be done separately on a scoring machine. The same separate machine used for scoring will also perforate. Both scoring and perforating can also be done while die-cutting (see p. 152) and on most folding machines.

6.1 A Polar 92 XT paper cutter (guillotine)
For cutting large sheets of paper and board before and/or after printing. It is also used for trimming printed items to give clean edges.

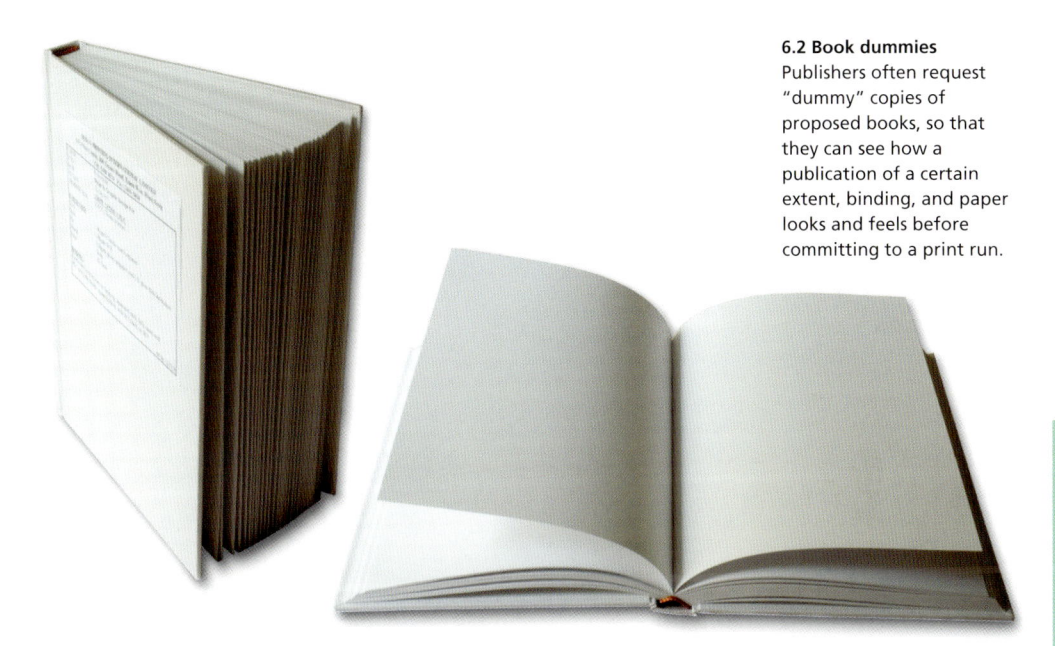

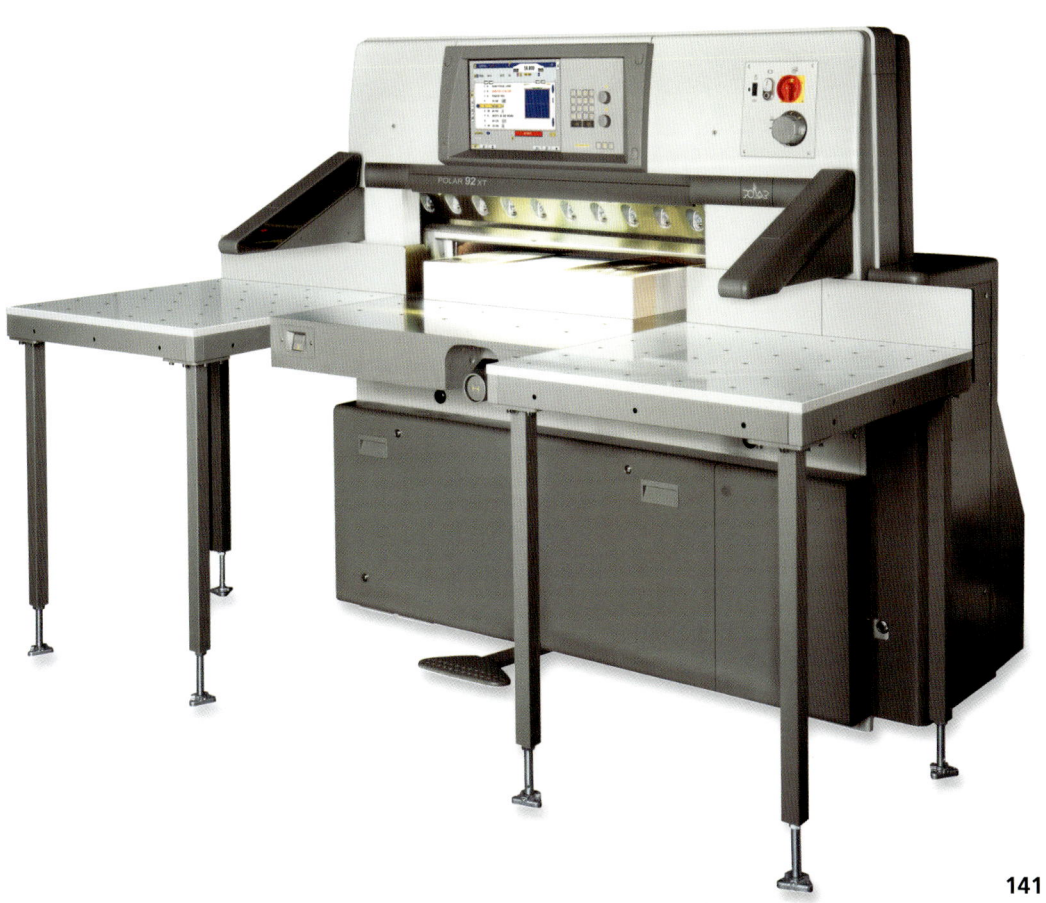

6.2 Book dummies
Publishers often request "dummy" copies of proposed books, so that they can see how a publication of a certain extent, binding, and paper looks and feels before committing to a print run.

FINISHING

Folding

Where an item has been produced on a web-fed press, the press will usually produce folded sections (known as signatures) of 8, 16, or 32 pages. However, with sheet-fed printing, the sheet has to be folded after printing on a folding machine. The flat sheets are fed in at one end and the machine delivers the sections folded in accordance with the imposition scheme used. Most folding machines process 10,000 sheets an hour, or more.

Folding machines fold the sheets using either a knife fold or a buckle fold (figs. 6.3, 6.4), or a combination of both—most modern high-speed folders use buckle folding. Various special folds are used for pamphlets—such as the the french fold (fig. 6.6) and the accordion (concertina) fold (fig. 6.7).

For books and booklets, the sheet should ideally be folded with the grain of the paper running parallel to the spine, so that the pages will open more easily and there will be less risk of a wave effect across the width of the pages. However, on occasion the printer will want the grain running in the other direction to avoid paper stretch, particularly in four-color work. The grain direction of the paper needs to be planned from the start.

Larger folding machines can deliver more than one folded section from a printed sheet, and it is common for two-up sections to be delivered to benefit from the economy of two-up binding. Folding machines can also add a glue line at the spine, so that self-covered leaflets of up to 16 pages won't require saddle-stitching (see p. 144).

Double-page spreads (or crossovers) may not line up when folded, so care is needed with images going across a spread. Also, where the paper used is thick, the inside pages of a section will be slightly narrower than the outer pages and allowance needs to be made for this. This is called shingling.

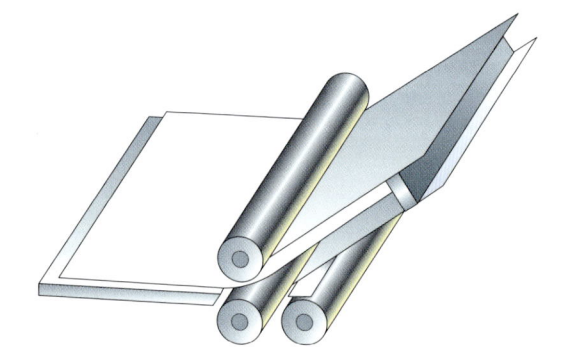

6.3 Buckle folding
The fold is achieved by passing the paper at high speed through two plates until it meets a stop, at which point it buckles where the fold is required

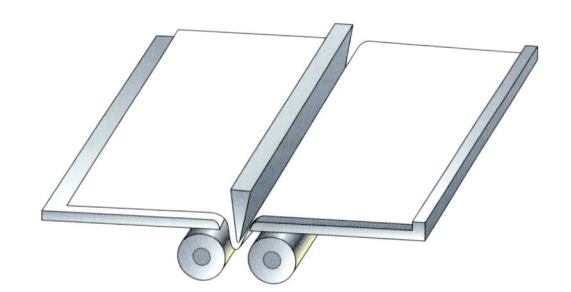

FINISHING

142

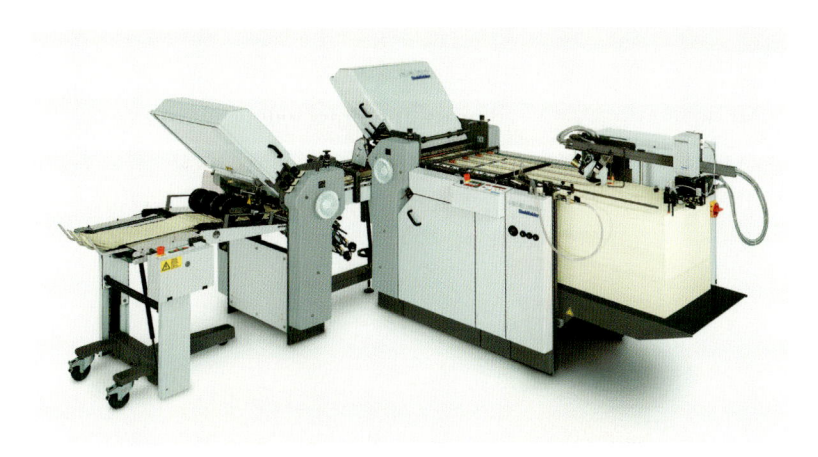

6.5 A Stahlfolder Ti52 Proline buckle folding machine

FINISHING

6.6 A french fold (left)
Often used for greetings cards. Only one side of the sheet has to be printed and the printed pages appear on the outside of the finished fold–unprinted pages are hidden on the inside.

6.7 An accordion fold (right)
Also known as a concertina fold. Used for publicity leaflets and maps

6.8 Saddle-stitched publications
if bulky, have the pages at or near the centre displaced and this "creep" or "shingling" may have to be allowed for by the designer or printer to prevent live matter being trimmed off the edge.

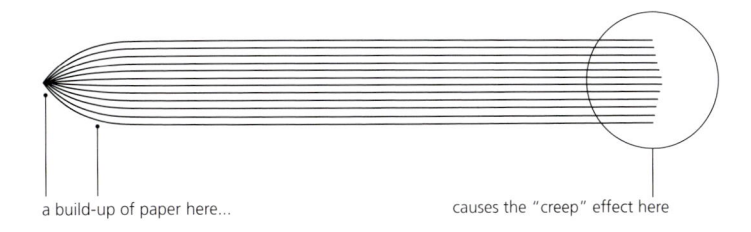

a build-up of paper here...

causes the "creep" effect here

Binding types and materials

How books and other publications are bound—and with what materials—are major consderations, because these decisions greatly influence the look and feel (and, therefore, the perceived value) of any commercial publication. Such decisions also impact on the total cost of a print job, and whether it is financially viable.

FINISHING

PAPERBACK BINDING

Brochures and magazines
A common method of binding brochures and magazines is wire stitching—which can be saddle-stitching or side-stitching (also called stab-stitching).

In saddle-stitching, the folded section or sections (inserted into each other, rather than side by side) are positioned on a metal "saddle" under a head that inserts wire staples (cut from a continuous coil of wire) through the spine. Stitching machines range from standalone hand-fed machines to high-speed saddle-stitching (McCain stitching) lines that gather the separate sections, insert them into each other, then stitch and trim in a continuous operation at up to 10,000 copies per hour or more. They can also deal with inserts on the run.

Side-stitching, also known as stab stitching, is used for thicker publications with more than one section. Here the folded sections are gathered in order and the staples are forced through the side about ¼in (6mm) in from the spine—very thick products need the stitches inserted at the back as well as the front. Obviously a side-stitched publication will not open or stay flat easily, and the designer should allow a wider back, or center, margin (or gutter). The stitches are hidden under the cover which is glued to score marks ¼in (6mm) from the spine. With improvements in the strength of perfect binding, side-stitching is now little used.

Perfect binding
Most paperback books (and many magazines and cased books) are "perfect" bound; this method is known also as "unsewn" binding. After folding, the folded sections are loaded on to a perfect binding line that first gathers the sections in the right order and then removes the back fold, trimming off about ⅛in (3mm) and grinding the cut spine to roughen it. The book block (which now consists of individual leaves) is then glued at the spine, both to hold the leaves together and to attach the book block to the cover. There are two types of adhesive in common use: PVA (polyvinyl acetate) and hot melt. PVA is stronger but takes longer to dry. Some binders use both in a two shot process, where PVA is used to bind the book and hot melt attaches the cover. PUR (polyurethane resin) adhesive is also being used increasingly and this gives a stronger bond, yet allows the book to open more easily.

The books are then trimmed using a three-knife trimmer to give a smooth edge all round. The trimmer opens the fore edge of the book block and trims the top and bottom edges. The finished books are then ready for packing.

Variations of this technique are known as "burst," "notch," or "slot," binding. With these methods, the spine of the section (or signature) is perforated (in effect, slashed across its width), either on the press or the folding or binding machine and the sections then go through a paperback binding machine, but do not have their spines removed to create individual leaves, as in the case of "perfect" binding. Instead, glue is forced into the notches to hold the sections together.

144

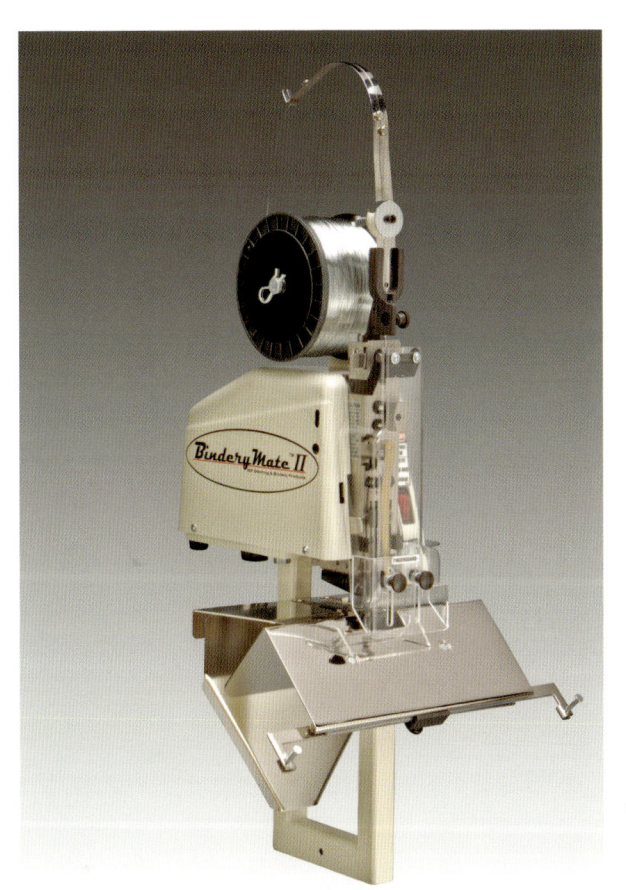

6.9 An ISP BinderyMate II wire-stitching machine
The wire from a large coil is cut into individual lengths which form the "staples". These are forced through the spine (saddle-stitching) or side (side-stitching) of a booklet and then clenched. Different gauges of wire are used, depending on how thick the booklet is.

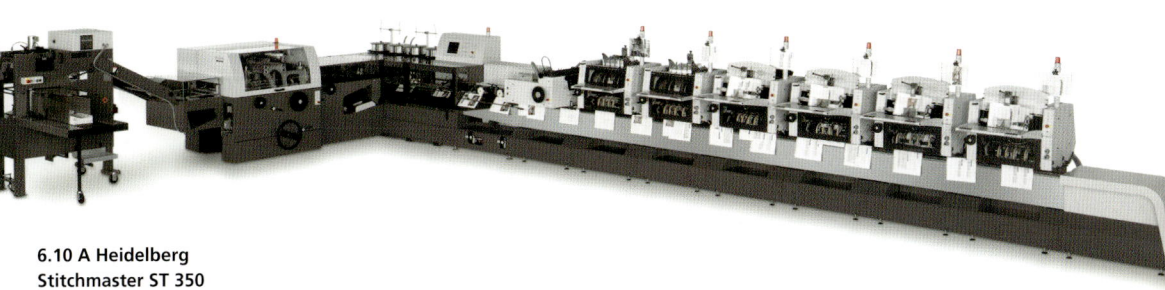

FINISHING

6.10 A Heidelberg Stitchmaster ST 350 high-speed stitching line
This first gathers the separate printed sections and the cover, inserts wire stitches and trims all three sides at speeds of 10,000 copies or more per hour. The end product can be either saddle- or side-stitched.

6.11 Applying adhesive for unsewn (perfect) binding
Applying the correct thickness of adhesive is a key factor in the strength of the bound publication.

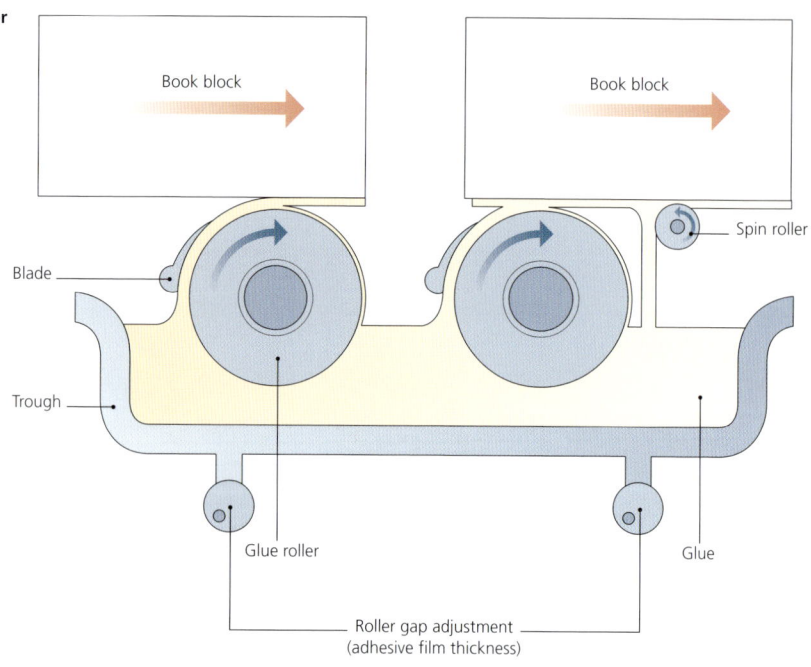

Book block

Book block

Spin roller

Blade

Trough

Glue roller

Glue

Roller gap adjustment
(adhesive film thickness)

6.12 A UK bookbindery
On the right is a row of automatic sewing machines and on the left a paperback binding line.

FINISHING

146

This is stronger than unsewn binding and less expensive than sewn. Notch-bound books also open more readily than perfect-bound titles. Adding flaps to the cover can enhance paperbacks—these have to be scored. Covers can be made of plastic, rather than cover card (board). Cover card stock ranges in from 10pt to 17pt (200gsm to 300gsm), depending on trim size and spine thickness. Side gluing up to the line of score marks can add strength—a four score consists of two scores for the spine and a score on the front and back covers ¼in (6mm) in from the spine. This creates hinges on the front and back covers that are glued to the first and last pages.

Sewn book binding

Some paperbacks are sewn. Although sewing is more expensive than perfect binding, it reduces the possibility of pages falling out and is preferred for gloss-coated or heavy, stiff papers. The pages also lie flatter. Sewn binding is used for products that will be handled regularly, such as textbooks, or high-quality art and photography titles. After gathering the sections in order, the sewing machine inserts threads through the spine of each section and then uses further thread to join the sections to each other to form the book block. The cover is then glued to the spine and the books are trimmed.

As well as sewing in sections, books can also be side-sewn where the sewing machine inserts threads through the whole book block ¼in (6mm) from the spine. This makes the book very strong and is used for educational books (library style binding); additional supporting tapes can also be added to the first and last signatures and attached underneath the endpapers to the board. Singer sewing is where the book (typically a children's book with 16 or 32 pages) is sewn with a continuous thread through the spine and consists of just one section. Another technique used is "thread-sealing," where, instead of sewing, plastic threads are inserted through the spines of the sections, at the folding stage, to hold the pages together and then the sections are gathered and the book block is glued at the spine to hold the sections together.

Spiral, wiro, and plastic-comb binding

These methods are used for manuals and shorter-run publications, or where the product needs to lie flat (computer manuals for example).

In spiral binding, holes are drilled through the cover(s) and all pages, which are then joined together using a wire or plastic spiral coil. Wiro binding is similar, but instead of a coil inlcudes a construct, the "fingers" of which go through slots in the sheets. Calendars and the like usually have wiro bindings. Plastic-comb binding is the plastic equivalent of wiro binding, but has a larger effect on the spine thickness—a consideration for mailing. It is a common, low-cost binding on some internal corporate documents.

HARDBACK (CASED) BINDING

The endpapers (usually made of uncoated paper) are glued onto the first and last sections, and the folded sections are collated. Where the paper is strong enough, "self-endpapers" (usually known as "self-ends") are sometimes used instead of separate endpapers; in other words, the first leaf of the first section and the last leaf of the last section act as endpapers and are glued down to the case. Endpapers can be printed either with a solid color or an, illustration to enhance the overall design.

If the book has illustrations (plates) printed on a different paper (usually coated) to the text, these can be incorporated either as sections of 8, 16, or 32 pages, or as "wraps and inserts," where four or more pages are wrapped around the outside or alternatively inserted into the center of a section—this is more expensive than having the illustrations in sections. More expensive still, and consequently, little used today, is "tipping" where a plate is printed on a single separate leaf and fixed to a text page by pasting along one edge.

The books are then sewn, as described above, and smashed (nipped) to reduce the swell in the back caused by the folding and sewing spread, and then trimmed to size. Although many hardback books are still sewn, an increasing number are perfect or notch bound, as the strength of these techniques has significantly improved.

FINISHING

147

The book block can be left with a flat spine ("flat back" or "square back") or can be "rounded and backed." Thin books are often square backed, as they are not bulky enough for rounding to have any effect. The rounding and backing operation gives a firm grip to the sections and helps to prevent the middles of the sections dropping forward. The next operation is "lining," where a strip of kraft (stout paper) is glued to the spine to help reinforce the joint when the case is applied—where more strength is required (e.g. reference books), a second strip of linen (mull or crash) is also glued on at this stage (prior to applying the kraft). Head- and tailbands (folded strips of plain colored or striped cloth inserted at the top and bottom of the spine beneath the lining), if required, are then applied. These do not really add any strength to the book, but look attractive and cover up the tops of the sections—their cost is minimal. A ribbon page-marker can also be applied. The book block is then cased in—glued into the case and pressed to make it firm and flat. Jackets, if required, are wrapped around the book (usually on the binding line).

Casemaking

For hardback books, the cases are made separately on a casemaking machine. This wraps cloth or imitation cloth around the three pieces of board (front, spine, and back) and glues them into place to make the case. Book cloth is often plain in color, but it can also have a design printed on it. The case can also be printed on paper and laminated—PLC (printed, laminated case), or PPC (printed paper case). A flat spine for square-backed binding is made with stiff board. A rounded spine is made with a thinner, more flexible board.

Foil stamping (blocking) is used to stamp such things as the title and publisher's imprint on the spine, and sometimes the front of the case. A die (brass) is made, very often reproducing part of the jacket artwork (see stamping p. 154).

Hand binding

Deluxe or very limited editions can be bound by hand, using leather or real cloth (as opposed to imitation). Here, all the operations described above for cased binding are carried out by hand. There is a shortage of skilled labor in this area and good craft binders are much in demand.

Binding materials

The covering of the case on most trade hardback publications is a reinforced paper (imitation cloth) that is dyed and embossed with a cloth effect (usually buckram or fine linen). However, many other more expensive covering materials are available, including plastic-coated paper, woven cloth ("real" cloth), imitation leather, reconstituted leather, or real leather. Cloth is made from cotton or rayon and comes in a wide variety of colors, grades, finishes, and thread counts. It can be aqueous coated or latex impregnated, depending on the intended application and market for the book, and be finished with a variety of different grained or embossed effects.

Boards for making the cases of hardback books come in a variety of thicknesses depending on the trim size and spine thickness of the book. The thickness of the board is referred to in either points or mm. A typical 6 X 9in (229 x 153mm) trim size book would be cased with 88 point (3mm) boards. Boards vary in thickness from 30 point through 144 point. In Europe and Asia, boards run from 2mm to 4mm.

The boards can be one ply or cross-ply. Cross-ply is pasted board (made of two or more layers of chipboard or oaktag pasted together) that is lower grade and tends to warp more easily. Binder's board is made from recycled, pulped materials, is one ply and usually has more dimensional stability.

6.13 Paperback binding line
On the left is the glueing unit and the conveyor belt on the right is transporting books to a three-knife trimmer. The long travel enables the books to dry before trimming.

6.14 Casemaking
The boards for the spine, front, and back panels are placed in position on the previously glued binding material (**1**), which is folded over on all edges to produce the finished case (**2**). This is now carried out automatically on high-speed, case-making machines.

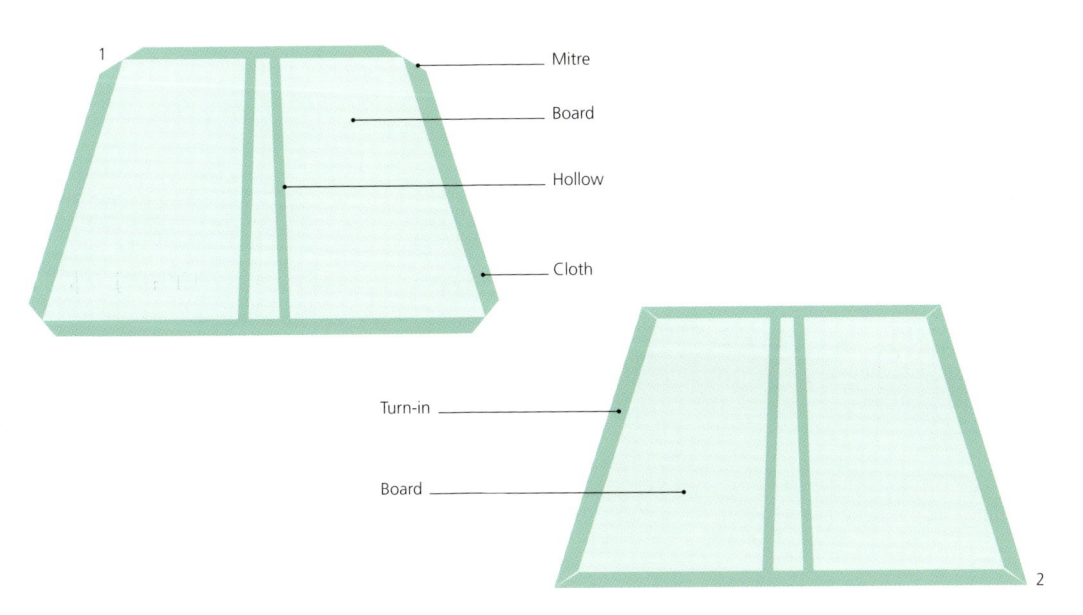

FINISHING

1

- Mitre
- Board
- Hollow
- Cloth

- Turn-in
- Board

2

149

6.15 Book-binding methods
These vary according to the nature of the job and the materials used. The various elements usually involved in the binding of a conventional, jacketed, hardback book (right) are endpapers (**1**), headbands (**2**), dustjacket (**3**), spine (**4**), case (**5**), metallic foil stamping (**6**), and tailbands (**7**). This form of binding is known as cased binding. Paperbacks are perfect bound, notch bound or sewn, before a preprinted cover is glued to the spine.

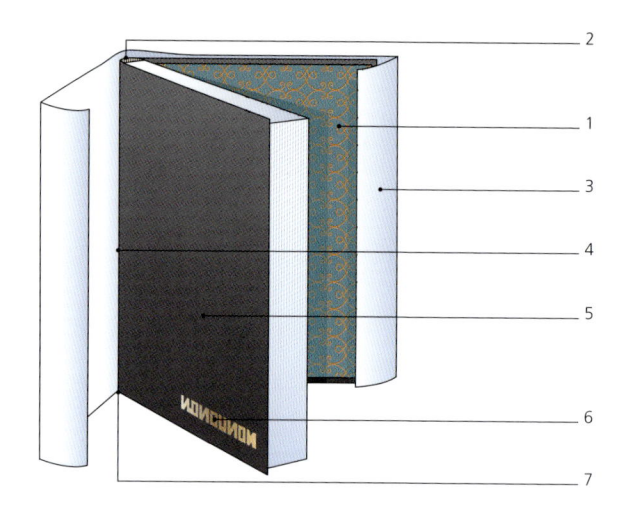

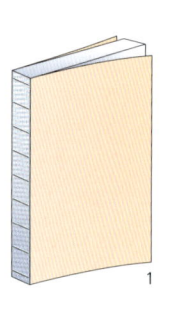

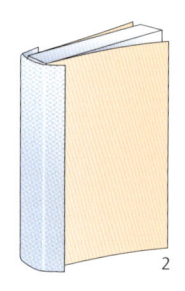

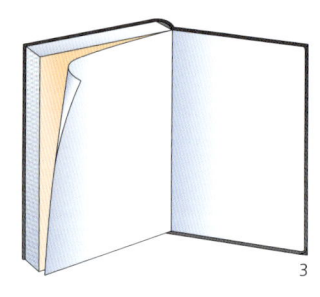

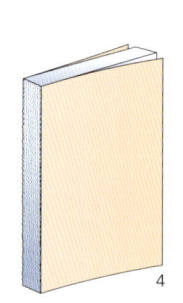

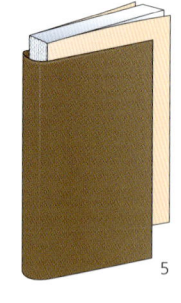

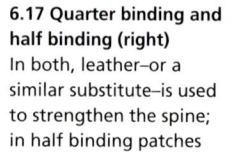

6.16 Cased binding and paperback binding
These are two conventional forms of binding for books. In typical cased binding, the sheets are folded into 16- or 32-page signatures to be collated (gathered) and sewn by machine. The edges are trimmed and the sewn back edge is coated with glue (**1**). The back edge is then rounded and backed and a gauze strip (if required) and a strip of kraft paper are glued to the spine to overlap on both sides (**2**). Finally book and case (**3**) are fed into a casing-in machine, which pastes the endpapers and applies the case to the book block. In perfect binding, the folded and collated pages have the spine edge trimmed off and roughened, enabling the binding glue to adhere strongly (**4**). The cover is glued firmly in place (**5**).

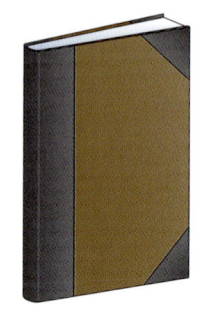

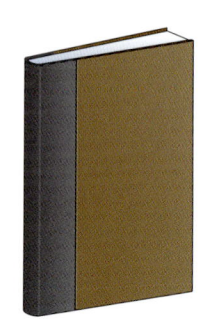

6.17 Quarter binding and half binding (right)
In both, leather–or a similar substitute–is used to strengthen the spine; in half binding patches are also used to reinforce the corners.

FINISHING

150

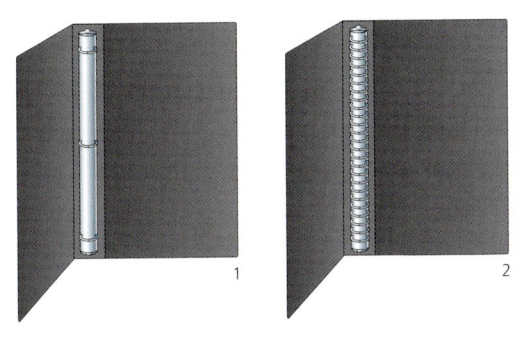

6.18 Ring binders

These enable the opened publication to lie absolutely flat. A loose-leaf post or ring binder (**1**) can have two to four rings riveted to a stiff or soft cover. It can then be sprung open and paper with the requisite number of punched holes is inserted. Multiple ring binders (**2**) use the same principle but have a larger number of rings.

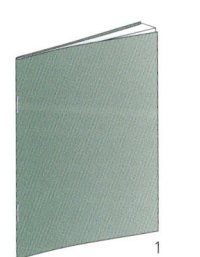

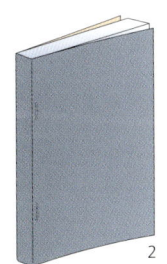

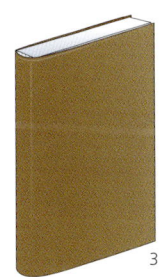

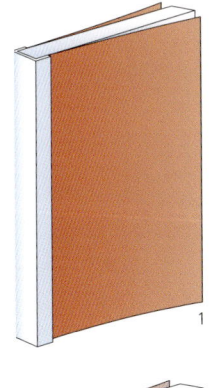

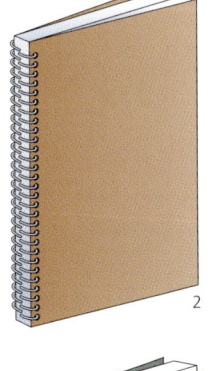

6.19 Keeping pages together

There are four main methods of holding pages together. In saddle-stitching (**1**), the booklet is opened over a "saddle" and stapled along the back fold through the center. In side-stitching with wire (**2**), wire staples are inserted from the front, about 1/4in (6mm) from the back edge, and then clinched at the back, not unlike a stapler. In unsewn (perfect) binding (**3**), the gathered signatures are trimmed along the back edge, roughened and bound with adhesive. In thread-sewn binding (**4**), the gathered signatures are sewn individually and then joined to each other by thread.

6.20 Mechanical binding can take several forms

A plastic gripper may be fitted tightly over the spine to hold the covers and pages together (**1**). In open-flat mechanical binding, holes are drilled through the covers and pages and a wire or plastic coil is inserted through them to hold the pages together. Examples of this method are wiro (**2**), spiral (**3**), and plastic comb (**4**). Unlike (**1**), these latter methods allow the pages to lie flat when the book is opened and so they are perfect for reference manuals and notebooks.

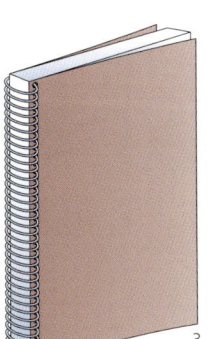

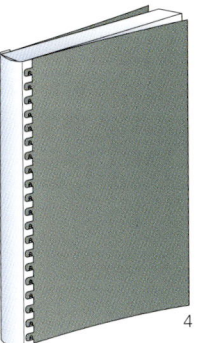

FINISHING

Other finishing methods

Here are some further finishing techniques for more specialist or unusual printing tasks, products, and publications—together with their supporting technologies. As always, it is worth discussing the pricing implications with your print supplier. (For more on working with your printer, please turn to page 158.)

Finishing on web presses
Web presses can be fitted with a variety of attachments to produce a finished product without further off-the-press operations being necessary. These facilities can include sheeting, scoring, perforating, wire-stitching, gluing, and envelope making. As with the folding machine, some web presses can add a glue line at the spine of 8- or 16-page leaflets to avoid saddle-stitching.

Collating
As well as the collating done in bookbinding in the gathering process, there are also collating machines for assembling individual sheets (8½ x 11in [approx. A4 size,) for example. These can be combined with booklet makers that fold, stitch and trim to produce a finished booklet in one operation.

Die-cutting
This is known also as "cutting and creasing." A forme is made (using a CAD system in conjunction with a laser) consisting of knives—blunt for creasing and sharp for cutting—and placed in the bed of a converted letterpress machine or a special die-cutting machine. The process is used mainly for cartons, where irregular shapes have to be cut out and the box corners scored. Laser die-cutting (where a laser beam cuts into the paper) is used in greetings cards and for business cards with cut out logos.

Round cornering
This can be done on a die-cutting machine or on a special round-cornering machine that has a tool shaped like a chisel with a curved cutting edge. This technique is often used for bibles, diaries, and small dictionaries.

Box making
Cartons are made up on special machines that glue the joints together.

Sealing/varnishing
Higher-quality jobs can have the printed area "sealed" with a varnish (printed on the press) that gives gloss and protection. Where the whole sheet is to be varnished (e.g. a paperback cover), this can either be done on a press with a separate varnishing unit added and with UV (ultraviolet) drying, or on a separate varnishing machine. Most paperback books and many cartons have this finish. "Spot varnishing" (spot UV) is used on cartons or books to give a thick layer of varnish and very high gloss to parts of the image (e.g. a title or product brand).

Laminating
Here gloss and protection are achieved by applying a sheet of clear film to the printed matter, with the application of heat. The process is more expensive than varnishing. Cellulose acetate is used for very high gloss, and oriented polypropylene (OPP) where

the laminate needs to fold without cracking. Matt lamination, giving protection without gloss is popular for book covers and jackets, but is more prone to scuffing or rubbing, as it is has a softer surface than a gloss lamination. Care should be taken if the color of the cover is dark, making this effect more visible than lighter colors. A "lay-flat" version of lamination is available for paperback covers to help prevent warping of the cover under various heat or humidity conditions.

Finishing for digital print
The increased use of digital printing—such as for print on demand and other short-run printing tasks—has resulted in the development of specialist binding and finishing machines designed for short-run jobs. These can perform most of the finishing and binding operations described in this chapter.

Loose-leaf binding
A growth area is the loose-leaf binding of reports, computer manuals, and "part works" (where readers collect installments each week or month). Plastic ring binders are popular; they are made by specialist suppliers, and come in a wide variety of spine diameters and colors. Other methods include plastic-slide or post binders.

6.21 Laminating machine
Lamination adds an attractive and highly protective layer to many types of publication.

Stamping and embossing

These finishing processes can add a touch of class to a printed publication, product, or package—however, the use of these techniques is also a matter of taste and fashion. In the 1970s and 80s, for example, they were popular on blockbuster novels, but today many publishers prefer a subtler approach. They are still commonly used on packaging.

Stamping (blocking)
Stamping (blocking) with foil is used on the cases of hardback books (see fig. 6.23) and also on book covers and jackets and cartons to make them stand out on the shelf. The metallic foil is often gold or silver colored, but can be many other metallic or solid, non-metallic colors. Holographic (patterned) metallic foils are also available. A die (brass) made from brass or alloys is produced from the designer's file with the image area raised above the background rather like a letterpress cut (block). On the blocking machine, the die is heated and pressed through metallic or colored foil on to the case material or printed jacket, cover, or carton. Stamping (whether foil or blind) is not suitable for fine detail or very small type, so the areas to be stamped should be reasonably bold.

Blind stamping (embossing)
Blind stamping raises an area of the paper or board (on a book usually the title or author) to make it stand out from the background. It can be used in conjunction with foil stamping to be particularly effective. For this process, two dies are needed—male and female, and these are heated before being stamped into the paper or board. Blind stamping is also often used for letterheads. Debossing is the opposite of embossing, so the area debossed is sunk below the surrounding paper, rather than raised above it. Hardcover book cases that feature a printed illustration should have the printed item placed inside a debossed panel to avoid them being above the level of the case covering material.

Cold foil stamping
This process is often used in packaging and labels for food, pharmaceuticals, and health and beauty products, for example. An adhesive is printed onto the paper by offset or flexographic printing and the metallic foil is then laminated onto the paper, adheres to the image area and is removed from the non-image area. The process uses normal printing plates rather than dies.

6.23 An example of a gold-foil-stamped title on a piece of packaging.

6.22 Finishing workshop at printers
The finishing area at Midas printers in China.

FINISHING

Packing and distribution

Although not technically a finishing process in terms of the printing itself, packaging and distribution—particularly from international suppliers—is a vital area to plan for and get right, ensuring that all of your hard work is not lost or damaged in transit, and that it arrives in time for you or your client.

Packing

This is an often neglected but vital area of the whole production process. Excellent printed products can be produced on sophisticated machinery and yet arrive damaged at their destination due to inadequate packing. If delivery is by the printer's own transport, the parcels can be shrink-wrapped on special machines, or work can be stacked on pallets and the whole pallet shrink-wrapped for protection. Where transport is being arranged by third parties, it is safer to pack the items in stout cartons, particularly if the work is being exported, where double walled cartons (made of two layers of corrugated cardboard) are recommended.

Most warehouses receiving printed material have detailed packing and delivery instructions, covering the type of cartons and pallets required, contents of carton labels, opening hours of the warehouse and usually a requirement to book in deliveries in advance.

DISTRIBUTION

Addressing and mailing

Many printers, finishers and book manufacturers are able to provide facilities for addressing and mailing; this particularly applies to magazines and journals, where the publisher asks the printer/finisher to address and mail subscription copies.

Addressing machines can range from those that simply apply a preprinted address label, to sophisticated computers that print out the labels while the copies are running through the machine. The address can also be printed directly onto the magazine. The more sophisticated machines can also batch the copies for different postal regions or countries. The labels here are often produced by ink-jet or laser printing.

Delivery

There is a wide choice of delivery options, whether it be the printer's own transport, overnight courier services, post or international couriers.

6.25 Shipping cartons
It is vital to enure that easily damaged publications and other print jobs are secure and protected in transit.

6.24 Warehouse
Avoiding the need to store vast quantities of material for freight and distribution is one of the attractions of on-demand printing.

FINISHING

157

Print buying

How do you select the right printer or prepress house for the job and work with them to get an outcome with which both parties are satisfied? The client wants the job delivered on time, at the right price, and to the required standard. The printer wants all these things as well, and yet a printing job can often be unsatisfactory to one or both parties. Although almost all printing is "bespoke" and each job will raise its own special problems, with good planning by the client, especially early on, most problems can be avoided.

When choosing a printer, what is required is a balance between price, quality, and service. Before considering these areas in detail, the area of choice of suppliers must be narrowed to those capable of effectively producing the job required. Printers specialize in one or more particular areas of printing, and there is obviously no advantage in sending the printer, or book manufacturer, a specification that his or her machinery cannot deal with. The printer's plant list will show the buyer if they are equipped to produce the job.

Price

Having chosen a group of suitable potential suppliers, the buyer will normally choose the one that quotes the cheapest price, as long as the quality and service are as good as those of the competitors: there is no point in saving a few percent on the price if the job is likely to be of poor quality, delivered late, or the printer's customer service is poor.

It is normally recommended that at least three competitive quotations be obtained for a printing job, unless the specification is similar to a previous job where the printer proved to be competitive with other suppliers.

Some buyers consider only the first price and do not give printers a chance to requote. Although this is the more ethical approach, many successful buyers negotiate prices down after the first quote; they may, for example, get a printer whose service and quality are good down to the price of a printer whose price is lower. There is obviously a limit to how far this process can go, as the printer is in business to make a profit, but, nevertheless, such negotiations can achieve big savings, particularly if a job is placed at a time when the printer has relatively little work, or if several jobs are placed together, so that the buyer is in effect getting a discount for volume. The buyer needs to very careful, however, to avoid gaining a reputation with suppliers for holding the equivalent of the wrong kind of auction on the price. This can eventually have a counter-productive effect.

Quality

Quality in printing really means fitness for purpose. A glossy promotional brochure needs to be of higher quality than a simple handbill. The use of modern presses with electronic controls means that quality is more of a "given" than in the past, but even so there are still some quality differences between printers. The best way to establish a printer's quality level with a reduced level of risk is by the recommendation of other customers. You can also see samples of work, and a visit to the factory is usually instructive.

Fine **Print** 4-COLOR PRINTING

QUOTATION

Client: T.Q.S Travel	Quote Number: 6251
Address: Block 4a	Creation Date: 08/07/2010
Riverside Avenue, Boston Massachusetts 01778	Produced By: Trevor Hopkins
	Phone No: (508) 261-8849
	Fax No: (508) 261-8481

Title: 32pp travel brochure

Trimmed Size: 8¼ x 11½ inches

Colors: 4C throughout

Repro: Supplied as PDFs by client

Stock: 90lb Coated Cartridge

Finishing: Trim and fold to finished size

Quantity:	20,000 copies	Run/on:	1,000 Copies
Cost:	$7,600	Cost:	$195
Comments: Wet proofs included in overall costs			

WORKING WITH THE PRINTER

7.1 Printer's quote
This is the minimum level of detail and clarity that you would expect from a good, professional print supplier.

Service

Service means meeting all the schedule dates and the final delivery dates and, if possible, making up time if the job runs late at any stage. It also means fast answers to queries and good attention to detail. Service is obviously of paramount importance on dated items such as magazines, reports, accounts, and so on. Where very fast turnarounds are required, one has to pay extra for the service, as the printer has to have sufficient staff (sometimes on night-shift, or paid overtime) and equipment to be able to respond rapidly to the customer's requirements.

Print buying

Print buying does not lend itself to the application of hard and fast rules, and a good print buyer is one who has learned from experience and has an instinct for the right supplier for a particular job. The real key to effective print buying, however, is to develop a good relationship with the printer. This can be achieved by continuity—in other words, by using a small group of suppliers who each receive a reasonable amount of work, rather than spreading the work thinly among a large number of suppliers. It is also important to develop "give and take"—whereby, for example, a printer may ask if a job can be delivered a couple of days late and, if the client can permit this, there is obviously a better chance of the printer returning the favor on a future job.

The printer's salesperson

Printers' sales staff, or "reps," vary enormously–from the superb to the appalling. A good salesman or saleswoman will start with a letter outlining his or her company's facilities, follow up with a telephone call to make an appointment, visit to explain how the company can help the buyer, provide production advice if so requested, estimate promptly and follow up with a telephone call to check how the estimate compared with those of competitors. Once working for the customer, the salesperson will act as the customer's representative in the factory and follow jobs through to completion. The bad salesperson will drop in without an appointment, be badly briefed on what the company can do, not fully comprehend the process, take a long time to give an estimate or sometimes not give one at all, and then either not follow up or, perhaps worse, pester the buyer daily.

Print management

This has established itself firmly, in the last ten years or so, as a method of placing print. Its origins are in "print broking" where a middleman would take a printing order from a client and place it with a printer who would pay commission to the broker. Print management is a much more sophisticated development of that concept. A print management company will approach clients (sometimes very large corporations) offering to handle all their print requirements from stationery and forms through to promotional print, or annual reports and manuals. They will do trial quotations to aim to prove that they can buy print cheaper (including their handling costs and profit) than the client going direct to a printer. They can also set up computerized systems to enable the client's staff to order printed items directly (up to authorized financial limits), rather than having to go through the client's central buying department. Print management is part of the trend for companies to outsource any operations that are incidental to their core business.

Buying paper

There can be advantages in the customer buying paper and supplying it to the printer, but in general it should only be considered for high-volume work such as books or magazines. The disadvantages are: the paper has to be paid for at a time based on the delivery date of the paper, rather than on the delivery date for the job as a whole, so that cash flow is affected; if there is a problem with printing on the paper you may end up with an unresolved dispute between the printer and papermaker, with the customer picking up the bill; the customer will not be able to buy the paper for less than the printer unless he or she is buying a very large quantity. Moreover, the customer can end up with excess stock that has to be paid for and stored, at a charge from the printer.

However, if a customer is buying a large tonnage of a limited range of papers, he or she can very often obtain a better price direct than by buying it through the printer, and can have better control and knowledge of likely price increases and availability problems. For contract work (e.g. books or magazines) the buyer will often work with both their contract holding printers and the paper mills to select the required grades, have the printer purchase the paper on their behalf, and store it for constant availability but at a price everyone finds cost-effective due to the higher tonnage involved for every making. Many book manufacturers and commercial printers have "just-in-time" arrangements with their mills or paper merchants for immediate availability of the required papers but in these situations the printer and publisher do not incur the inventory capital carrying cost.

PRINT MANAGEMENT

Advantages
- Ability to get good prices by pooling the print requirements of their clients to get discounted deals from printers in return for high guaranteed annual turnover
- Print buying and management carried out by skilled print professionals, whereas a client buying print direct may have a buyer who is not a print specialist
- Client can hand over responsibility for all print requirements and have one point of contact, rather than having to deal with several suppliers for different types of print

Disadvantages
- Possible loss of control in dealing via an intermediary rather than direct with printer and not possible to develop a relationship directly with a printer
- "Bespoke" nature of print work means that it is difficult for client to be sure that initial anticipated cost savings are actually achieved

7.2 Preflight
If expensive corrections are to be avoided at the prepress stage, after artwork has been supplied to your printer, it is best to preflight your original files before you create PDFs.

Outsourcing (outwork or subcontracting)

A printer will sometimes quote for the whole operation but place part of the work with another supplier. This applies particularly to specialist finishing and binding operations, for which the printer may not have the necessary equipment. This is not usually a problem, as long as the printer takes complete responsibility for the outsourced supplier. Some buyers may want to know with whom the outsourced portion of the project is being placed, possibly to avoid inadvertently using a supplier who has given problems before.

Typesetting

In buying typesetting, the same principles apply as in buying print, but the following additional points should be taken into account.

Today's typesetter performs a very different role than in the past. Most copy is provided on disk or transmitted by email or by FTP (file transfer protocol) directly to the typesetter's Web site. Many manuscripts have already been coded by the publisher, sometimes to conform to one of several standard designs that the typesetter holds on behalf of their publisher customer in various macros on their system. The typesetter now carries out an H&J (hyphenation and justification) check and then completes the page makeup before providing proofs back to the publisher, again often via electronic form. Rarely does the typesetter carry out the first step in the typesetting process, namely the keyboarding. This has become the role of the author who provides their manuscript on disk to the publisher, whose editor also carries out their role with a computer and an editing software program before transmitting it to the typesetter. "Author's corrections" is a contentious area, as it is always difficult to judge if the charge for corrections is fair and some less scrupulous typesetters will put in a low quote for the job but then overcharge for the corrections in order to make a good profit. Some typesetters have a standard charge for corrections of so much per line, and here it is comparatively easy to check the correction bill, while others prefer to charge by the hour and it can be difficult to assess the charge, so it becomes a matter of trust between the customer and typesetter.

Prepress

Proofing, making PDFs, and backup archive duplicate files can be quoted by the printer as scale prices, based on the size of the job. As with typesetting, there can be difficulties over the charges made for changes and extras unless these are specified and discussed earlier in the process. The easiest way for suppliers to deal with this is to have standard charges for extras, either per item or per hour. All of this is part and parcel of the planning stage of the job: think about and anticipate what extras the job may demand, and establish the costs for additional services upfront, otherwise your supplier may adopt a less competitive pricing approach if a lot of unscheduled extra work is demanded at short notice, causing problems at the printers' end with previously scheduled jobs and other clients.

International suppliers

The market for print is increasingly a global one, with printing being done where the supplier has the best combination of price, quality, and service. The recent developments in digital prepress and computer to plate technologies have served to make it much easier to place work abroad, if there are advantages to doing so.

With earlier technology, printing abroad meant sending parcels of film by courier and receiving blues (ozalids) back by courier, with the expense and delay thus incurred. Files can now be sent instantly anywhere in the world by email or FTP and the printer can send "soft proofs" back electronically. These soft proofs are the equivalent of plotter proofs and are for position only rather than color quality. When printing abroad, you can use a prepress house in your home country to make the PDF file and produce a contract quality digital proof and send it to the printer with the file. Alternatively, you can get the digital proofing done by the foreign printer or prepress house and sent to you for approval. This means that you still need to use a courier to send or get back the digital proofs. However, likely future developments in remote proofing mean that quite soon it will be possible for everything to be transmitted electronically, apart from the physical delivery of the finished printed item.

For typeset proofs the same technology applies, and page-proof files are often sent in digital form for printing out at the publisher's offices. Final, approved PDFs can be transmitted via FTP directly to the appointed printing plant from the typesetter, to anywhere in the world that is equipped to receive files in this manner.

Shipping times (by sea) are around four to five weeks from the Far East to the USA or Europe and about three weeks from Europe to the USA—these times are not just to the port, but include inland transport to the client's warehouse. Using airfreight can bring this down to three or four days, but is very costly where the printed item is heavy (such as a book). Air couriers are used for advance copies or a small quantity if there is a special requirement (e.g. the opening of an exhibition). Within Europe, delivery by truck takes two to four days. If, however, the work you are placing abroad is typesetting or design, then no physical transport is required so no cost or delay are incurred.

7.3 Book-printing factory in China
This plant employs many workers to put together novelty children's books by hand.

7.4–7.6 Midas printing plant, Hong Kong
The building, reception, and showroom show how important overseas customers are to Chinese printing businesses and the economy, alongside local customers.

WORKING WITH THE PRINTER

165

7.7 Cargo ship
If you are placing large or heavy orders with a print supplier based overseas, you will have to build into your planning the time and cost implications of putting the job on a ship that may call at several international ports. Air freight is almost certainly either impossible, or extremely expensive.

The type of printing work that is often placed abroad tends to be books or packaging that don't have the same time constraints as commercial or advertising work. The main reason for printing abroad is that labor costs are much cheaper. It therefore tends to be labor-intensive jobs that are placed abroad—examples are high-quality art or photography titles, children's novelty books produced in China or Singapore, or complex typesetting for academic books, where India has become a specialist source.

Assuming you are placing work abroad on price grounds, how do foreign suppliers measure up on quality and service? Most printers abroad working for the export market will have equipment every bit as up-to-date as suppliers in your home country and the electronic controls on presses should enable them to reach the desired standard of print quality. Large foreign suppliers have usually gained international quality standards that ensure inspection procedures to catch any defects in printing or binding. As regards service, exporting suppliers will have customer service staff, who (as well as having good technical knowledge) are fluent in the language of the client's country. There can be problems with the time difference–depending where you print, you may not have any office hours in common, meaning that all communication must be by email, although Far East printers often have export staff working earlier or later shifts to suit the client country. The foreign supplier may also have a sales presence in the client's country, which will ease communications. Where using sea or air freight, it is essential that shipping and packing instructions are correct and complete in the documentation, including the required method for shipping—Ex-works (EXW), FOB, or CIF as these differ in levels or accountability and cost to each party in the contract.

Ex-works

The client is responsible for everything once the printed materials are available at the printer/binder's shipping dock.

F.O.B.

The printer's responsibility ends once the printed items are loaded onto the ship—hence F.O.B. (Free On Board).

C.I.F.

The printer includes in their quoted price the cost of the Insurance and the Freight. These are often quoted as a separate line item to the cost of manufacturing the order. The C.I.F. arrangement can be on the basis of arrival dockside in the destination country, or from door to the door of the client's warehouse.

If you are arranging shipment on the basis of Ex-works or F.O.B. you will need to secure the services of a customs broker and freight forwarding company to handle the various and complex steps to clear the shipment and ensure the correct documents are prepared at the right time.

For shipments coming into the USA, the US Customs now require a special document confirming the pallets have been fumigated against insect infection. Shipments without this are subject to rejection and possible return to the originating port.

It is important to be clear at the outset, whether the job is to be invoiced in the currency of the client's country, that of the printer's country, or even a third currency (e.g. quite often Far East suppliers sell to European clients in US$). Most foreign printers are happy to quote in the client's currency. If not, the client needs to beware of currency fluctuations that could increase the cost of the job. With large jobs, it may be worth the client considering buying currency forward, so the invoiced cost is known in advance.

Specifications

The specification is the key tool used by any print buyer or production manager. It defines the physical attributes of the printed object and is used to communicate these to in-house colleagues such as editors, designers, and warehouse staff, and outside suppliers including prepress houses, printers, and customs brokers, or freight forwarding agents.

Before drawing up the specification, the following questions need to be asked:

- How durable does the job need to be?
- Who will be using it and under what conditions?
- What is the quantity of the first printing and are reprints likely?
- How quickly is it needed?

These points all need to be resolved by the client before the printer is contacted. The printer can be asked to quote on alternative specifications, but this should only be done if there are good reasons for it, rather than simply trying to postpone a decision. Let us assume that all the necessary questions have been answered and the point has been reached where a specification can be drawn up and sent to suppliers for quotation. The first considerations are typesetting (where not done by the client) and prepress. These might be done by the printer or by separate trade houses.

Typesetting specification

If the typesetter is not quoting from actual copy (manuscript) he or she needs to know the number of words, number of pages, typeface, type size, type measure, layout, whether there is any art (photographs or line drawings) to be placed in the pages, the number and type of proofs and what final product is required. The proofs will normally be page proofs (that can be sent electronically as PDFs) and the final product is usually a PDF. Although a typesetter will give a price without seeing the copy, he or she will usually reserve the right to requote on seeing the manuscript. Particularly difficult or dirty manuscripts are referred to as "foul copy" in the typesetting industry and subject to penalty composition charges. A good example would be keyboarding from photocopied material with tiny point size type that has been badly copied.

Prepress specification

Many jobs will have high-res scans supplied by the client, but where the prepress house is to scan originals, the specification should include the number of originals to be scanned, whether they are transparencies or flat artwork and their appearing size. Also specify if you just want high-res scans or also require low-res for the designer to use in page layout applications, with the prepress house or printer dropping in the high-res scan at a later stage.

For quotes for proofing and making PDFs, specify what files will be supplied (application–state which, and/or PDFs), the page size, whether illustrations bleed, whether proofs are to be supplied as single pages or imposed to the printer's requirements, and the number and type of proofs required. It is critical to specify who does what and when in the prepress stages of production to avoid misunderstandings and additional costs.

7.8 Marked-up printout
It's advisable to include a marked-up laser printout of your work for your supplier wherever they are based, to accompany the job on disk, or sent separately if the files are sent via FTP. A markup would include written instructions about images, cutouts, drop shadows, tints, and so on.

169

Printing and finishing specification

Opposite is an example of an enquiry form.

❶ Origination

Under Origination, the printer should be advised what the client is supplying. This could be complete PDF files for the job or page layout (e.g. Quark or InDesign) files with high-resolution files of images. If the job has not been proofed to a "contract" (graphic-quality) standard, then the printer should be asked to supply a graphic-quality digital proof, as an office quality color laser proof will not truly show the color values in the files. If a graphic quality proof already exists for the job, then the printer need only supply a plotter proof or blue (ozalid) for checking that the job has been imposed correctly. Simpler jobs (particularly black and white), where PDFs and digital proofs are supplied may not require any proofs from the printer.

On occasions, the client may require a press proof printed on the press and paper being used for the final job. This is expensive, as the printer has to make plates and make-ready the press exactly as for the final job. This sort of proof might be required if, for example, a promotional item is planned for distribution nationwide and several people in the client company need to approve it in its final form before the printing of the main run. Another, book-related example might be a publisher co-publishing a title with a museum, and staff at both locations need to approve proofs of the high-end reproduction from paintings or photographs.

❷ Trimmed Page Size

The trimmed page size is probably the most important single item in the specification, as this determines which printing and binding machines will fit the job and therefore has a direct bearing on the price.

The chart on page 172 shows the economical page sizes one can get out of a printing press with a sheet size of 43 x 63in (1,100 x 1,600mm), depending on how many pages are printed to view (that is on one side of the sheet). To make the best use of the machine, the job should be printed as near to the maximum sheet size as possible; the price of the job will increase considerably, if you ask for a size that is just slightly bigger than the page size given. For example, a page size of 7 $^{11}/_{16}$ x 10 $^{1}/_{2}$in (266 x 195mm) will fit 32 pages to view. However, if you choose a size of, say, 7 $^{7}/_{8}$ x 10 $^{1}/_{2}$in (266 x 200mm), only 24 pages can be printed to view, requiring a third more plates and make-readies and a third greater number of sheets to be printed, folded, and gathered; all this will add greatly to the cost, even though the size is only fractions of an inch bigger than the more suitable one. Exactly the same principles apply to smaller machines. The printer will be happy to give you relevant information about the presses.

The number of pages printed at a time will also affect the binding or finishing. For example, if you print 24 pages of a book to view, it is more economical to bind in 24s rather than 16s, giving fewer sections to fold, gather and sew. If you are using a large size (bigger than 8 $^{1}/_{2}$ x 11in (or European A4), then check with the supplier the maximum size that can be finished or bound.

7.9 A typical enquiry form for printing and finishing work

ENQUIRY FORM

From: _____ To: _____

Date: _____ Job title: _____

❶ Origination: supplied by client as:
Proofs required: Wet ☐   Digital ☐

❷ Trimmed page size: Upright ☐   Oblong ☐
Bleeds ☐   No bleeds ☐

❸ Extent: _____

❹ Pages: printed in _____ colors on _____
Cover: printed in _____ colors on _____
Laminated ☐ varnished ☐

❺ Paper: _____

❻ Packing: _____

❼ Delivery to: _____
by: _____

❽ Quantity: _____ and 1,000 run on _____

❾ Price to be valid until: _____

❿ Extras _____

WORKING WITH THE PRINTER

Pages to view	Maximum page size (mm)	Maximum page size (inches)
20	309 x 266	10 ½ X 12 ³⁄₁₆
24	266 x 261	10 ¼ x 10 ½
32	266 x 195	7 ¹¹⁄₁₆ x 10 ½
48	193 x 178	7 x 7 ⅝
64	193 x 133	5 ¼ x 7 ⅝

7.10 Maximum trimmed page sizes
Obtainable from a press size 43 x 63in (1,100 x 1,600mm). These sizes allow for bleeds.

7.11 Oblong and upright formats
Upright (or European portrait) an upright rectangular format, and oblong (or European landscape) a horizontal rectangular format.

WORKING WITH THE PRINTER

After the size should come the description "oblong" (or landscape) or "upright" (or portrait) (fig. 7.11). In the US and most European countries, this is also indicated by the width being given first, but in the UK, the height is given first, so it is always best both to state whether the job is upright (portrait) or oblong (landscape) and show it by the order of the dimensions. It is also important to state here whether the job bleeds (i.e. images extend to the full height or width of the page), as this requires a slightly larger sheet size to accommodate the trimming of the images. In book production it is wise to check first with the bindery on their maximum width for an oblong (landscape) book using automated binding equipment, in order to avoid very expensive hand binding.

❸ Extent

The extent (number of pages) obviously depends on how the designer can fit in the copy and pictures but, in order for it to be economical to manufacture, it should be divisible by 4, 8, 12, 16, 24, or 32 pages, depending upon what sheet size is being used; the printer can advise you on this. An example might be a booklet whose extent could be either 16 or 20 pages. It might well be that 16 pages fit exactly on to the particular machine being used, and that the extra four pages will need a separate working involving new plates and make-ready. This means that certain operations nearly double in cost for only a 25% increase in extent. This is the area where the client and the printer need to work closely to give the job an economical extent.

❹ Printing

Specify the number of colors to be used, both for interior pages and cover/jacket, if required. The shorthand for this is:

- 4/4 Four colors both sides of the sheet

- 2/2 Two colors both sides of the sheet

- 1/1 One color (normally black) both sides of the sheet.

It is possible to have any combination of the above, for example, 4/1, 4/2, or 2/1. Although you can print in three colors, this is unusual because most printing machines for multicolor work are two-color or four-color, so that printing in three colors does not make the most economical use of the equipment. With four-color work, if none of the inks are process colors it is important to specify they will be black and three PMS (Pantone—see p. 40) colors, or all PMS color inks that cost extra compared to process inks.

7.12 Signatures (left)
The total number of pages of a finished document is normally divisible by four, or eight. A signature is a group of pages—often 32—printed on a single sheet which, when folded, will be in the correct order.

This book has an extent of 224 pages, which is equal to 14 signatures made up of 16 pages in each.

Quantity	Total Cost	Unit Cost
1,000 A6 flyers	$90.00	$0.09
2,500 A6 flyers	$105.00	$0.04
5,000 A6 flyers	$115.00	$0.023
10,000 A6 flyers	$175.00	$0.017
15,000 A6 flyers	$240.00	$0.016
20,000 A6 flyers	$310.00	$0.0155
25,000 A6 flyers	$380.00	$0.0152
50,000 A6 flyers	$685.00	$0.0137
100,000 A6 flyers	$1,020.00	$0.0102

7.13 Unit cost vs. price
This table shows the relationship between unit cost and price, illustrating how the unit cost decreases when larger quanties are printed. This is part of the reason for short-run or minority-interest publications often being comparatively expensive compared to mass-market items. Pricing them at mass-market levels would lose the publisher a lot of money.

❺ Paper
Unless you specifically require a particular brand of paper or board, it is best to describe the type of paper or board (for instance, "matt blade-coated cartridge" or "gloss coated two sides") and the desired weight, leaving the printer to choose the brand, as he or she may stock a particular brand or have an arrangement to buy it at an advantageous price. In this case, you should ask for a printed sample with the estimate—and, better still, a blank dummy (a book made up in the size, extent, type, and weight of paper required but unprinted). If the client is supplying paper, the printer should be asked to state the sheet or reel size and quantity required (including spoilage [wastage]) and the grain direction, if sheet-fed.

❻ Packing
You must find out the packing and delivery requirements of the warehouse to which the job is being delivered, as labeling, parcel, or carton and pallet specifications vary, to suit their racking system. Printed products can be packed in paper parcels, shrink-wrapped parcels, single- or double-wall cartons, depending on the weight of the contents and whether they will be sent out as full packages to further recipients and, therefore, have to make more than one journey.

❼ Delivery
The delivery date and delivery address should be provided.

❽ Quantity
When stating the quantity, always ask for a "run-on rate" (the cost of an extra number of copies printed at the same time as the main quantity). The purpose of this is twofold: if the client decides to print slightly more or fewer copies, it saves getting a new estimate; secondly, the final delivered quantity is hardly ever exactly the number ordered and a quoted run-on rate enables the invoice to be checked. However, calculations based on the run-on rate (up or down) must be done with care, as they can be misleading if the total quantity has changed markedly in either direction. For example, if a job is increased from 40,000 to 80,000 copies, a calculation based on the run-on rate could be seriously wrong, as the printer may switch from sheet-fed to web-fed offset at 50,000 copies, giving a much lower run-on rate above this quantity.

Because most printing methods give lower unit costs for larger quantities (as the design, prepress and make-ready costs are spread over more copies), there can be a temptation to print more copies than required, which should be resisted. Instead, for example, when printing a short run, consider if digital printing is more economical than offset.

❾ Validity
This is important, as there are periodic increases in labor and paper prices.

❿ Extras
Extras can include optional items (e.g. the extra cost of matt lamination rather than gloss or a more expensive paper). Ask for these to be shown as separate prices, enabling you to decide whether to select these options for the final job.

Book production specifications

An example of a specification for a black-and-white cased book is shown opposite. Here all the above general points on specifications apply, but there are some additional considerations.

Endpapers are normally on uncoated cartridge paper of 80 or 90lb (115 or 135gsm) paper that adheres better to the case than does coated. Sometimes, however, the endpapers may have been printed in a four-color process, and they will normally then be coated, as the printability takes precedence over the adhesion qualities. Self-endpapers can save money, but some strength will be lost.

Printing 4/1 (four colors one side of the sheet and one color the other) can give a good spread of color throughout the book at a lower cost than printing 4/4 (four colors throughout), and can also save in origination costs. Another way of achieving color scattered throughout the book is by the use of wraps and signature inserts; this practice saves money on printing, but it does inevitably add to the binding cost.

Cover board for paperbacks is normally coated one-sided (C1S), meaning that the inside has a rougher surface that helps the glue to adhere to it and the book block; cover board with a smooth or coated inside surface can cause binding problems. The boards from which the case is made should be binder's board for all but the cheapest books, where pasted oak board (strawboard) can be used. The reason for this is that pasted oak board can warp in extremes of temperature and humidity. This consideration is important, because at least some copies of most titles are exported. You need to specify the thickness of boards in points for US manufacture and millimeters for overseas binding. Typical board thicknesses for books are 80, 88 or 98 point in the USA and 2.5 to 3mm elsewhere.

When asking for the basic printing price, it is useful to ask about the costs of various extras. Although these extras may not in the event be required, it will save you having to ask for the prices separately should they become so. These extras can include the cost of a complete language change of the black plate for printing a foreign edition at the same time as the original run (in a co-edition, the cyan, magenta, and yellow plates are common to all languages) and the cost of an imprint change (the cover/jacket, title page and title-verso [imprint page]) for another edition in the original language. Many publishers of quality illustrated books supply text in layout as a fifth-color version of black to enable easy foreign-language translations. If a reprint is expected fairly soon after the first printing, it is worth asking the printer to quote a reprint price at the same time.

The printer's estimate

Having sent out the specification to one or more printers, you should carefully check the estimate on its arrival. The printer may have changed some of the details of the specification to suit the equipment better. In particular, the printer may have changed the size—although, if so, the customer should have been alerted to this separately rather than simply by a different size appearing in the estimate. Other things to watch for are that the weight and type of paper are as given in the specification, and that the paper sample or dummy (if supplied) is acceptable. The validity should also be checked against the specification. If the printer breaks the price down into component parts, the client cannot thereby assume that he or she can use the printer for some parts of the job and another supplier for other parts, as the prices may be based on the printer getting the whole job.

There is a difference between an estimate and a quotation. Usually an estimate is just that, an indication as to the likely cost of a job based on sometimes initial rather than final specifications. A quotation, however, is more specific in both respects and has a deeper legal connotation. It is a firm offer to carry our certain work for a guaranteed price and a supplier can be held more accountable to a quotation. Any variance to the initial specifications is subject to a revision of the first quotation and often a subsequent revision to the purchase order.

7.14 A printing and binding specification For black-and-white cased bookwork, to be sent out to printers to request competitive quotations.

BOOK SPECIFICATION

From:	A publisher
To:	A printer
Date:	08/07/2010
Author/Title:	A book
Origination:	Text supplied as PDFs, jacket as PDF with digital proof. Printer to supply plotter proofs of text and jacket
Trimmed page size:	5¾ x 8⅜in upright (213 x 146mm portrait)
Extent:	160 pages
Printed:	1/1
Paper:	50lb (80gsm) Antique Wove Cream
Endpapers:	Plain on 80lb (115gsm) offset cartridge
Case:	Black imitation cloth over .088 (3mm) boards, foil stamped in gold on spine
Jacket:	Printed 4/0 and matt laminated on 100lb (150gsm) gloss art paper
Binding:	Burst, separate plain endpapers, rounded and backed, head and tail bands, jacketed
Packing:	In double wall cartons of on pallets
Quantity:	10,000 and 1,000 run on
Delivery:	To publisher's warehouse
Extras:	Imprint change in black to jacket and prelims and blocking change on spine
Validity:	Six months

WORKING WITH THE PRINTER

Quality control

With so much design and production work now done digitally in-house prior to involving an external supplier, quality control can be a contentious area when dealing with printers as, to a large degree, it depends on you supplying them with everything they need. However, sometimes errors do occur with digital files that were correct when leaving the customer's desktop, and mistakes still happen at the proofing, printing, and finishing stages, which remain the printer's responsibility.

The print buyer's control of quality was mainly that of checking material going to and from the printer. However, whereas in the past the print buyer saw the originals, now normally only electronic files are supplied which means that the control of the quality of the images is mainly an editorial/design responsibility. Even when digitally proofed, the original photographs or artwork that were supplied as high-res scans may not be available, so the quality control of images has to take place at an earlier stage in the workflow. Despite this, modern systems and processes mean that color is measured at all stages (design, prepress, and press), which is more accurate than judging by eye.

To avoid prepress and proofing problems it is worth putting a prepress or repro house, or anyone who is originating the scans (sometimes this can be the author/photographer), in contact with the printer to secure a profile "footprint" of the press that will be used to print the job. This is achieved through the use of the ICC profiling method that is now in international use.

Where a job is very critical or has a very long run, it may be passed on press. When the job has been completed, the buyer should ask for advance copies to approve before dispatch (if time allows) so that, if there are any queries, checking and, if possible, correction can be done. On critical jobs, advance printed sheets can be supplied, for approval prior to finishing. Opposite are the particular points to look for.

7.16 Checking the binding
This can be the most expensive and problematic area for printers to put right, as it can mean restarting a job from scratch if there are errors in the trim size of the paper, or in the binding process itself.

7.15 Running sheets
These are checked, sometimes randomly, by printers to ensure that quality remains consistent throughout the run.

QUALITY CONTROL CHECKLIST

- **Setoff**
  This is where the ink from one sheet smudges on to the underside of the following sheet during printing, and is particularly noticeable on covers where the inside is blank. It is caused by not using sufficient anti-setoff spray, or sufficiently quick-drying inks, or problems with the paper.

- **Color variation**
  This occurs where the printer does not maintain consistent color throughout the run and with the use of modern press control equipment should rarely be a problem nowadays. The press operator pulls a sample sheet at regular intervals during the press run and checks this against the approved proof and signed off press sheet if someone is attending for a "press check."

- **Bull's eyes/frog eyes (hickies)**
  These are small areas of unwanted solid color surrounded by an unprinted "halo" area, and are caused by specks of dirt, paper debris (linting) or ink skin on the plate or blanket cylinders. These can be avoided by regular washing of the blanket. These should be picked up by regular checks on press and affected copies discarded.

- **Bad register**
  This is easy to spot as normally the color(s) out of register protrudes beyond the edge of the four-color set, creating a blurred or fuzzy visual effect making the subject look out of focus.

- **Binding faults**
  These are often the most expensive to put right, as very often a problem here means the job has to be started again completely from scratch. Perfect binding always has to be monitored closely, particularly on heavy, coated papers. Binders have testing equipment for page pull and flex strength and test copies at regular intervals during the run. Inaccurate trimming is sometimes a problem, as is marking on coated papers, where the paper is marked by ink rubbing in the finishing or binding processes. Printing a seal over the printed image can help to avoid this.

Scheduling and print orders

Setting aside for the moment all of the technologies and mechanical processes needed to produce a finished printed item, perhaps the most vital aspect of print production to master and manage effectively is scheduling. It is here that the success of the job truly lies. Scheduling is not just a matter of printing; it needs to accommodate and anticipate proofing, error fixing, packaging, and distribution timescales, and enshrine these in a formal contract.

All but the simplest print jobs should have a schedule drawn up giving the deadlines for the various stages. When preparing the schedule, the buyer should verify with his or her colleagues that the in-house dates are feasible before checking with the printer as to how much time will be needed for the different stages. Where possible, contingency time should be built in to allow for any corrections and second proofs that might be required, or other unforeseen problems that may occur. Don't forget that one day's delay in getting material to a printer may not translate into a day's delay in delivery—if a job loses its place in the queue, the next job may be a big one, meaning that your job is delayed by more than the delay in supplying material.

As well as the delivery date, it is important that the schedule allows for timely proofs where required (e.g. proofs to be submitted to a client's presentation). The key to scheduling is ongoing communication with all the parties involved.

The printing order
Once chosen, the printer should be given a written order for the work, detailing the specification, price, and delivery date.

Details such as warehouse opening hours are important as well—no point in delivering a job at 4.00 pm on a Friday, if the warehouse closed at 2.00 pm! Also, give a contact person at the warehouse and phone and email details. Giving detailed packing instructions is even more vital in bookwork than in commercial work, as many publishers' warehouses are highly automated and give very precise instructions on labeling, type, and size of cartons, type, and size of pallets, and maximum height of books on a pallet. Failure to follow these instructions can lead to charges for repalletizing—sometimes the load can even be turned away from the warehouse for the printer to repack or repalletize. An essential instruction is to have the books packed flat and not on end.

The printing order should state acceptable overs and unders—the printer aims to deliver the required quantity, but because of the many stages a job has to go through, there is usually an allowance (e.g. +/- 5%).

The printing order is a legal document, indicating acceptance of the printer's "quoted" price and forms the basis of a contract between client and printer. It is therefore important that the details are clearly spelt out, to avoid any problems at later stages.

Using the Internet
A lot of data is transmitted via the Web between client and printer—this used to be known as EDI (Electronic Data Interchange), but that acronym is now rarely used. As an example, the printer may have a Web site with a blank specification template giving headings for the buyer to fill in the details of the job. The price is then calculated by the printer's estimating department and emailed to the client. Where a job is fairly standard, the estimate request form can be interactive, meaning that the price is automatically calculated by the software referring to the printer's price scales and quoted instantly, so that the client could try out different specifications and get immediate feedback.

On simple jobs, the client can indicate their acceptance of the estimate, now legally deemed a quotation, and this acceptance acts as the order. On more complex jobs the order can be sent separately. Using the Internet dramatically reduces paperwork and administration costs for both client and the printer.

Some systems have templates for standard items such as letterheads or business cards, so that the client can fill in personal details (phone, email address, and so on), and immediately order the item without having to supply a file.

Once the job is placed, some printers offer clients the ability (via a Web site) to track jobs and see exactly what stage a job has reached and the confirmed delivery date. The use of Job Definition Format (JDF) that is starting to be introduced by printers means that all stages in the printing process from the client's order, via the printer's customer service staff to the individual presses and finishing machines can be linked electronically and feed information up and down the workflow.

The days when you used to ring your contact at the printer to check on progress of a job and he would wander onto the factory floor to check progress are—on the whole—long gone.

Legal considerations

The business relationship between client and printer is governed by the laws of their country (where the client and printer are in different countries, they must agree which country's laws apply) and most printers have terms and conditions that will cover the following areas:

- **Price variation due to increased cost** (this can apply particularly to paper, where the paper mill or merchant may impose price increases at short notice)

- Sales tax (VAT)

- Client's acceptance of proofs

- Ownership of files

- Variations in quantity

- Ownership of goods and payment

- Claims

- Insurance

- Liability

- Insolvency

- Illegal matter (e.g. libel)

As these terms and conditions will apply in the event of a dispute, it is important that the client reads the "small print" and comes to a separate agreement about any items they disagree on—or the client can ask the printer to agree to the client's terms and conditions.

It is fortunately only rarely that disputes between printers and customers reach the stage of going to court. They can usually be settled by negotiation or, failing that, some form of arbitration, where the parties in dispute agree to accept the verdict of an independent third party.

Checking invoices
On completion of the job, the client checks the invoice and approves it for payment. This is done by reference to the quotation and the printing order and acceptance of any extras incurred on the job.

The international perspective
While the laws governing printing and publishing—and, in particular, intellectual property—vary from territory to territory, they are struggling to keep pace with the implications of global technological change and the Internet, which has challenged the notion of intellectual property in an era when digital content can, in effect, be "stolen" an infinite number of times, while leaving the owner still in possession of the original item. Companies such as Google have stated an aim to digitize and make available the content of books via its search engine. However, another area that ought to be factored into your thinking applies to the use of overseas print suppliers. In certain territories—such as China—the prevailing political climate means that print suppliers can be prosecuted if local authorities believe they are printing material that might be regarded as seditious, obscene, or critical of the authorities—including images of political protest.

7.17 Lawyers
Forward planning and consideration of potential legal repercussions is vital when committing anything to print.

Glossary

by Tony Crouch, with Chris Middleton

A note on US and British spelling and terminology.
The spelling follows US style. Where a single meaning is covered by more than one word it is normally defined in terms of its first occurrence, be it British or American, and then cross-referenced.

A

A sizes The finished trimmed sizes of paper in the *ISO International Paper Sizes* range. See also International Paper Sizes on p. 214.

AA/AC (US/UK) See *Author's Alterations/ Author's Corrections*.

APR Asahi Photopolymer Resin A *letterpress* or *flexographic* plate made from a clear and flexible *photoploymer* liquid.

ASCII (American Standard Code for Information Interchange) A digital text file format used to transfer data. It does not include any formatting.

Acid-free paper Paper with a pH rating of 7 or higher rating of alkalinity. Acid-free paper has a much longer life expectancy than paper with a higher acid content.

Accordion fold (US) A series of parallel folds resembling an accordion when opened. **(UK)** Concertina fold.

Achromatic A method of *color correction* used on a color *scanner* to achieve an extended degree of *undercolor removal* (UCR). In conventional UCR, most of the color and tone is still contributed by the three *primary colors*, with the black lending only deeper shadow tones. With achromatic reproduction the very minimum amount of color required is computed and the black is added to produce the required depth of color.

Acrobat Adobe-patented technology that allows documents (text and graphics) created on one computer system to be read on and printed out from another system. The heart of the system is *PDF* (Portable Document Format) technology, from which application files or PostScript code are processed through Acrobat Distiller. The end user requires only the reader component. Used extensively for both proofreading and transmitting final files. All formatting, fonts, text, and images are included.

Adhesive binding A binding method used for magazines and books whereby an application of either hot- or cold-melt glue is applied to the roughened spine edge of the publication. Usually ⅛in (3mm) is lost on the spine margin during the grinding process to make the paper receptive to the glue.

Air-brushing A term that originated with the manual use of a spray to modify a photograph. Now part of several software programs that achieve the same end result via digital means, e.g., *Photoshop*.

Aliasing When "*jaggies*," or visual stair-stepping effect, becomes apparent in an image. Caused by a low-resolution file. Can occur when an image is enlarged beyond its capacity to be viewed as smooth edged.

Anti-aliasing The addition of increasingly lighter pixels to a jagged (stair-stepped) edge to smooth the visual effect.

Alphabet length The length of a *lower case* alphabet in a particular font. Assists *casting off*.

AM Screening Conventional screening in various screen rulings featuring a display of dots in different sizes.

Ampersand The character "&," meaning "and."

Angle bar (US) see *Turner bar*.

Aniline A category of liquid inks used in *flexography*.

Antique A paper finish denoting little or no calendering. Bulks highly but usually not suitable for *halftone*. reproduction. See also *Wove(n)*.

Application file A data-based file prepared in the native format of a software application, e.g., InDesign.

Aqueous coating A coating applied after initial printing, but usually in-line from a water-based solution to further enhance the visual printing effect.

Archiving Storing of text and images for easy retrieval in the event of reprinting or repurposing in other media.

Art(work) Material for illustration on the printed page, e.g., photographs, maps, line drawings, and so on.

Ascender The portion of a lower case letter that extends above the x-height, e.g., b, d, and k.

Assembly (1) Combining all of the items, text, and images to prepare a printing *plate*. **(2)** See also *Flat*.
Author's alterations/corrections (US/UK) Corrections made to the original content (text and illustrations) provided by the author at any stage in the proofing process and sometimes charged back to the author.
Author's proof The proof provided to the customer.
Autopaster A *flying paster*.
Azure A gray- or blue-shaded paper.

B

B sizes The *ISO International Paper Sizes* used primarily for posters, wallcharts, etc., where the difference between each A size represents too large a jump. See p. 215.
BF Bold face. See *Bold*.
BPIF British Printing Industries Federation. The employers' body for printing in England, Wales, and Northern Ireland.
BPOP Bulk Packed on Pallets **(UK)**.
Back/spine The binding edge of a book or booklet. *Cased* books are backed by machine.
Back margin The white area between the spine and the commencement of the type area. See also *Gutter*.
Back step (collation) marks Black numbers or letters on the spine of a *signature/section*. When the signatures are *gathered*, the marks appear in a staggered sequence on the spines indicating if any are out of order.
Back to back/backup (US/UK) (1) Aligning the reverse side of a previously printed sheet to match the type area. **(2)** Preparing a security, second copy of a document, file, or series of files in electronic form.
Backing/release paper The component of a self-adhesive material that acts as the carrier for that material. The silicone-backed material facilitates the easy release of the surface paper, e.g., labels.
Backmatter/endmatter (US/UK) The final pages of a book, e.g., bibliography, glossary, and index.
Bad break A poorly hyphenated final word on a line of typesetting.
Banding An undesired printing effect when the graduation from one tone to another is not smooth, causing a band effect at the transition point.
Bank paper A thin, lightweight writing (air mail) or typing paper.
Bar code Unique graphical identifier printed on publications and packaging. Bar codes can be read on a variety of devices ranging from handheld to large computers for stock control and security purposes. The two most common types are the American *UPC* (Universal Product Code) and the *EAN* (European Article Number).

Baseline An invisible (in print) line for the alignment of all capital letters, *x-height*s, and arabic numerals.
Basis weight The weight in pounds of 500 sheets (a *ream*) of standard size paper, usually 25 x 38in.
Belt press A letterpress machine for printing books (Cameron belt press) and lottery tickets. Flexible (Grace letterflex) plates allow books of variable page length and trim size to be printed.
Bible paper Very lightweight, highly opaque paper used to print dictionaries, bibles, and encyclopedias.
Binary The counting system system based on 0 and 1 used by microprocessors to represent the on/off electrical charges of every computer calculation. Binary calculations are stored in strings of *bit*s (binary digits).
Binder's brass/stamping die (UK/US) Brass, magnesium, or copper used to stamp the type and image on the *case* spine or side panels. **(US)** Also stamping die.
Binding A generic term applied to books and other publications on completion of the printing stage.
Bit Binary digit, i.e. a 1 or a 0, the heart of all digital systems. 24-bit describes computer data stored in strings of binary digits (binary words) that are 24 characters long.
Bitmap Any image formed in monochrome or color by *pixel*s in a rectangular grid. Contrast with *vector* graphics.
Black printer The black printing film and plates used in *four-color process* printing. May have to be altered to accommodate alternative languages.
Blad Book Layout and Design. A small booklet featuring the front cover of a book plus sample pages to provide advance promotion or sales interest at trade book fairs, and to help secure commitments for reviews.
Blank (1) A partially printed sheet held in stock for subsequent printing with current information or an alternative language. **(2)** A blank page in a publication.
Blanket A rubber sleeve that wraps around the *impression cylinder* on an *offset* press, transferring the image from the *plate* to the paper.
Blanket cylinder The cylinder of an *offset* machine. The blanket is wrapped around the cylinder, carries the image from the *plate cylinder* to the paper or printing surface.
Blanket-to-blanket press An *offset* press upon which the blanket is carried. This press can print both sides of the sheet in one pass, known as *perfecting*. The sheet passes between two blanket cylinders each carrying its own image from a separate *plate cylinder* to the paper or printing surface.
Bleed (1) When an illustration or image is designed to run off the page, or edge of the paper. A term also used by book binders to describe overcut margins. **(2)** Ink that changes color or mixes with other colors. This is sometimes caused in *lamination*.

Blind (1) Book *cases* or covers that that are stamped (U.S.), or blocked/embossed (UK), or without the use of ink or *foil*. **(2)** Term applied to a *litho* plate that has lost its image.

Blister card/pack (US/UK) A bubble of clear plastic adhered to a backing board stretching over the product.

Block (UK) (1) A binding term describing the impression or stamping of type or a line image on the cover. This can be achieved with metallic or pigment-based *foil*, or gold leaf. **(2)** In printing, a *letterpress block (cut,* US*)* is the etched copper or zinc plate mounted on wood or metal, from which an illustration or text is printed.

Blocking (UK) To make an impression on paper or board from a *block* specially hardened and heated for the application of *foil*, or which may be used *blind*.

Blowup A photographic enlargement.

Blues/blueprint (US) An economic proof prepared by contacting film in a *vacuum frame* with a specially coated paper developed in an ammonia-based vapor. The result may be blue, black, red, or brown; one- or two-sided; or negative or positive. Also known as "browns" or "Vandykes" **(US)** and as ozalids, diazos, or dyelines **(UK)**. Falling into disuse as digital *CTP* replaces film.

Blu-Ray (disk) Emerging DVD-like disk offering a storage capacity of up to 50GB (double-sided), written by a blue laser, which has a shorter wavelength than the usual red.

Blurb Promotional text on the back cover of a book.

Boards There are many different types of board:

   binder's (US) The best quality of book-binding board. Used for *case* binding and made from a solid sheet of fiber not prone to warp. **(UK)** Grey (sic) board.

   bristol A high-quality cardboard that may be made stiff by pasting two or more sheets together.

   chip A lower-quality board made from *mechanical wood pulp*/ground wood and other waste materials. It is used for rigid boxes, cartons, and showcards.

   cloth centered A *triplex board* in which the the center sheet is cloth for added strength.

   duplex Paper or lightweight card of two qualities or colors, and either made on the machine, or bonded together as a separate process.

   grey (UK) See *Board/binder's* **(US)**.

   ivory A high-grade board of one or more laminations of identical quality.

   mill A high-grade, brown-colored board, traditionally made from rope and other materials. Very hard and tough. Used for covers of superior books, less likely to warp than straw *board*.

   paste (UK) Two or more laminations of paper, for visiting cards etc.; pasted together **(US)** Two or more layers of *chip board* used in cased bindings.

   pulp Manufactured from pulp as a single sheet on a *Fourdrinier* or *cylinder* machine.

   straw Traditionally made from straw and today from pulp or waste materials. Lower cost than *binder's board*, and more prone to warp on casebound books.

Body copy/body text The main text of type as distinct from *display* matter.

Bold A *font* that is heavier in weight than regular text type. Available in most typeface *families*.

Bolt Any folded edge of a section other than the binding/spine fold.

Bond The most commercially used paper for letterheads, stationery, and photocopying.

Book block The printed, gathered sections/signatures of a book or publication ready for the application of glue, prior to paperback binding, or casing in hardcover books.

Book cover/jacket Printed paperback cover or dust jacket for a casebound book.

Book paper Usually a wood-free paper made specifically for books, magazines, and journals. Available in a variety of weights, shades, and finishes depending on whether the content includes line art or photographs.

Bottom out (US) The arrangement of type to prevent *widows*. See also *Orphans*.

Bound book A paperback or hardcover *cased* book, whether adhesive, notch-bound, or sewn.

Brace A curly bracket sometimes joining several lines of type.

Brass (UK) See *Binder's brass*.

Brightness A papermaking term to define the level of blue light reflected by the paper. Contrast with whiteness, the degree of which is achieved by varying the chemical mix in the pulp.

Broadside/broadsheet Any sheet in its basic size (i.e. not folded or cut). In newspapers the large format is equivalent to *THE DAILY TELEGRAPH* (UK) and *USA TODAY* (US), and double the size of tabloids such as *THE DAILY MAIL* (UK) and *THE NATIONAL ENQUIRER* of Florida (US).

Broke Paper Paper spoiled in the making process and which is returned to the beaters to turned back into pulp.

Bronzing A process for obtaining a metallic finish by the addition of a hand- or machine-applied bronzing powder to a wet, adhesive ink.

Brown line/print (US) See *Blues/blueprint*.

Buckram A heavyweight binding cloth with a surface chemical application. Suitable for legal and library or reference book bindings.

Bulk The relative thickness of a sheet or sheets, e.g., a bulky paper and a thin paper may have the same weight.

Bulk factor (US) The number of pages of a paper equal to one inch. **(UK)** Volume.

Bulking dummy See *Dummy*.

Bull's eye/hickie A printing defect caused by dust or lint, usually from the paper or board's surface causing a white spot on the printing surface that should be carrying ink.

Bullet/bullet point (UK) A heavy, centered dot (•) used to make a piece of text stand out, or to identify items in a non-numbered list.

Bumper cartons One-piece-fold mailing cartons with the ends folded tightly to form the bookends, thereby keeping it in place during transit. Usually reserved for high-end, and heavy, individual titles.

Burst binding An *unsewn binding* method whereby the spine fold is burst with perforations during the folding, enabling the glue to adhere to each *leaf* without having to grind off the usual 3mm, or 1/8in.

Buyout (US) Sub-contracted work not handled in-house, e.g., typesetting, or binding.

Byte Computing term usually denoting a fixed sequence of eight bits (binary digits).

C

C sizes The C series within the *ISO International Paper Sizes* range, used to make envelopes or folders to take the standard A sizes. See p. 215.

CCD (Charge Coupled Device) A type of photosensor used in digital cameras and some scanner for the creation of color separations.

CD Compact Disk. Common, low-cost storage format for storing approximately 700MB of digital information.

CIF An international shipping term signifying Cost, Insurance, and Freight, which will be paid for by the supplier and then often rebilled to the customer.

CIP Cataloging in Publication. Program provided by the British Library and the US Library of Congress. Unique entries contain data concerning the publication, including the ISBN, author, and subject matter. CIP details appear on the copyright page of a book or journal.

CIP4 International Cooperation for the Integration of Processes in Prepress, Press, and Postpress. The standards organization for color and job information.

CMYK Abbreviation for Cyan, Magenta, Yellow, and BlacK, or Key, used in four-color process printing. Combined they approximate colors in the spectrum, within the color gamut of printing inks.

CMS Color Management System.

CRC Camera-ready copy. Pre-digital page layout systems, CRC was pasted-up text and art ready for shooting on camera to be turned into plates for printing.

C/T A color transparency.

CTF Computer to Film. See *CTP*.

CTP Computer to Plate. The prepress or imaging process in lithographic printing where a finished digital layout or image file is output direct to a printing plate, rather than to film. Most book and magazine publishers now use this system, which is more efficient and usually more accurate than *Computer to Film* (CTF), although there are some disadvantages.

Calender A stack of steel rollers used to create various levels of paper smoothness, ranging from Antique, through English, to Smooth finish, depending on the number of rollers through which the paper will pass. The calendaring stack is at the "dry end" of the papermaking machine.

Caliper The thickness of a *substrate*, or the device used to measure it.

Cancel page A page that is *tipped* in to replace one containing an error.

Cap height The vertical space taken up by a capital letter. The top may be below the top of the font's ascender, while the foot will always align with the *baseline.*

Caps Abbreviation for capital letters.

Caption A text description accompanying an illustration in a magazine, newsletter, or book.

Carbonless paper (NCR) No Carbon Required Paper that has been coated with microscopic chemicals allowing the transfer, under written or typed pressure, of whatever is being written on the surface onto the sheet below. Variants exist for the use of *bond* paper as the top sheet.

Caret A proof reader's insertion mark on a typeset proof.

Cartridge A strong, opaque paper, usually off-white with an *antique* finish. Can be matte coated.

Case (1) In binding, the cover for a book using cloth, paper, or synthetic material, or a combination of these, over *board.* Can be one or three piece. **(2)** In the hand composing of type, the sectional trays where the type is kept. California case (US).

Case binding The binding of a printed book block into a *case* or hard cover (a casebound book).

Cast coating A high-gloss surface finish to paper. Can be one- or two-sided, as in C1S or C2S. Made by drying the coating with a heated drum that has a chrome surface.

Castoff The estimated length (page count) of a typeset publication from the author's manuscript. The length can vary depending on the chosen typeface, point size, line length *(measure),* and *leading.*

Catch-up Image in what should be a non-image area of a *plate.* Attributable to a water/ink imbalance.

187

Cell Tiny indentations in the surface of a *gravure* cylinder to hold ink.

Cellulose The basic fibers used in papermaking. Obtained primarily from wood *pulp*.

Center line/centered A line of type with an equal amount of space at each end. Contrast with *ragged right* or *ragged left,* or *justified* composition.

Centerfold See *Spread*.

Center point A full point (a period, or full stop) centered on the x-height.

Chalking A drying problem with offset printing leaving a loose pigment on the surface of the paper.

Character Any letter, numeral, symbol, or punctuation mark in a *font* of type.

Character set The complete suite of letters, numerals, symbols, and punctuation marks, plus any special characters, in a *font*.

Check digit The final numeral of a *bar code* to assist the computer in verifying the accuracy of the bar code.

Chemical wood pulp Pulp prepared from wood chips, treated with chemicals to remove resins, leaving cellulose material. Used in the preparation of higher grades of paper, e.g., *freesheet,* or *woodfree*, or to improve mechanical pulps if the two versions are mixed.

Check/Cheque paper (US/UK) Paper that has been sensitized or specially enhanced to provide security printing and assist in the prevention of forgeries.

China clay Material used for *loading* and *coating* high-grade matte or gloss-coated papers.

Choke See *Spreads*.

Chromo An ultrasmooth paper, cast coated on one or both sides.

Club line See *Orphan*.

Coarse screen A halftone screen of up to 35lines per cm (85 lines per inch). Used to reproduce photographs on *newsprint* or similar grade papers.

Coated paper Paper that is coated either one or two sides in matte, semi-gloss, or gloss finish.

Cockling A wave effect on paper caused by changes in the humidity while in transit or storage. Can result in severe problems on press.

Cold melt An adhesive used in binding (like PVA) that does not require heat to melt it. *PUR* glues are the most commonly used.

Cold set Printing by *web offset litho* that does not require heat for drying the ink. It has limitations on the fineness of a halftone screen and suitable paper.

Collate A check of the *gathered sections* of a book or publication to verify they are in the correct sequence.

Collation marks See *Back step marks*.

Collotype A planographic process of printing. Gelatine is applied to a sensitized plate onto which the type and images are exposed, and without a screen. This is a slow and expensive process. It reproduces flowers and art with a high fidelity of color balance and detail.

Colophon A statement detailing the typeface(s) and the materials used to prepare the publication. Often includes information concerning the designer and people or companies involved in the production. Placement is usually at the back of the publication.

Color control bar A strip at the back edge of a sheet consisting of color and grayscale measurements to assist the press operator in determining a variety of controls are working correctly for the job on press.

Color correcting The process of reviewing prepress proofs and making correction marks/comments on them for the next stage in adjusting the color. The actual correction can be carried out in *Photoshop*, or by a supplier using a scanner. Images are usually reproofed.

Colorfast Color gamut. See *Light fast*.

Color Matching System See *Pantone Matching System*.

Color profile Establishing a profile on a prepress device, or for a printing press that conforms to an agreed set of parameters throughout the system.

Color Rotation System (US/UK) The sequence in which the *four-color process* inks are laid down on the paper or material being printed.

Color separation In color reproduction the method whereby an original image, e.g., a transparency, print, or digital file, is separated into the primary colors, plus black. This can be achieved on desktop computers running programs such as Photoshop, or on high-end scanners. Once approved, the separations are converted into film or go direct to plate from the digital file.

Color separation film The *negative* or *positive* printing film produced by a *process camera* or *scanner*. Today film is fast giving way to *Computer to Plate (CTP)* technology.

Color separator (US) Also known as a prepress house, or a repro house **(UK)**. The facility where all material for publication is prepared for print.

Color swatch(es) A set of color reference guides, e.g., the *Pantone* Color Matching System®.

Comb binding A method of binding a publication. Small rectangular holes are punched into pages and covers followed by the feeding of the plastic "comb" which comes in a wide variety of diameters and colors, through the holes. The spine of the comb can be printed.

Coming and Going A specialized *imposition* arrangement whereby pages are printed, usually on a web offset press, *head to head*, allowing for two copies of the publication to be printed simultaneously from one plate. The folding is usually on-line via a double parallel fold, with trimmed signatures at the end of the press. Originally a single cylinder, sheet-fed, printing both sides from the same plate.

Compositor Typesetter. A now outdated role from the days of hot metal printing. In digital layout systems it is usually part of the overall design and production process.

Comprehensive (US) Also known as a Comp. In non-digital systems, a layout of text and images for approval prior to the preparation of a finished *mechanical*.

Compression See *File compression*.

Concertina fold (UK) See *Accordion fold*.

Contact frame See *Vacuum frame*.

Continuous tone An image, such as a photograph, composed of graduations of tone from black to white. Contrast with *line* work, such as drawings.

Contone see *Continuous tone*.

Contrast The variance between the highlights and shadow areas of an image.

Control strip A *color control bar*.

Convertible press A printing press that can print either a single color on both sides of a sheet of paper or board in one pass, or two colors only on one side.

Copy Author-supplied text and supporting material ready for editing and production. Can be supplied as *hard copy* or in electronic form.

Copy editor Person employed to edit an author's text for grammar, spelling, and errors so it is ready for publication.

Copy preparation Also known as markup. Designer's or typographer's instructions for typesetting indicated on the copy, or on a separate document, prior to typesetting.

Copyfitting See *Castoff*.

Copyright The right of the legal party in the contract (author, photographer, artist, or publisher) to control the use of the work being reproduced. International agreements exist to protect the copyright holder. However, intellectual property rights are an increasingly complex area in the Internet age, with local legislative systems often at odds with the global, file-sharing impetus of the Internet.

CorelDRAW A PC-based vector drawing application, within which bimap images can also be traced and turned into vectors. See also *Illustrator* and *Freehand*.

Corner marks Serve as the location in finishing for where the sheet is to be cut or trimmed.

Corrigenda A list of corrections printed in a book—as opposed to an *erratum slip,* which is printed as a separate piece and either tipped in to the publication, or made available as a loose *insert*.

Covering The process whereby a cover is affixed to the spine. Sometimes it wraps for 3mm or ¼in around the sides of a book with a softcover (limp) binding to strengthen the spine.

Cover stock A generic term for paperback cover material.

Crash (1) The numbering of a multipart set of forms on *carbonless paper* using the *letterpress* printing method. The top sheet is printed with a heavy *impression* enabling the same number to appear on subsequent sheets in the set. **(2)** A heavy muslin cloth used for lining with glue to the spine of a book block during binding. **(3)** A finish to paper with a coarse, linen style surface. **(4)** When a computer system or component fails.

Crease See *Score*.

Cromalin DuPont-patented high-quality, off-press, four-color proofing system from color separations, used to provide a good indication of final color reproduction.

Crop/cropping The removal of unwanted areas in an image, allowing only a desired portion to be seen. Images can be permanently cropped within software such as Photoshop, or for a specific purpose/effect by moving the entire image around within a smaller picture box in a page-layout program, so only a portion of the image is visible.

Crown A standard printing paper 15 x 20in (384 x 504mm).

Cursor The moveable pointer on a computer screen.

Cut (US) See *Block*.

Cut flush A binding style where the book block and the cover are trimmed flush to each other. Usually achieved with a *guillotine,* or in-line with a *three-knife trimmer*.

Cut in Index Also known as a *thumb index*. An index to a book, e.g., dictionary, where the alphabet divisions are cut into the fore edge of the book in a series of steps.

Cut line See *Caption*.

Cut marks (US) Printed marks on a sheet to indicate the edge of a page to be trimmed. **(UK)** *Trim marks*.

Cutoff The maximum length of a sheet that can be printed on a *web-fed* press and equivalent to the circumference of its *impression cylinder*.

Cutout (1) An image that has been cut out of its original background. **(2)** A display card that has been die-cut to form a unique shape.

Cutting and creasing A *letterpress* operation typically carried out on a *cylinder press*. It creates special shapes in die-cutting for packaging, or when book covers need to be creased to provide a tight fit on the spine. For each job a *forme* is prepared on a wood base with sharp metal rules conforming to the desired shape. These rules are just above type height.

Cyan The special shade of blue in the four-color process inks, known collectively by the abbreviation *CMYK*. The pigment shade may vary from country to country.

Cylinder machine A paper machine, mostly used for making boards.

Cylinder press A letterpress machine in which the sheet to be printed is carried on a cylinder and brought into contact with the raised surface. Mainly used for *cutting and creasing*.

D

DAM Digital Asset Management. Now print production is largely digital, DAM describes the strategy of managing these digital assets collectively and individually on central servers and in terms of version control, archiving, and easy retrieval for reprints and new editions. A logical DAM strategy can be an asset in itself, as searchable databases can be built from text and images.

DAT (Digital Audio Tape) A compact but linear form of digital storage using tape cartridges. DAT backups are often run at the end of each day within publishing houses. Falling into disuse in favor of more easily searchable and accessible alternatives that degrade at a slower rate.

DCS2 (Desktop Color Separation) A robust format for transmitting five EPS files—one for each color image, plus a master file—from the prepress stage to the final output device, preventing any intervention or changes.

DIN Paper-size standard developed in Germany, which subsequently became an ISO standard everywhere but the U.S.A. and Canada. See pp. 214-215.

DPI (Dots per inch) A measure of the output resolution of a laser printer or imagesetter. See also *pixels per inch*.

DPS Abbreviation for double-page spread. See *Spread*.

DTD (Document Type Definition) A specialized coding system that prepares documents for *XML* searching and display. It identifies the various elements in the document and establishes a hierarchy by the use of machine-readable tags. The results are invisible to the end-user.

DVD (Digital Versatile, or Video, Disk) Common, low-cost digital storage and archive format with a nominal capacity of 4.8GB. New disk technologies such as Blu-Ray offer storage capacities of 25–50GB.

Damper rollers Rollers on a *litho press* that bring water or damper solution to the printing plate, sometimes by way of the inking rollers.

Dandy roll The cylinder on the "wet end" of a papermaking machine that impresses a design or logo into the paper for promotional or security purposes.

Data Any information, especially that stored digitally.

Database Searchable, updatable, and retrievable data held in a systematic manner within a digital system.

Deckle The machine width of the wire on a *Fourdrinier* papermaking machine.

Deckle edge The ragged or frayed edge on the edges of a sheet of handmade paper.

Delivery On a *sheet-fed press* the mechanism that takes the sheet from the printing unit and stacks it in an orderly manner on a skid ready for folding.

Demy Standard size of pinting paper 22½ × 17½in (572 × 445mm).

Densitometer The optical instrument used to measure the intensity of tone on film or reflection copy as well as the ink reading on printed images.

Density The weight of tone or color in any image as measured by a densitometer. The printed highlight can be no brighter than the base paper or board, while the shadow can be no darker than the quality of the ink and the volume of ink the printing process will permit. A greater range in the color gamut is achieved on photographic film or transparencies.

Descender The part of a lower case letter falling below the X-height of the character as in g, q, and p.

Descreen Removal of the original screen value on a previously printed image or film to prevent the creation of a *moiré* pattern. The image is then rescreened to the desired new halftone screen value. Can be applied to one-color or four-color images. Also see *rescreen*.

Device Graphic denoting the publisher's emblem that may form part of the *colophon*, or appear on the base of the spine of a book. Also known as a mark or symbol.

Diacritic A typesetting term applied to a mark placed over, under, or through a letter to distinguish it from one of similar form, or to indicate pronunciation or stress.

Digital printing (DP) An *impression* printed from a digital prepress file via plateless application of text and images using ink-jet, or fused toner (electrophotgraphy), or liquid ink. Some presses image directly from the file to the press.

Diazo See *Blues/blueprint*.

Die See *Binder's brass/die*. **Die cutting** The use of a *die* to cut holes or irregular shapes in display work or on book covers.

Digital press A printing press that is capable of receiving data from a DTP system and printing on paper or other substrates using xerographic, ink-jet, or offset printing processes, without the need to prepare printing plates.

Digital printing The use of either ink- or toner-based technology to print on paper or other materials without the use of *plates*. Applies to both *sheet-fed* and *web* digital presses.

Die stamping An *intaglio* process whereby the image is in relief on the surface of the material, either in color or blind (without ink).

Dingbat An ornament typeface, used for symbols and directional devices on the page.

Diplomatic edition The faithful following in typesetting of an original manuscript, complete with all errors, markings, and rewrites by the author.

Direct to plate (or *CTP*: Computer to Plate) The process of transmitting digital layouts and instructions from a file to the plate without the interim step of creating film.

Directory The list or catalog of all the files, jobs, or documents stored on a computer, drive, or disk.

Dirty copy Manuscript containing numerous revisions and changes making keyboarding more difficult, and thus more expensive. Also known as penalty copy.

Dirty proof A proof with numerous corrections or changes marked on it.

Discretionary hyphen Also known as a soft hyphen. This specially noted hyphen in a computer file will disappear in the event of editing or reformatting.

Disk drive Any device that can store data from a computer, either internally, or by cable, modem, or wi-fi.

Display matter Type used for display matter as distinct from *body type* in main text. Used extensively in advertising type and headings, chapter openings, and so on.

Distributing rollers The rollers on a printing press that distribute the ink from the ink *duct* to the printing plate or *forme* inking rollers. They thin the ink from roller to roller and help to deliver a smooth ink film, so arranged as to help prevent a *ghosting* effect on the printed piece.

Doctor blade A thin, flexible metal blade on a *gravure* or *flexograhic* press that removes surplus ink from the surface of the printing cylinder before an *impression* is made.

Dongle Small piece of removeable hardware that connects to a computer or *phototypesetter,* usually via USB (Universal Serial Bus). It authenticates a specific piece of *software*, or prevents unauthorized software and *fonts* from working. An anti-mumping and anti-piracy device. Dongle-protected software can still be copied, but will not work on another machine without the dongle attached.

Dot See *Halftone*.

Dot etching The process by which tonal corrections are made to *halftone* film negatives or positives.

Dot for dot (1) (UK) The use of pre- *screened prints* on *artwork* enabling them to be reproduced without the photographs needing to be screened. **(2) (US)** Printing color work in perfect *register.*

Dot gain An on-press condition where the dot size of an illustration or text increases, making type appear heavier and images less clear. Some papers, such as newsprint, are more absorbent and thus can cause increased dot gain. All presses have a dot gain capacity, and software can compensate for the problem.

Excess pressure exerted on the *blanket,* or use of an overly worn blanket during the press run can also add to dot gain.

Double coated Premium-quality *coated papers* receive two or more coatings on each side.

Doublepage spread See *Spread.*

Doubletone ink A printing ink producing a secondary tone as it dries.

Doubletruck See *Spread.*

Double wall Refers to cartons that have two walls of corrugated fiberboard to protect printed matter or books in transit. Recommended for heavy items or cartons that may have to make more than one journey. Compare to *single wall.*

Download When data is transferred from one computer or data device to another, often from a server, such as a Web server, to a "client" desktop computer.

Draw down A strip of ink spread on a sheet of paper with a pallet knife and allowed to dry in order to show the resulting final color.

Drawn-on cover A paper or board book cover that is attached to the *sewn* or *adhesive bound* book by the application of glue to the spine.

Driers (1) The components in a printing ink or varnish allowing it to dry through reaction with oxygen in the air, or via absorption. **(2)** On a printing press the drying mechanism after the application of ink to the paper or board. The drying may be via *UV (ultraviolet)*, infrared radiation, or gas heat.

Driver Software that allows a computer to interface with all the functions of a peripheral digital device, such as a printer or scanner.

Drop A gap, or the space between the top trim of a page or column, prior to the commencement of the type area, expressed in mm., inches, *points*, or lines of type.

Drop cap An upper case character appearing larger than the text point size, but dropped into the main text type. It may occupy several lines of text type and is often used as the very first character of a chapter in a book, or at the beginning of the first line of a magazine feature, for example. It signifies the beginning of a piece of text.

Dropout To expose by the use of *filters* to prevent an item from appearing on the final printed version.

Dryback The reduction of the initial gloss of ink as it dries to its final condition.

Dry litho See *Waterless offset.*

Dry offset See *Waterless offset.*

Dry proof Any proof that is prepared off press. Cromalin, Matchprint, Epson, Approval, Waterproof, etc., all fit into

this category of proof. Various systems use powders, films, ink-jet, or thermal transfer to achieve the proof.
Duct The reservoir on a printing press that contains ink, or the *damper* water solution for transfer to the plate.
Dummy A sample copy, often blank, submitted for approval of the client, and prepared with the actual paper and cover materials to be used in the final production. In book publishing, dummies are supplied on request to indicate the bulk, binding style, extent, and "feel" of a printed item, so that clients can have a good indication of what the final item will be like. Also a complete mockup of a project showing the position of the type and illustrations.
Duotone Two *halftone plates* made from the same original image, usually a black-and-white photograph, but to different tonal ranges. When the image is printed a duotone will have a greater tonal range than is possible from one-color reproduction. One color in a duotone is usually black; the other can be any color.
Dupe Abbreviation for "duplicate."
Duplicate A film or printing *plate* that is an exact copy. Duplicating film will produce one positive or negative directly from the original.
Dyeline See *Blues/blueprint*.

E

EAN (European Article Number) See *bar code*.
ECF Elementally Chlorine Free. A method of pulping without the use of chlorine as a bleaching agent.
EPS (Encapsulated PostScript) A file format often used for images generated in object-orientated drawing applications, e.g., *Illustrator* or *Freehand*, and also for scanned images. Contains a *postscript* file, which describes the image, and a preview image for display on a computer screen.
EXW A shipping term, Ex-works, whereby the customer assumes all costs and responsibility for the goods from the supplier's shipping dock.
Edges, sprinkled Book edges colored with a brush full of liquid ink, or an *airbrush*. Used as decoration for books —in paperbacks to hide the edge discoloration of an inexpensive paper. Rarely used today.
Edition A number of identical copies printed at the same time, either as the first edition, or (following subsequent changes and updates after the first edition) as a revised, expanded, or new edition.
Electro/type A duplicate *letterpress* block/cut made by 'growing' a layer of electrolytic copper on a mould taken from the original type or block/cut. Used to distribute the same image to a wide variety of printing locations.

Em The area occupied by the capital letter M. It will be wider or narrower than square, all depending on the style of the letter in a specific typeface. An em space is twice the width of an en space. Ems and ens are referred to, respectively, as "muttons" and "nuts."
Embossing, blind The process of raising or recessing an image using an uninked block.
Emulsion Normally, a light-sensitive coating on film or a printing *plate,* but it may also include *encapsulated* aromas or flavors in promotional printing.
Emulsion side The matte side of a film that is placed in contact with the *emulsion* of another film or *plate* when printing to ensure a sharp image. As in "right-reading emulsion down."
Enamel paper (US) A *coated* paper.
Encapsulation (1) In printing or papermaking, a chemical may be enclosed in a microscopic capsule, such as perfumes for promotional printing or coloring chemicals for *self-copy papers.* **(2)** Method of packing in a *blister card/pack.* **(3)** Sealing a printed item in an airtight plastic covering (usually by small, local, short-run printers).
Endmatter (UK) See *Backmatter* **(US)**.
End of line decision In typesetting *hyphenation* and *justification (H&Js),* the decision made by a keyboard operator or by a computer as to where a line should end.
End notes Notes to the main text which are placed either at the end of the chapter, or collected by chapter at the end of the book's main text.
Endpapers Lining paper used for the front and back of a casebound book. They adhere to the first and last signatures of the book and attach to the front and back covers of the *case.* Also known as endsheets.
Engraving (US) See *Block* **(UK)**.
Erratum or Errata slip See *Corrigenda*.
Ethernet A high-speed *network* protocol used to interconnect some computers.
Even working Mainly used in book work. Planning the imposition to work with an even number of signatures so as not to have an extra signature containing blank pages.
Extenders See *Ascenders* and *Descenders.*
Extent The complete number of pages in a printed work, which will normally be a multiple of four or eight.

F

F&C/F&G Folded and Collated/Gathered. Sheets of a book that have been folded and *gathered* and/or *collated* in preparation for binding.
FOB A shipping term meaning Free on Board. The customer assumes all responsibility dockside for the freight cost and insurance with attended risks.

FPO (For Position Only) A low-resolution image in a digital document to indicate the size and placement for the eventual high-resolution image.

FTP (File Transfer Protocol) A data transmission and communication protocol for sending large amounts of data between remote locations, either via a Web browser, or using dedicated FTP software. (Compare with HTTP [Hypertext Transfer Protocol], used to allow remote computers to connect to a Web site.)

Fade-out halftone (US) See *Vignette*.

False double See *Spread*.

Family A group of related *fonts*, including *roman, italic, bold, extended* and *condensed*, all derived from the same typeface design.

Feathering Also known as carding. The addition of extra vertical space to assigned *leading* on lines of text.

Feeder The part of a *sheet-fed* press or folder that transfers the sheets of paper to the printing/folding units.

Feet/foot margin The white area at the bottom of a page between the type area and the trimmed edge.

Feint Lines, usually ruled and printed in a pale blue on account book pages and in school exercise books.

Felt side The side of a paper on the reverse of the wire side of the papermaking machine on which it is formed. Also known as the top or right side.

Figure (1) An illustration; often abbreviated to fig. **(2)** A numeral, as opposed to a letter.

File compression The use of specific algorithms to make digital file sizes smaller, either with a noticeable loss of quality ("lossy" compression), or by using perceptual algorithms that only discard data that will not be missed, or which is unnecessary ("lossless" compression). The difference between the resolution of computer screens and printed items means that low-resolution images appear to be much higher resolution on screen, but will reproduce poorly in print. Therefore images for the Web can be highly compressed, enabling much faster download speeds. Different file formats—e.g. *JPEG*—use different codecs (compression/decompression methods).

File server A dedicated, secure central computer holding all the files being used by workers on a networked system. It reduces the need to hold massive amounts of data on local computers, and data can also be better managed and backed up from a single location.

Film assembly/stripping (UK/US) The bringing together of all the elements of film on a *foil* or *goldenrod* during the imposition stage.

Film composition See *Phototypesetting*.

Film lamination A polypropylene or other synthetic film laminate applied in one of a variety of finishes (gloss, matte, silk, lay-flat) to the printed surface of a dust jacket, paperback cover, or item piece. Used both for visual effect and protection.

Finish The surface given to a grade of paper from *calendering, coating*, or *embossing*.

Finishing (1) All operations performed after printing. **(2)** The hand lettering or ornamentation on the cover on a handbound book.

Filled in The effect on a halftone, or the counters on letters such as "e," being blocked in with an excess of ink.

Firmware Programs integrated on a *chip* to form the core component of the system's *hardware*.

First and third A printed sheet on which the printed matter appears on pages 1 and 3 when folded. Achieved by printing it on both sides, as opposed to a *french fold*.

Fit (1) See *letter fit*. **(2)** See *Register*.

Fixed space The space between words or characters not variable for justification purposes. Used in *ranged* left, *ragged* right, *centered*, and *tabular* typesetting.

Flat (1) An assembly of *imposed* film or photographic paper, as in *CRC*. **(2)** A *halftone* of inadequate contrast, maybe lacking in *density*.

Flat back Bound sections or signatures having a square spine, as opposed to a *rounded* and *backed* spine; normal in *limp bindings*, but less common in *case binding*. More common in short-extent children's books.

Flat color Area of printed color with no tonal variations.

Flat wire stitching See *Stabbing*.

Flexiback/Flexibind (UK/US) A binding style with sewn signatures. Often used for guide books.

Flexography A relief printing process using rubber or plastic plates on a *web-fed* press and solvent-based liquid inks. Mainly used for packaging, and for some newspapers.

Floating accents Special accents or diacritics that can be positioned, or "floated," over the required character.

Flop When an image is reversed (or flipped) from its intentional appearance, usually in error.

Floret/flower Typographic ornament. Also printer's flower.

Flush See *Cut flush*.

Flush left/right Type that aligns vertically to the left or to the right. Also described as *ranged* left or right. Contrast with *ragged left* or *right*.

Fly fold A single fold providing a four-page leaflet.

Flying paster The part of a *web-fed* press that joins a new reel of paper to the nearly completed web of the current roll on press. It avoids the need to stop the press and apply a new roll.

Foil (1) Film with either a metal or color pigment used to *block* type and images on book covers and packaging. **(2)** Clear, stable film used as a backing during *film assembly*.

Foldout The page(s) of a book or publication *imposed* to facilitate a series of folds that combine to reside at least ⅛in (3mm) in from the *fore edge*. The foldout is bound inside the publication to prevent it being trimmed off during *finishing*. As a result, three or more pages, often in *accordion fold*, can be viewed as a *spread*.

Folio (1) A page number, and consequently a page. **(2)** A large book in which the full size sheet only needs to be folded once before binding.

Follow copy An instruction to the *compositor* to set the type exactly per the *manuscript* without any corrections for errors of fact, style, grammar or spelling. Also see *Diplomatic edition*.

Font Software which contains the data necessary to generate the characters or glyphs for a particular typeface.

Foolscap See p. 217.

Footer Recurring information at the foot of a page in a book or magazine, often repeating the title, subject matter, or chapter heading. Also see *Headline*.

Fore edge The edge of a book or publication where it opens for reading. As opposed to the *back*, spine, or binding edge.

Form/forme (US/UK) In *letterpress* the forme comprises all the type and *blocks* in a *chase* ready for printing.

Former On a *web-fed* press the folding element that makes the initial fold, parallel to the *machine direction* of the paper.

Fount (1) A fountain or *duct* on a press. **(2) (UK)** A set of type characters of the same design, now more commonly referred to using the US *font*.

Fountain The part of a printing press containing the ink, sitting at the top of a *unit*. An array of *keys* controls the flow of the ink onto the rollers.

Forwarding In hand *case binding* the stages in book making after sewing the signatures, but before *finishing*.

Four-color press A press that prints one side of a sheet in four colors in one pass through the machine.

Four-color process Color separation from original art, transparencies, or files followed by printing the three primary colors, *cyan* (C), *magenta* (M), and *yellow* (Y), plus *black* (K, standing both for "key plate" and also instead of "B" to distinguish it from blue).

Four-color inks The pigmented inks used to reproduce the four-color process.

Fourdrinier A papermaking machine on which the pulp is held on a moving wire before moving onto a series of heated rollers to dry. The liquid pulp begins with over 90% water and finishes with 5% humidity. Further treatments may include calendaring, coating, and sheeting.

Four-score When the cover for a paperback publication is scored four times, two for the spine, and two typically ¼in (or 5mm) in from the spine edge acting as a hinge when the book is opened. Also see *score*.

Freehand An object-orientated drawing program made by Macromedia. Used to generate diagrams, logos, and technical illustrations. See also *Illustrator*.

Freesheet (1) (US) A paper made only from *chemical pulp* and excluding *groundwood* or *mechanical wood pulp*. **(2) (UK)** A local newspaper without a cover price whose only revenue is from advertising sales.

French fold (1) A sheet of paper with four pages printed on one side only, then folded twice with right-angle folds into quarters without cutting at the *head*. The inside pages are blank with an image appearing on pages 1, 2, 3, and 4, but actually on pages 1, 4, 5, and 8 of the *imposition*. **(2)** A dust jacket that has a fold over at the top and bottom to provide extra strength. Usually reserved for large art books.

Frog eye (US) See *Bull's eye*.

Front lay See *Lay*.

Frontmatter (US) The pages of a book prior to the main text, including contents, imprint page, etc. **(UK)** Prelims.

Frontispiece The illustration placed facing the title page in a book. Maybe printed on text stock or *tipped in* as a separate page printed on coated stock.

Fugitive color An ink that is no longer stable on press. Can be affected by light, moisture, or atmospheric conditions.

Full/whole bound A *case binding* known as a one piece, i.e., the same cloth or binding material covers the entire *case*. Contrast to a three-piece case or *half bound* and *quarter bound*.

Full color Interchangeable term for *four-color process*.

Full out Type that is set to the specified full *measure*.

Full point/stop (.) (US) A period.

Furnish In papermaking, the mix of raw materials.

G

Gatefold Two parallel folds towards each other, in which the fold can be opened from the left and right.

GSM or G/M2 (Eur) Abbreviation for grams per square meter. A method of indicating the substance of paper on the basis of its weight, regardless of the sheet size.

GUI Graphical User Interface. The visible interface on most software that allows users to interact with data represented by icons, menus, and windows, using a mouse, keyboard, and other control surfaces. A concept pioneered by Xerox, popularized by Apple, and subsequently by Microsoft.

Gather To place in the correct page sequence the signatures or sheets before binding. See also *Collate*.

Ghosting (1) When an image re-occurs in a faint appearance by mistake alongside the required image. **(2)** Due to ink starvation the image is reproduced to a lighter (and unacceptable) degree.

Grain (1) In photographic film, the structure of its light-sensitive *emulsion*. **(2)** In paper, the direction of fibers during the papermaking process. See *Machine direction*.

Gravure A printing process. The ink resides in cells below the surface of the roller containing the text and images. A *doctor blade* removes any excess ink before the ink is sucked out of the cells onto the paper. Also known as photogravure **(UK)** and rotogravure **(US)**.

Gray level Original continuous-tone images are reproduced in 256 levels of gray. When an original image is scanned the scanner allocates a gray level to each pixel.

Grayscale A line of gray tones in varying percentages ranging from white through black and used by printers as a measure to an industry standard.

Grey board See *Board, gray*.

Gripper The part of a *sheet-fed* press taking the paper from the *feeder* and passing it to the printing units, continuing to move it in *register* through the units, and finally to the *delivery* portion of the press.

Gripper edge The allowance of extra space on a sheet of paper for the grippers to hold it.

Groundwood paper/pulp Paper or pulp manufactured from *mechanical wood*.

Guard book A book with *guards* at the spine edge to allow the placement of ephemera, samples, or patterns.

Guards Narrow strips of paper or linen projecting from the spine approximately 10mm or approximately ¼in wrapped around the first and last signatures to add strength to the hinge. Also called *reinforcing*.

Guide, front/sides Guides, lays or gauges at the front and side of a *feeder* on a press to which paper is fed prior to printing. They assist the paper reaching the printing units in the correct *register*.

Guillotine Machine to trim paper or board before or after printing. Often computerized to enable a programmed sequence of cuts.

Gutter The margin closest to the spine of a publication.

H

H&J See *Hyphenation* and *justification*.

HSWO Abbreviation for Heat-set Web Offset.

H/T Abbreviation for *halftone*.

HTML (Hypertext Markup Language) A markup language used to format digital text and graphics for use on the Web, in which links can be embedded.

Half bound A binding style also known as a *three-piece case*. The spine and wrap around on to the side panels are covered in one material/color, and the remaining side panels with another. This may be a combination of two cloths, two papers, or one of each.

Half up Art prepared 50% larger than final reproduction size. Allows it to be reproduced at 66%, thereby reducing any initial flaws in the original.

Half-sheet work See *Work* and *turn*.

Halftone/screen An original photograph reproduced on press following the prepress application of a screen value in a series of dots varying in number per square inch depending on the paper to be used. See also *contact screen*.

Hardback/Hardcover (US/UK) A generic term for a *casebound* book whether constructed as a *one-piece* or *three-piece case,* and regardless of *notch, adhesive,* or a *sewn book block.*

Hard copy Printed page(s), as opposed to digital files.

Hard disk/drive The central storage component of a computer, where all files, including software, are permanently stored for access. External hard disks can be used for additional storage, and backup. The storage capacity of a computer is distinct from its *RAM*, which is additional temporary storage space accessed by the computer when needed for complex processing tasks.

Hard sized paper Paper, usually a writing quality, with a maximum of *size*.

Hardware The electronic components of a computer, as opposed to the programming *(software)* or the intermediary *firmware*.

Hash Symbol used in computing to stand for the word "number," but in UK typography it is used primarily by proofreaders to indicate a space.

Headbox The part of a *Fourdrinier* paper machine that sits at the top of the "wet end" and contains the pulp, accompanied by another chemicals or ingredients destined to become part of the paper.

Head or Top The edge of the paper above printed matter.

Head to head/to tail An *imposition* plan that facilitates the binding of the publication. Note: if two paperbacks are being printed and bound in this fashion the cover imposition must allow for this.

Headline The display line(s) of type denoting the title of a news story, article, and so on. Followed by a white space before commencement of the main text. In the US, *running heads* **(UK)** are referred to as headlines.

Head margin The space between the top of the printed type area on a page and the *head trim*.

Head/tail band A narrow band of plain or striped sewn cotton, glued to the top and bottom of the *book block's* spine in a *casebound* book. They cover the ends of the signatures or sections. Primarily a cosmetic, inexpensive addition with minimal addition to the binding strength.

Head trim The usual allowance is 3mm or ⅛in (or twice this between pages) for the removal of folds and clean edges. *Bleeds* must compensate for this.

Heat-set drying A method of quickly drying the ink on a web press. Achieved by the paper passing through one or more *driers*.

Hexachrome Also known as Hi-Fi color printing when two additional inks are used with the CMYK—usually a green and an orange to heighten the visual impact on selected images.

Hickie/Hickey See *Bull's eye*.

Highlight The lightest portion of a *halftone*. See also *Density*.

Holding line (US) See also *Keyline* **(UK)**.

Hollow The space at the back of a cased book's spine between the *case* and the *book block*. Not visible on a *tight-back case*.

Horizontal format (US) Rectangular page or sheet with the shortest dimension on the spine. **(UK)** Landscape.

Hot melt An adhesive for book binding. Pellets are melted and the glue is applied to the *book block*.

Hot metal typesetting Outmoded method typesetting method used in *linotype* and *monotype* machines. A liquid of alloy, lead, tin, and antimony was heated and forced into a *matrix* to create each character.

House style Standard spellings, writing styles, and abbreviations used by different publishing houses. House style guides are usually given to writers and editors.

Hue The part of a color that is its main attribute, e.g., its redness or blueness, as compared to its shade (lightness or darkness), or its saturation.

Hyphenation and Justification/H&J A system, usually software-generated, that determines the accepted end of line breaks in justified typesetting. Preprogrammed word-break dictionaries with publisher's approved exceptions or alternative are core to such a system.

I

ICC (International Color Consortium) An internationally recognized and accepted method for achieving consistent color management throughout the prepress and printing stages. Scanners, monitors, proofing devices, and printing presses can all be calibrated to conform to a device-independent ICC standard.

ICC Profile When a device has been calibrated to conform to a given ICC standard and will operate with similarly calibrated devices.

IPH Impressions Per Hour.

IR *Infrared.* See also *Radiation drying*.

ISBN International Standard Book Number. A unique (once 10- and now 13-digit) serial number that identifies a book from all others, with its title, author, and publisher, plus a check digit.

ISDN (Integrated Services Digital Network) A rapid data (and voice) transmission system, now being gradually superseded by other broadband communications systems.

ISO International Standards Organization, which oversees the adoption of many types of internationally accepted working methods, protocols, and technologies.

ISSN International Standard Serial Number. A unique eight-figure number that identifies the country or publication of a magazine or journal and its title, referring to the run of a publication instead of a specific edition.

Illustrator An vector drawing application made by Adobe, and now a component of the company's Creative Suite (CS). See also *Freehand*.

Image area The printing or ink-carrying areas on a printed sheet/page.

Imagesetter A device using either a solid-state or gas laser to record text and images at high resolution on special paper, film, or direct to plate.

Impose/Imposition The arrangement of pages to fit the press being used and to provide the correct margins such that when the sheet is folded after presswork, the pages appear in their correct sequence.

Impression (1) When the printed text and image appears on the paper regardless of the printing method employed. **(2)** All the copies of a publication or a book edition printed in one order.

Impression cylinder The part of a printing press that brings the paper, or board, or other substrate surface, for printing into contact with the printing *plate,* or cylinder.

Imprint The printer's name and location of printing. Often a legal requirement for overseas printing to comply with customs, i.e.,country of origin. As distinct from a publisher's imprint which comprises their name and often a 'mark' or symbol, appearing inside and on the spine of a book. For example, the imprint (UK) copyright (US) page contains the printer's and the publisher's name, an ISBN, credits, and the British Library (UK) Library of Congress (US) CIP (Cataloging in Publication) information.

Incipit notes A system in typesetting in which sourced content is not flagged in the text, but is identified in a section at the back of the book by page number and the opening phrase, from the content being sourced.

Indent (1) Short line (or lines) of type set to the right or left of the standard margin, often used at the beginning of new paragraphs, and to draw attention to specific pieces of information within a larger text. **(2)** The special making of a paper order from the mill for a particular publication or book. May require several weeks or months to acquire.

InDesign A page layout application made by Adobe. It combines text and images to a highly sophisticated degree for output, and is the centerpiece of the Creative Suite, linking seamlessly with Photoshop, Illustrator, Acrobat, and other component programs.

Inferior characters Letters or numbers smaller in point size than main text, and set on or below the *baseline*.

Infrared See *Radiation drying*.

Ink-jet (printer) A type of printing device generating images on paper or other substrates by spraying tiny droplets of colored inks. Often used at the low end by design studios to produce a comp or initial proof from a DTP system, and by photographers for making prints. High-end ink-jet equipped commercial printers can reproduce images up to 150-line screen quality.

In-line A term used in the *finishing* stage, following presswork—e.g., folding, gathering, but not comprising a separate operation.

Inner forme The half of an *imposition* where the pages fall on the inside of a sheet in *sheetwork,* e.g., pages 1 and 2 of a four-page job. The reverse of the outer *forme*.

In proportion (1) An *artwork* piece to be enlarged or reduced in the same percentage during reproduction. **(2)** Instruction that one dimension of artwork is to be enlarged or reduced in the same proportion as another.

Input Data or datastream entering a device for subsequent processing and formatting.

Insert (1) A signature/section of a book printed separately, often on a different paper—e.g. uncoated for the main text and coated for an illustrative insert—and bound into the book between signatures, as opposed to *wrap*. **(2)** A piece of paper or card placed loose inside a book or magazine by hand or machine. A blow-in.

Insetting To place a signature/section inside another.

Intaglio A printing process whereby the image is below the surface of the plate or cylinder, as in *gravure*.

Italic Letters in a type family that slope forward, as distinct from *roman* upright letters and numerals. Text or individual words are set in italic, *thus*, for emphasis or reference purposes, and also occasionally when foreign-language words are used during the course of a text. If the italic type formatting function (rather than the italic version of a font) is used within a page layout application such as QuarkXPress, it is not a true italic and may not reproduce. Within InDesign, false italics can be created by sloping highlighted text by a few degrees.

Integrated A book in which text and illustrations are printed together on the same paper.

International Paper Sizes The accepted standard range of metric paper sizes adopted by *ISO* (the International Standards Organization). See p. 214.

Intertype See *Line caster*.

iPod Apple-manufactured portable media player that is often used as a pocket-sized hard disk by many people for storing images, layouts, text, and other digital files.

J

JDF Job Definition Format. An *XML*-based "job ticket" standard that permits easy exchange of information and specifications between the various parties involved in the production of a printing job.

JPEG (Joint Photographic Experts Group) One of several bitmapped compression methods for storing images in a *lossy* format. In some applications, quality can be set on a scale from high (for print), to low (for Web, or layout positional purposes). Resaving JPEGs recompresses the file, losing further data.

Jaggies The visible stair-stepping (*aliased*) effect on raster images and type, that should instead appear as smooth edges and curves. See *aliasing* and *anti-aliasing*.

Jaz (disk) Once-popular portable storage medium used by designers, publishers, and photographers. Now largely replaced by DVDs, portable drives—including media players such as the iPod—and broadband networking.

Jobbing General printing not related to any specific category.

Joints The hinges on a *case* binding. Also known as a French joint.

Justification See *Hyphenation* and *justification*.

K

K (US) Key (or blacK). Indicates black in the four-color (CMYK) process, preventing confusion with "B" for blue.

K or KB Kilobyte or 1,000 *bytes*. A computer measure of storage capacity in which one byte is equivalent to one character or code.

Kaolin Clay, a natural mineral used for coating paper.

Kerning The adjusting of the space between individual characters in a line of type, nowadays within programs such as InDesign and QuarkXPress.

Key/line (1) Any *block, forme, plate* or *artwork* fitting into the *register* with other colors. **(2)** A line on *artwork* indicating an area for *tint laying*. **(3)** A component on aprinting press that controls the degree of ink flow onto the rollers. Adjustable by the press operator, usually by computer control.

Kiss cut A light touch of a knife blade on label stock with peel-off to the required size. Sufficient pressure is applied to allow the label to easily detach from the backing sheet without cutting into it.

Kraft (1) A synonym for the *sulphate* process. **(2)** A brown wrapping paper.

L

LAN See *Local area network*.
LC Abbreviation for **(1)** *lower case* **(2) (US)** Library of Congress.
LED See *Light-emitting diode*.
LWC Light Weight Coated Paper.
Lacquer A generic term covering a variety of on- or off-press varnish effects. See *UV coat, Lamination*.
Laid paper A consistent pattern of lines applied to the wet end of papermaking about 1mm apart, crossed at 90 degrees with lines 1in (25mm) apart. Impressed by a *dandy roll* and visible after the making. Used mainly for stationery.
Lamination (1) The application of a transparent gloss- or matte-finish thin film from a variety of materials, e.g., polypropylene, mylar. Available in a lay-flat finish for paperback books to prevent warping of the cover. **(2)** Manufacture of paste *boards* (see *board, duplex*, and triplex) by pasting sheets or reels together.
Landscape format (UK) See *Horizontal format* **(US)**.
Laser An electronic device producing an exceptionally thin beam of light at a given frequency, used in many imaging systems to record text and illustrations onto photographic materials, or printing plates. Also used to write information onto CDs and DVDs.
Laser printing A variant of electrostatic printing. Text and images are created by the modulation of a *laser*'s on/off capability as dictated from the computer-fed digital file. See *xerography*.
Laser printer A device which prints text and images on paper. It creates the image on a xerographic drum and transfers it to paper using powder toner.
Latin The standard alphabet used in the majority of European (Romance) languages. Comprised of *upper case/lower case* characters. Other alphabets are Greek, Cyrillic (Russian) and the Oriental languages, Arabic, and Hebrew.
Lay, front side (UK) See *Guide, front/side* (US).
Laydown See *Impose*.

Layout The complete text and any illustration(s) ready for reproduction or printing.
Leading The vertical space between lines of type, expressed using the point system—10 on 12 point (meaning 10pt type with an additional two points of leading added). Originally, leading was a literal term describing thin strips of metal used in *hot metal* typesetting as spacing. Today, leading is set within page layout programs, such as InDesign and QuarkXPress.
Leader A type character having two or more dots in line. Used to assist the eye's movement across blank space to the next type item, especially on lists, tables, and so on.
Leaf A single sheet within a publication.
Lenticular printing A series of optical-grade, ribbed plastic lenses that sit above two printed images giving the impression of movement, or a 3-D effect. Also known as auto-stereo images. Not to be confused with a hologram.
Letter fit The adjustment of space between letters achieved by *kerning* or reducing/increasing the *set* to give a different visual effect from the standard set.
Letterpress printing Text and images printed from a raised surface.
Letterspacing The consistent spacing between letters, numerals and characters when typesetting. See *letter fit*.
Library binding A reinforced binding for books to add strength for a required long and active life for the book. Used also for large format, heavy titles.
Ligature Two or three letters joined together to make one typeset character, e.g., 'fi', 'fl', 'ff', and 'st'.
Light box/booth A transportable box or a fixed booth using Kelvin 5000 bulbs, suitable for color matching under industry-standard lighting conditions. Used to view and approve color proofs, original transparencies, or art.
Light-emitting diode (LED) A semiconductor that produces light when powered.
Light fast An ink or colored material whose color is not easily affected by light, specifically sunlight. Often used for point of purchase and window display printed matter, e.g., showcards.
Light pen A light-sensitive stylus used, for example, within some CAD (Computer Aided Design) systems, text editing, or for reading *bar codes*.
Limp binding/cover A flexible book cover, as distinct from a stiff board cover, or *case*. Bible and guide books are often bound this way. The book block is usually sewn. Also known as *flexibind*.
Line art Artwork entirely in black or white, i.e., having no tonal values.

Line block/cut (UK/US) A relief block produced from *line art* or a drawing and used for *letterpress printing* having a raised surface.

Line caster Now defunct *Hot metal* typesetting machine that produces lines or *slugs* of type, as in *Linotype*.

Line copy See *Line art*.

Line drawing A drawing prepared with black ink and printed in single tone.

Line gauge (US) A template-like tool used for measuring the leading of a page of text. Not commonly used anymore. Also known as a type scale (UK).

Line original See *Line drawing*.

Linen finish A visual effect impressed onto paper that simulates the look of linen cloth. A form of embossing achieved in the off-line paper making process. Often used as a covering over board for casebound books.

Linen tester A magnifying lens used to check *halftone* dot patterns. Also see *Loupe*.

Lining figure Numerals that are the same height as the capital letters in any given typeface.

Lining, first/second Following the application of *mull* (gauze) by glue to the spine of the book block a sheet of kraft paper is glued to the *mull* before the *case* is applied.

Linotype See *Line caster*.

Literal (UK) A typographical error **(US/UK)**. Also known colloquially as a *typo*.

Lithographic printing A printing process where the image and non-image areas are on the same surface plane of the plate. As water and grease do not mix, the surface of the plate is treated to attract ink and repel water.

Loading Clay or other mineral filling used in the *furnish* of paper making to provide a smooth and opaque finish. Also used in *coating*.

Local Area Network Usually abbreviated to LAN. Expression for a group of computer devices connected via the same server(s)—such as within an office or building. Wide-area networks (WANs), are usually between separate locations.

Lock on See *Spread*.

Logo/type Graphical symbol, or stylized piece of typesetting, representing a company or organization.

Long grain The direction of fibers on the web of the paper-making machine. Also known as the *machine direction*.

Loose leaf Individual sheets of paper placed in a binder for easy removal or addition.

Loose line A typesetting term applied to a line where the space between words is excessive.

Lossless A method of compressing data that retains all of the original data quality. See *File compression*.

Lossy Data or file compression method that involves a noticeable loss of quality. See *File compression*.

Loupe A magnifying glass, sometimes illuminated. Used by printers and customers to check registration, trapping, moiré patterns, and halftone and color reproduction. Also see *Linen tester*.

Lower case Small letters (not caps).

M

MB See *Megabyte*.

MF paper Abbreviation for machine finished or mill finished. A calendered paper, but not super-calendered.

MG Abbreviation for Machine Glazed papers. Refers to paper that is rough on one side and highly polished on the other, the smoothness being achieved by the use of a chromed and heated cylinder to dry the *web*. Commonly used for posters.

MICR See *Magnetic ink character recognition*.

Ms See *Manuscript*.

Machine direction The length of the paper and the direction in which the majority of the cellulose fibers are oriented during the papermaking process.

Machine finish A calendered paper that is smoother than English finish, but still uncoated.

Machine readable Typeset or typewritten characters that can be read by a machine, e.g., *OCR* or *MICR*.

Macintosh (Mac) The trade name of the personal computer introduced by Apple Computer in the mid-1980s. Although Macs hold a minority share of the computer market overall, they remain the dominant platform within graphic design and publishing. The Macs popularized the *GUI*—a concept originated by Xerox—and were the first desktop computers capable of displaying foundry-based typefaces on screen. The switch to Intel processors in 2006 brought the Mac platform significantly closer to the PC as a computer system.

Magenta The red pigment based ink used in *four-color process* printing.

Magnetic ink character recognition A form of *machine readable* character.

Make-ready The preparation of a printing press, folding machine, or bindery line for the main run.

Make-up The arrangement of type and images into columns or pages. Precedes *imposition*.

Makeover (US) Materials and labor lost when a job has to be reprinted at no cost to the customer. A printer error.

Making A special order of paper, usually to a specific and non-standard size, or with a special shade or weight. Often with a minimum quantity to qualify for an order. Also known as *indent*.

199

Manilla A strong paper, originally made from old manilla ropes.

Manuscript (1) Written by hand. **(2)** The complete text of a publication, as submitted by the author.

Marbling A decorative multicoloring applied to book edges and commonly used on endpapers in bookbinding.

Margins The space around the text and images (type area) on a page. Head, spine, fore-edge and foot margins.

Marked proof The returned proof from an author or proofreader with required corrections or approval.

Mark-up Directions to a typesetter or prepress house for the composition treatment to a manuscript.

Masking The area of an illustration required for reproduction with extraneous material "masked" out.

Masthead (UK) See *Flag* (US).

Matrix Also matrice. **(1)** In typefounding and *hot metal*, a copper *mold* from which type was cast for hand composition or on *monotype* or *slug* casting. **(2)** In *phototypesetting* the negative on disks, film strips, grids, or drums from which the image is generated. **(3)** The horizontal and vertical rows of dots used to form a character on a dot matrix printer (now rarely used).

Matchprint A proprietary prepress proofing system prepared from film, or in digital form. A *dry proof.*

Measure The length of a line in *typesetting*, normally determined in *picas* or *points,* but sometimes in inches or millimeters.

Mechanical (US) See *Artwork* (UK).

Mechanical paper (UK) Any paper containing a proportion of *mechanical wood pulp.* Groundwood (US).

Mechanical wood pulp (UK) Produced by grinding wood mechanically, a pulp used in lower-cost papers, such as *newsprint.* It can be combined with *chemical wood pulp* to produce higher-quality papers.

Medium **(1)** The substance (usually linseed oil or a varnish) in which the pigment of printing ink is carried. Also known as a vehicle. **(2)** The weight of a typeface midway between light and bold. **(3)** A standard size of printing paper (18 x 23in; 455 x 585 mm).

Megabyte 1,048,576 bytes.

Menu A choice of functions available within a software package, as displayed on a computer screen.

Metallic inks Inks whereby the regular pigments are replaced by very fine metallic particles, typically gold or silver in color.

Metamerism Color perception by the human eye can vary depending on variances in the lighting conditions. Color proofs should always be viewed under consistent light, i.e., K 5,000 for accurate assessment.

Microprocessor The data processing component of a desktop or laptop computer.

Micron 10 and 20 dots assigned in stochastic or FM screening for process color reproduction. 10 micron is finer, but it is more difficult to adjust color in track when on press, and special equipment is required to bake the plates prior to exposure.

Middle space A type space having a width of one quarter of its own body *point* size.

Middle tone The range of tonal values between highlights and shadows. Also see *Density.*

Mill board See *Board, mill.*

Modem (Modulator-Demodulator) A device that allows computers to access communications networks for the uploading or downloading of data.

Modern typefaces (1) Numbers that are the same size as the capitals with no part below the *baseline.* **(2)** A family of typefaces with contrasting thick and thin strokes and hairline serifs, e.g., Bodoni.

Moiré The undesired screen pattern caused by incorrect screen angles of overprinting halftones.

Monochrome A single color.

Monotype A typesetting system in *hot metal* that set one character at a time.

Mold (US) Mould (UK) In *hot metal* that part of the typecasting or *typefounding* system in which the *body* of the type was formed.

Mull An open-meshed gauze-like fabric, glued to the spine of *cased* books to provide extra strength.

Mullen tester A machine that determines the burst strength of any given paper.

N

NJ Non-justified typesetting.

Negative Exposed photographic film or image in which all the tonal values are reversed.

Network A group of interlinked computer or communications devices through which information can be exchanged, either via cables, hubs, and routers, or wireless protocols via a wireless hub.

Neutral See *Blank.*

Newsprint A relatively inexpensive paper made for newspaper presswork – mostly from *groundwood/ mechanical* pulp. With its high acid content, it quickly yellows when exposed to daylight.

Nip The point between any two rollers (typically on a press) where a substance can be drawn into that system. As well as being a point of danger for the operator, nips can be used to draw a *web* of paper through a press.

Nipping A pressing that takes place in bookbinding after the *case* has been applied to improve its formation and strength on the joint or hinge.

Non-woven A paper-based bookbinding material. Sometimes strengthened with latex and often embossed with linen or patterns to simulate cloth, leather, or other natural finishes.

Notch (burst) binding A form of *adhesive binding*. Pages are not cut into individual leaves, as in *paperback binding*, but instead the printed sheets are notched with slots to facilitate the penetration of glue.

O

OCR See *Optical character recognition*.

OEM Original Equipment Manufacturer. Any company that builds products or components which are used in products sold by another company, or which are bought by another company and "rebadged" under the purchasing company's name for sale at a profit.

OS See *Operating system*.

Oblong Rectangular. See *Horizontal format* (US).

Octavo A standard book format obtained by folding a sheet three times at right angles to create eight leaves. (UK). Sometimes abbreviated to 8vo or 8mo.

Oddment A signature/section that has to be printed separately when a job does not comprise an *even working*, i.e., complete signatures.

Offprint An article in a journal printed for separate distribution. May or may not be included in the main run.

Offset (1) A mainly *lithographic* method of printing, in which the ink is transferred from the printing plate first to a *blanket cylinder*, and then onto the paper or other material—rather than printing direct from plate to surface. **(2)** When the pages of a previously printed book are photographed into bitmap form and the file is used to print a new *edition*. Also referred to as "shoot from the book." Often used to bring previously out of print titles back into print.

OK press (US) An indication that a job has received approval to all corrections and is ready for press. **(UK)** *Pass for press*.

Old-style face Typefaces from a period between Venetian and Transitional, e.g., Bembo. Capitals tend to be shorter than lower case ascenders and slightly more contrast in the stroke weight.

Onion skin A lightweight airmail paper that has a crinkly finish.

Opacity A state of a material that determines its relative ability to inhibit the transmission of light. In papermaking this determines *show through*, i.e. whether or not text or images printed on one side of the paper can be seen from the other.

Open ink An ink that can be left on a press without it drying on the rollers.

Open time (US) Available press or binding time attributable to a break in the schedule. **(UK)** Standing time or down time.

Opening Any pair of facing pages, which may or may not form a double-page *spread* (DPS).

Operating system (OS) The *software* or *firmware* that controls and underlies all of a computer's other operations. Common desktop computer operating systems are Microsoft's numerous versions of Windows, the different versions of Apple's OS X, and Linux.

Optical character recognition The use of a scanner to scan a printed text and turn it into an editable text file.

Optical media A disk, such as a DVD, encoded by light.

Orange peel A fault in *lamination* caused by excessive *setoff spray* in the printing that prevents complete or permanent adhesion.

Original Any *artwork* or copy to be reproduced in print.

Origination (UK) All the preparatory stages prior to presswork: graphic design and layout; typesetting; generation of halftones and any color separations; proofing and pre-flighting; and transmission of the application and PDF files to the printer.

Orphan An unacceptably short line length on the last line of text on a page, or paragraph, which needs correcting. Contrast with *Widow*. Also known as a *club line* **(US)**.

Otabind™ A proprietary binding method for soft cover books that provides for a lay-flat effect when open. Uses cold-set glue and offers a printable spine.

Outer forme The opposite to an *inner forme*.

Outside sort A *pi character*.

Outwork (UK) See *Buyout*.

Overdraw See *Spread*.

Overlap cover The cover on a *limp binding/soft cover* that extends beyond the trimmed edges of the pages (which have to be trimmed before covering).

Overmatter Typesetting that will not fit in the available type area space. Options are to edit to fit or cut.

Overprinting (UK) To print a second image (not always in an additional color) on a previously printed sheet.

Over-running To turn over words from one line to the next (or for several successive lines) after an insertion or other correction. The opposite is to run back.

Overs The percentage of additional copies above the agreed contract quantity. The percentage is negotiable and may be chargeable. The opposite of *unders*.

Ozalid See *Blues/blueprint*.

ENDMATTER

P

PC (Personal Computer) A generic term that describes any desktop home or office computer, but in general usage refers to computers running the Windows operating system, distinguishing them from (Apple) Macs.

PCB Printed Circuit Board.

PCF Paper made with the process known as Processed Chlorine Free. Often combines virgin pulp with some recycled content of varying percentages.

PCW Post Consumer Waste. The content in a paper that includes a given percentage of pulp from previously printed, de-inked publications. Can vary from 30% to 100% PCW pulp. Contrast with *Virgin pulp*.

PDF Portable Document Format. Adobe Systems technology that enables layouts (for example) to be viewed on screen and printed outside of the original application that created them, and without the need to have the original files and fonts. When a PDF is made of a document, by using Adobe's Acrobat Distiller on the original QuarkXPress or InDesign file (for example), all of the fonts and images are embedded into the file, which can then be published online, or sent as an email attachment, or via *FTP*. Printers can produce separations from prepress-quality PDFs, while low-resolution PDFs have relatively small file sizes but are of sufficient quality to be viewed on screen (using the free Acrobat viewer) or published on a Web site. When combined with CTP, the workflow from origination through to printed article can be relatively swift and manageable.

Ph A measure of the level of acid or alkaline content of paper on a logarithmic scale with 0 representing the extreme of acidity and 10 of alkalinity. Neutral Ph is level 7.

PIA Printing Industries of America.

PLC Paper Laminated Case. Instead of a cloth over board, paper is printed, laminated, and glued over the board.

PMS Pantone Matching System.

Packager A company that sells book ideas to publishers, who will then commission an agreed quantity of the book from the packager and publish it under their imprint when the packager delivers the completed book. The packager does not publish or distribute the book, and is guaranteed the sale of the printed quantity at an agreed unit cost, while the publisher sells at the full cover price for a profit.

Padded board A foam-backed binding board used for a cushioned effect in *case* binding.

Page One side of a *leaf*.

PageMaker The first page make-up application designed by Aldus. Since absorbed into the Adobe InDesign software with numerous modifications and upgrades.

Page makeup The organization of text and graphics into the desired design and format.

Pagination Making a publication into its paged form with page numbers, includes any blank pages.

Pallet/Skid A pallet contains cartons and is accessible by a fork-lift truck from all four sides, whereas a skid is accessible only from two sides.

Pan(chromatic) film A film used in ordinary photography and in reproduction, that is sensitive to most of the visible spectrum.

Pantone Pantone Inc's. proprietary check standard for color reproduction and color reproduction materials. Each color bears a description for its formulation in percentages, for use by the graphic arts and printing industries.

Paper A material made mainly from *cellulose* and usually, less than 110lb/200gsm, or 15 points, in card weight. Additional chemicals are added for strength, shade, and opacity or coating.

Paper sizes See tables on pp. 214 onward.

Parallel folds More than one fold on the same axis, as in *accordion* or *gatefold*.

Pass (for press) (1) Client's instruction to printer approving the project for press. See *Ok press* (US). **(2)** When a sheet or roll of paper is running through the press, i.e., one pass, two passes.

Paste board See *Board, paste*.

Pasteboard A virtual memory area within computers that holds text and images (or image elements) that have been cut out of a document or file (as opposed to deleted) before being pasted into a new location, or application.

Paste-up Becoming a little-used term as most page make-up now takes place on a computer screen using an application file. Refers to the pasting down in layout position of text and illustrations on to paper layout sheets ready for graphic arts camera work. Also known as *CRC*.

Peculiar A *pi character* in a type font.

Perfect binding See *Adhesive binding*. A binding method, most popular in magazine publishing, in which all of the sections are glued into a separate cover, with a flat spine, rather than wire-stitched/saddle-stitched, or sewn, for example. Magazines with extents shorter than, say, 80 pages (depending on the weight of paper) may be too slim to be perfect bound, and will have to be wire-stitched (or, to similar effect, stapled).

Perfected sheet (1) A completed sheet of paper printed on both sides or **(2)** in one pass on a perfecting press.

Perfecting The printing process whereby the sheet/roll is printed on both sides in one *pass*.

Perfector The category of printing press that achieves printing on both sides of the paper in one *pass*.

Perforating on press When required perforations are made to the paper while it is still on the printing press, usually by means of special attachments.

Perforation Very small holes or slots in continuous lines made through the paper or card. Can be done to achieve easy removal of part of the form or document, or to facilitate easier folding of heavier-weight paper or card.

Period (US) Punctuation mark indicating the end of a sentence (.) See *Full point* (UK).

Peripheral Any device not essential to a computer's operation, but connected to it for a specific additional function, e.g., a printer, scanner, or external drive.

Photoengraving A photomechanical method of making *relief* plates for *letterpress* printing.

Photogravure See *Gravure*.

Photolithography The combining of photography and the *litho* printing process to produce a printed image.

Photopolymer A light-sensitive polymer or plastic used either as a coating for *litho* plates, or as a relief printing plate for *letterpress* or *flexo* work, in which case it may have the non-image areas developed away by a solution of alcohol.

Photoshop The "industry standard" software program (Mac and Windows) for image editing, manipulation, creation, and preparation. Manufactured by Adobe and part of the Creative Suite. Once completed, images should be saved out of Photoshop's native PSD format into a different format, such as *TIFF* or *JPEG*.

Phototypesetting The setting of type and sometimes images as well on film or photographic paper.

Pi characters (Pies) (US/UK) (1) Any character such as fractions or musical symbols, not normally included in the regular *font*. Also called a special sort. **(2)** A mixed or disordered collection of printing type.

Pica A unity of typesetting measure. One pica equals about 1/6". Twelve *points* equals one pica in the Anglo-American system with 6 picas to the inch.

Picking Damage to the surface of the paper, card, or board during presswork.

Piece accents (US) See *Floating accents*.

Pigment The mineral, vegetable (often soy) or synthetic material that gives color to an ink.

Pixel (Picture Element) The smallest element of a picture captured by a scanner or displayed on a monitor.

Pixels per inch/per centimeter The measure of resolution of a scanner, scanned image, or monitor screen. The ppi or ppm system is used to describe the resolution of a scanned image to distinguish from the frequency at which it is printed. The accepted ratio for conversion is 2:1, e.g., 300 ppi = 150-line screen.

Planning (UK) *Imposing* or *film assembly*.

Planographic See *Lithographic printing*.

Plastic Comb Binding See *Comb binding*.

Plate Metal, plastic, or even paper, image carrier used to transfer ink to paper in *letterpress* and *litho* printing, or to the *blanket* in *offset litho*. In color separation for full-color or two-color printing, a separate plate is made for each process color.

Plate cylinder (1) The cylinder on a press that holds the printing *plate* in position. **(2)** An illustration in a book. Can be printed with main text, or more usually, separately on a different (perhaps coated) paper, and tipped in.

Platen (1) A small *letterpress* machine in which both the paper and type, or *plates,* are held flat and brought together in a parallel, or near-parallel, motion. **(2)** A large *cutting* and *creasing* press that may be integrated with printing units in the production of packaging.

Platesetter A laser operated device that records text and images directly from the file to the printing plate.

Plucking See *Picking*.

Point (US) (1) One thousandth of an inch. **(2) (US)** Used to refer to the thickness of board, e.g., 98pt board.

Point system Type measurement systems. **(1)** Anglo-American, in which the point is 0.013837 of an inch or 0.351457mm. 12 points make a Pica Em. **(2)** Didot, in which the point is 0.376065mm. 12 points makes a *Cicero*.

Polyvinyl alcohol (PVA) A *cold melt* adhesive used in book binding.

Polypropylene film A lamination film in gloss or matte finishes.

Portrait A vertical format, the shorter dimension being at the width.

Positive A photographic reproduction on printing film, made from a *negative,* or on a *duplicating* film in which the highlights in the original are clear and the shadows are deep.

PostScript The device and resolution-independent page description language, which is used to describe the appearance of a page prepared on a computer to a laser printer, imagesetter, or digital press.

PostScript file A data file containing all the information required to print a single or stream of pages. Contains all picture and text data and may also include fonts.

Posterization The condition of using a limited number of gray levels creating a special effect to a halftone, i.e., reduced number of tonal shades.

Preflight Before a completed application file is sent for proofing/printing one of several desk-top programs can run a series of checks to ensure the content is correct and all fonts and additional items are included. Printers also run preflight checks prior to platemaking.

Prelims (UK) See *Frontmatter*.

ENDMATTER

Presensitized plate A *litho* printing plate on which the surface is coated at the factory, as opposed to a wipe-on plate, and even older plates that required careful operator coating prior to use.

Press proof A proof prepared on a press with ink on paper, often the actual paper to be used on the final pass, as compared to a prepress proof. A machine proof.

Primary colors Used in the *four-color process* printing, comprising cyan (blue), magenta (red), and yellow, plus black, to reproduce four-color separations.

Print down To use a *vacuum frame* to transfer a photographic image from one film to another, or to a printing *plate*.

Printer A computer output device. Available in a variety of options, e.g, toner based, dye sublimation, ink-jet, laser, and so on.

Printout The output from a *printer,* usually laser driven using ink-jet, toner, or dye transfer, on to plain or a sensitized paper. Can be one or several colors.

Print to paper The instruction to a press operator to divide all the paper supplied equally among the *workings* of a job, rather than produce a specified number of copies.

Printability The ability of a specific paper from a particular making to successfully accept the ink without causing on-press problems, especially *picking*.

Printer's error (PE) Any error in typesetting that is the typesetter's responsibility, not the client's.

Printer's flower / ornament Decorative items in typesetting, also known as Arabesques. Available through the ages from *hot metal* to transfer lettering and now in digital composition.

Printing cylinder See *Plate cylinder*.

Process color See *four-color process*.

Progressive proofs A succession of proofs utilizing all of the inks in the *four-color process*, shown individually and in gradual combination.

Proof The representation on paper of the final printed product. This can be at any interim stage, or at final *layout*, showing text and images in paged form. Some proofs can be used for color reproduction checking, and others purely for positional purposes.

Proof correction marks Standardized symbols used to mark errors in text or illustrations on proofs that require correction. Usually, these are marked by hand by a *proofreader*, or an editor, but software exists to allow these to be marked electronically on PDFs. Corrections will then be "taken in," either by the project editor, on interim, internal proofs, or at the printer on completed layouts.

Proofreader A person who reads typeset proofs and marks appropriate corrections.

Proportional spacing System used in typesetting by which all the letters in the alphabet occupy an appropriate amount of space for the best fit within that typeface's design, with an 'm' being wider than an 'i'.

Protocol The set of codes that control a computer system's internal communications, or its communications with other systems.

Pull A proof prepared on a proofing press, usually in *letterpress* printing.

Pulp The raw material used to make paper and board, consisting of a variety of ingredients. See *Chemical* or *Mechanical/groundwood pulp*.

Pulp board See *Board, pulp*.

PUR A cold-melt binding glue that retains "memory" enabling it to remain flexible through many openings, not crack and to assist a lay-flat binding.

PVA See *Polyvinyl alcohol*.

Q

QuarkXPress A page make-up application produced and marketed by Quark Inc., which is used extensively in the graphic arts and printing industry. It has many XTensions with special features beyond the basic program. QuarkXPress runs on both Mac and PC platforms. It used to be the dominant layout application, but is now facing incresing competition from Adobe InDesign.

Quarter bound A book whose spine covering and often around the beginning of the side boards is one material and the remaining covering of the sides is another. This can be combination of cloth and paper, or all paper of two colors. (US) A three-piece *case*. See also *Full* and *Half bound*.

Quarto A page size typically about A4 and obtained by folding a sheet once in each direction. See p. 217.

Quire stock (UK) See *Sheet stock*.

Qwerty The standard typewriter-like keyboard layout used for computers, wordprocessors, and *phototypesetting* keyboards. Attributable to the arrangement of the initial six letters on the top left hand side of the keys.

R

RA See *International paper sizes* table on p. 214

RAM Random Access Memory. The temporary memory accessible by a computer for processing tasks. Increasing the amount of RAM (by adding a new RAM "chip" in blocks of 256MB, 512MB, or 1GB, for example) allows computers to process complex, or multiple, tasks faster.

RC Resin Coated. A term used for photographic papers.

RFQ Request for a Quotation.

RGB (Red, Green, Blue) The additive primary colors used to create the image on a monitor. Most scanners capture their image in RGB values with a subsequent conversion to *CMYK* for print reproduction. A device-dependent color space with a color gamut in RGB that is greater than that of *CMYK* inks and, therefore, cannot be exactly matched. Used for scanning and color separations

RIP (Raster Image Processor) A computer device which converts the *postscript* data describing pages into bitmap format for imaging on an *imagesetter, platesetter, digital press*, color photocopier, or other imaging device. Often includes specialized technology for the rendering of different types of halftone screen. Also used in *phototypesetting* and electronic page composition systems, processing the digital information passed to them relating to individual letters, numerals, and images both line and halftone, before preparing pages for output in the correct position and orientation. "Rip," as a verb, has (inaccurately) come to mean the processing of any digital file—such as video or music—onto a hard disk from an external device, such as a media player.

RIP (2) Rest in Proportion. An instruction to reproduce one side of an *artwork* in the same proportion as the side marked.

ROM Read Only Memory. Stored data on disk or within an area of a computer that only permits the reading of information and not the writing or modification of it—as in a CD-ROM.

ROP Run Of Paper/Press/Print. In newspaper and similar work, color printing carried out at the same time as the main run, rather than supplied to the newspaper preprinted for inclusion with its distribution. The term is also used synonymously with *print to paper*.

Radiation drying Accelerated drying of specially formulated inks or varnishes by *ultra violet* or *infrared* radiation. UV cures and IR dries. Units are attached to the back end of a press.

Ragged right/left Use of a fixed word space in typesetting to prevent the type from aligning vertically on either the left or right hand side. Also known as unjustified composition. The opposite of *flush left*, or *right* typesetting.

Range To cause type or illustrations to line up on or to a certain point, either vertically or horizontally.

Raster (graphic) A *bitmap*. An image formed from a grid of *pixel*s, or points of color, on a computer monitor, or printed onto a surface. Contrast with *Vector graphics*.

Raster image processor See *RIP*.

Rasterize To turn into a bitmap.

Ream 500 (originally 516) sheets of paper.

Rebind (1) A second binding from stored, printed sheets of a book. **(2)** The removal of a damaged or faulty binding and replacing it.

Recto A right-hand page.

Reduction (1) To reduce *artwork* in size during reproduction either to improve the sharpness or to enable it to fit the available space. **(2)** To dilute an ink or varnish to give it less *tack* on the press.

Reel-fed See *web-fed*.

Register/Registration To print two or more impressions that fit together without overlap or causing a moiré effect. Also to *backup* accurately if printed on opposite sides of the sheet with the intention of maintaining register and preventing possible show through.

Register marks Marks on sets of overlays, *artwork,* typeset pages, film, *plates,* or *formes* so that when they are superimposed during printing the rest of the work is in *register*.

Reinforcing See *Guards*.

Release paper A silicone-coated paper used as backing with some adhesive materials, allowing the latter (e.g., a label) to be peeled off when the adhesive printed material needs to be used.

Relief process Where the printing surface is raised, as in *letterpress*.

Remake (UK) To remake a printing plate or film due to an error. **(US)** *Makeover*.

Repkover™ A softcover binding with lay-flat pages when opened. The book block can move freely within the cover.

Repeat See *Ghosting*.

Reprint Any printing of a work (with or without corrections) subsequent to the initial printing.

Repro house (UK) A prepress house, who take application files or PDFs from clients and ready them for print production, making color separations, and so on.

Rescreen When a previously printed halftone has to be treated as an "original." To avoid the creation of a moiré pattern with conflicting screens the image is first de-screened and then re-screened. See *Descreen*.

Resist A coating on the surface of a printing *plate* used in order to stop or impede an etching solution.

Rest in proportion See *RIP (2)*.

Retouching (1) Hand treatment on litho film *negative* or *positive* to change tonal values or correct imperfections. **(2)** In a digital context the modification in *Photoshop* of an original image to comply with the photographer's or designer's preference for the final visual effect.

Reverse out When type or an image appears in white out of a black, or other color background.

Reverse reading See *Wrong reading*.

Reversing see *Reversal*.

Revise (1) To make a revision or correction at any

proofing stage to comply with the author's, designer's, or editor's instructions. **(2)** To make a correction on a *forme* on press.

Right reading Paper or film in *positive* or *negative* that can be read in the usual way, i.e., from left to right.

Right side see *Felt side*.

River A series of word spaces (usually occurring in badly *justified* typesetting) that form a noticeable pattern of white space down many lines of type.

Roman The standard characters of a *font* in which the letters are upright, as opposed to *italic* sloping.

Rosette The locations on a color separation where all four colors intersect.

Rotary A printing press in which the text and images are contained on either a *litho* plate, a *letterpress wraparound* plate, or a *gravure* cylinder or *plate*, and on which the text and images are transferred to the paper by a rotary, as compared to a reciprocal motion.

Rotogravure See *Gravure*.

Rough An unfinished design/layout. Also know as a *comp* **(US)**.

Rounded corners A *finishing* or binding operation whereby a special die is used to round the corners of the book block or other item—at times before it is *cased* in.

Rounded and Backed The *cased* bookbinding operation on a machine that shapes the spine of a book block after sewing or *adhesive binding* to make the back become convex (and thus the fore-edge becomes concave) and at the same time forms a shoulders against which the *case* boards fit for a stronger end result. The opposite of a *square-back binding*.

Royal A standard printing paper size, 19 x 25in, (480 x 636mm).

Ruling A process used to prepare *manuscript books* and note pads in which a liquid ink is "ruled" onto the paper by special pens or disks.

Run (1) To print. **(2)** To start up a computer program.

Run in (US) Instruction that two paragraphs should be set as one without the customary break.

Run on Sheets or signatures printed in addition to ordered initial quantity.

Runability The resistance of paper to curling/waving, or *web* breaks and other problems associated with the paper, as opposed to *printability*.

Runaround To lay out type on a page whereby the line beginnings or endings follow the shape of an illustration, which may be regular or irregular.

Running head/foot Recurring lines of text—usually a book or magazine title, or a chapter heading—at the head or foot of every page of a publication. Also see *Headline*.

S

Saddle (wire) stitching Similar in effect to stapling, achieved on a saddle-stitching machine which feeds a continuous wire to form staples of the required length to be fired into the publication and folded on the inside.

Sans serif A category of typeface without the *serif*s, e.g Helvetica.

SC (1) Supercalendered paper (see *Calendered*). **(2)** Abbreviation for small caps.

SGML (Standard Generalized Markup Language) A meta language used for coding a digital manuscript to facilitate eventual searching of the document.

SPH Sheets per hour through the printing press.

SRA see Paper sizes table on p. 214.

SWOP Standard Web Offset Printing **(US)** A standard for printing color on web offset presses. An alternative is a *sheet-fed* color space with more density than the high speed *SWOP* version.

Scale To calculate the percentage of enlargement or reduction of an image. To resize an image in proportion.

Scamp (UK) A rough layout.

Scanner An electronic device used to read a hard copy of an image (or piece of text) and digtize it and turn it into an editable file for importing into a software application. Scanners can be small desktop devices or very large machines, both operating with *lasers* as the light source. The two basic versions are flatbed or drum. Either transparencies or flat *reflection* copy can be scanned depending on the size of the original.

Score To make a crease in a board enabling it to be folded along the intended line. Can be achieved either by the roller or creasing method, roller being the fastest.

Screen (1) See *Halftone screen*. **(2)** The material used in *screen printing* that contains the text and images.

Screen angle When *halftones* are printed in one or more colors there is a risk of a *moiré* pattern appearing on the printed sheet. If the angle used for each screen is not correctly selected the result can create a moiré effect In the *four-color process*. The angles are commonly black 45 degrees (as in monochrome), *magenta* at 75 degrees, yellow at 90 degrees and *cyan* at 105 degrees.

Screen clash See *Moiré*.

Screen printing As in silk-screen printing. Instead of using a *plate* or *cylinder,* a stencil is photographically prepared on a screen or mesh. The traditional silk screen is now nylon. Ink is squeezed through the screen and on to the paper or *substrate*. *Halftones* of a very coarse screen can be reproduced. Results are often viewed at a distance, e.g., posters and billboards although the same process is used for a variety of applications requiring a heavy ink lay down, e.g., t-shirts.

Screen ruling (or frequency) A measure of the quality or fineness of the dot structure used to reproduce a halftone image or tint expressed in lines per inch or centimeter. Do not confuse with *PPI*.

Screen tester A device used to ascertain the fineness of the *halftone screen* that has been used.

Screened negative / positive print Any film or print of a color or monochrome subject that has been reproduced using a *halftone screen*.

Script A typeface that imitates any handwritten style.

Scrolling The ability to move the text and images up or down on a computer screen.

Scumming Effect caused in litho printing when the non-image areas of the *plate* do not repel the ink resulting in a dirty image being printed.

Sections/Signatures A folded press sheet. Paper is folded to form part of a book or booklet. Sections/signatures normally comprise sheets folded to make 4, 8, 16, 32, or 64 pages.

Search and replace When every instance of a specified word or group of words can be found in a document, and replaced with a different word, group of words, or spelling/formatting. Used in editing and correcting to prevent the need to change each occurrence by hand.

See/show/look through (UK/US) (1) The appearance of paper when held up to the light. **(2)** In less opaque papers, the printed image on one side being partially visible on the reverse.

Self-copy paper A form of carbonless paper in which all the chemicals needed to create an image are *encapsulated* in a single sheet.

Self cover A publication whose cover is the same paper or material as the inside pages.

Self ends A binding in which the *endpapers* are part of the first and last *section* of the book, as opposed to being *tipped in* separately. Rarely used.

Separated artwork Artwork prepared as a series of *overlays*, each one providing the portion of the overall *separation* for the relevant color to be printed.

Separation See *Color separation*

Serif The small ornamentations/terminating strokes on individual letters/characters of serif typefaces, e.g., Garamond or Baskerville, as opposed to *Sans serif* (such as this typeface, Frutiger).

Setoff Ink marks on the underside of a sheet caused by the still-wet ink on the sheet on to which it drops at the *delivery* end of a press. Often attributable to insufficient drying powder.

Setoff spray The fine powder used at the *delivery* end of *sheet-fed* printing presses to assist the avoidance on the ink from one sheet touching that of another thereby causing *setoff*.

Set solid Type which has been set without any *leading* or line feed between the lines. The result is usually difficult to read.

Shadow See *Density*.

Sheet stock Printed sheets held in storage by the printer awaiting future binding.

Sheeter The machine used at paper mills or trade converter to splice rolls into sheets ready for *presswork*. Some litho sheet-fed presses have a roll stack at the front end to sheet immediately prior to printing.

Sheet-fed press A press on which the printing *plate* surface is fixed around a cylinder and is fed with single sheets, as opposed to a *web-fed* press.

Sheetwork Pages imposed on two separate *plates* or *formes*, one to print each side, each *backed-up* sheet producing a *perfected* copy.

Shore hardness Scale of hardness, most commonly measured on the Shore Mfg Co's 'A' scale in which the hammer with a diamond point strikes the material being calibrated, e.g., an *offset blanket* or *flexographic* printing plate, with a greater degree of bounce being recorded for the harder materials.

Short grain See *Machine direction*.

Show through See *See through*.

Shrink and spread See *Spread*.

Shrinkwrap (1) Individual publications or books shrink wrapped for security or protection. Convenient shrinkwrapping applies to as many copies as possible within the capacity of the shrink wrapping machine. **(2)** The wrapping of items in a layer of heat-sealed plastic film to protect them during transportation or display. In ocean freight of books it reduce the effects of humidity changes.

Side notes Short lines of text set in the *margin*.

Side sewing/stitching To stitch through the side of a book or booklet from front to back at the binding edge (spine) with a thread or wire. A method of binding leaves as well as *sections*. The publication will not lay flat and extra spine margin should be allowed for.

Sign-off sheet (US) The document used by printer's for a customer to sign approval for printing/binding to proceed.

Signature Interchangeable term for *Section*.

Signature numbering A consecutive number or letter printed at the foot of the first page of a *Section/signature* to enable the binder to check the correctness of the sequence and completeness of a binding. The letter or number may be accompanied by a rule on the back of each section so that when they are folded and *gathered* these appear in a stepped pattern, one out of sequence indicating incorrect gathering.

Silk screen See S*creen printing*.

Silver print (US) See *Blues*.

Singer sewing Machine sewing of single sheets on their edge (unfolded) into sections. They are then sewn onto tapes or webbing to produce a book or pamphlet in a *library binding*.

Single-color press A printing press that can only print one color at each pass.

Single wall Refers to cartons for shipping printed matter or books. Constructed with one wall of fiberboard in varying strengths, e.g., 200lb to 275lb test, depending on the weight of the items. Compare to *double wall*.

Size A resin, starch, or other synthetic ingredient included in the *furnish* of papermaking to bind the *cellulose* fibers and *loading* together to provide resistance to ink penetration and strength.

Skid See *pallet*.

Skiver A leather binding material made from splitting sheep or goat skins.

Slitting Cutting a sheet into two or more parts on a press or folder, instead of on a *guillotine*.

Slot binding see *notch binding*.

Slug A complete line of type from a *line caster*, e.g., *linotype* machine.

Slug line A line on a color proof that indicates if any of the colors are clogged (filled-in) on the proof.

Slug setting see *line caster*.

Small caps Type *fonts*, especially those used for book typesetting which include an extra alphabet whose *cap height* of the *roman* font is the same as the *x-height*, but without the strokes being thinner than the rest of the font, as occurs when ordinary capitals are reduced to their x-height. There are no true *italic* small caps.

Small offset Traditional classification for *offset* presses below A2 in size – Usually A4 or A3(UK).

Smash (US) See *nipping* (UK).

Smyth sewing Also known as section sewing. Signatures are individually stitched with nylon thread through the fold to each other. A sewn book has the advantage of lying flat when opened as compared to a notch bound or side sewn publications.

Soft proof A digital proof, usually provided as an email attachment, for viewing on a monitor screen.

Software The programs that enable the computer's *hardware* to perform specific tasks.

Solid A typesetting term for set solid.

Sort (1) A single character of type. **(2)** A computer instruction to rearrange data in any selected order.

Spell checker A computer *program* that compares a text file with a spelling dictionary and identifies any words that are deemed as not correctly spelled. A programmed exception dictionary can override the initial decision.

Spine The binding edge of a book. Also see *Back*.

Spiral binding A publication bound with spiral width of varying diameter and often coated with a colored plastic. Pages are first punched with small holes to accept the coiled wire. Facilitates a lay-flat effect when opened.

Splice To join a *web* of paper on a press.

Split-duct working When small areas of color are to be printed at some distance from each other, two or more colors can be printed on a *single color press*. The effect is achieved by confining the colored inks to just that part of the ink *duct* that supplies the image.

Spoilage (1) Printed matter lost during the press run or binding stages due to imperfections in the process. Not suitable for inclusion in the final delivered quantity. Printers allow for spoilage the extent of which can lead to *overs* or *unders*. **(2)** See *Makeovers*.

Spot color When a color is printed using a specific color of ink, usually from a special guide, in coated or uncoated version, instead of creating it via a build of percentage tints from process color inks.

Spot varnish The application of a gloss or matte varnish to a specific area on the page or cover. Can be a press varnish applied in-line or a separate pass.

Spray See *Setoff spray*.

Spread (1) Reproduction. A variety of terms, e.g., "lock-on," "overdraw," and "spread and choke," are used to describe the need to make two adjoining images slightly thicker than on the original *artwork* to facilitate *register* in two or more color printing. **(2)** A double-truck/page spread (DPS) **(US/UK)** occurs when an illustration occupies two opposing pages. Strictly speaking, this only occurs on the *center* spread of a signature—elsewhere it is a "false double"—however the term is commonly used in book and magazine publishing, advertising, and design

Square back See *Flat back*.

Squared up (US/UK) A *halftone* illustration that has been trimmed to a square or rectangular shape.

Squares The 3mm or 1/8in proportions on the cover of a *cased* book and beyond the trim book block pages.
Stabbing See *Side sewing/stitching*.
Stamping (US) See *Blocking*.
Standing time (UK) When a press or bindery line are idle awaiting work. See *Open time* **(US)**.
Standing type Type matter kept in a *chase* or stored in locked up pages for reprinting by *letterpress* and, by extension, film flats, or *CRC*.
Step and repeat The repetition of text and/or images in a planned interval.
Step index See *Cut-in index*.
Stereo/type A duplicate *relief* printing plate cast in metal usually copper, zinc, plastic, or rubber from a *matrix* or mold.
Stet Leave as set. Instruction to return to the original intention in a typeset proof and to ignore a previous correction or deletion mark.
Stitch To sew, staple or otherwise fasten pages together by a nylon thread or wire in binding.
Stock (1) Any material to be printed on. **(2)** See also *Sheet stock*.
Stochastic screening Also known as *FM*, or random dot screening. Unlike *AM* screening where dots are placed in a pre-determined line screen per inch, e.g, 150 lpi and vary in size, with stochastic screening the microns at either 20 or the even finer level of 10 micron dots are the same size and vary where they are positioned, i.e, clustered heavily in shadow areas and fewer in highlights.
Straight matter /text Copy to be set to a consistent *measure* and without any complex typographic commands or *tabulations* or equations.
Strapping Strong metal bands applied to pallets to keep the cartons from shifting during transit.
Strike through Action of an ink's *medium/vehicle* causing discoloration on the reverse side the paper via penetration.
Strip and rebind To take unsold casebound books (for example), strip off the covers, and then rebind them as paperbacks to achieve further sales.
Stripping (1) To insert, i.e., "strip-in," any correction in film or paper during *phototypesetting*. **(2)** To glue a strip of cloth or paper to the back of a paperback book or pad as reinforcement. **(3)** To remove any waste material from between cartons and other work after *cutting* and *creasing*. See also *Film assembly*.
Subscript /inferior characters Any letter, numeral or character appearing below the baseline in typesetting. The opposite of *superscript*.
Substance See *GSM / G/M2*
Substrate Interchangeable term with *stock*.

Suitcase A method of managing fonts in which all the elements needed to display and print a *font*, or font family, are included within a single, protective file.
Sulphate A *woodfree (freesheet)* pulp produced by cooking the wood chips in a solution of sodium hydroxide and sodium sulphide.
Sulphite A *woodfree (freesheet)* pulp produced by cooking the wood chips in a solution of sulphurous acid and one of its base salts, e.g., calcium, sodium, magnesium, or ammonia.
Super-calendered (SC) See *Calender*.
Superscript/superior characters Any letter or numeral smaller than the text-size and are positioned above the *x-height* of the type *body*.
Supershift A second bank on a keyboard providing access to another *font* or set of characters.
Surface sizing When size is applied to the surface of the paper in the making process. It reduces the likelihood of the paper causing picking or linting on press.
Surprinting (US) See *Overprinting*.
Swash characters Italic letters with exaggerated strokes. Not all letters in the alphabet are available as a swatch character and only in some fonts.
Swatch (book) Samples of binding cloths, inks, endpapers, head/tail bands, or text papers to show the designer and print buyer the available selection.

T

TCF Totally Chlorine Free. Pulp ready for paper making that contains no chlorine in the bleaching process, thereby no creation of the toxic dioxin. Alternatives such as hydrogen peroxide or ozone are used. A term reserved for virgin pulp, i.e, no recycled content.
TIFF (Tagged Image File Format) A high-quality bitmap file format for images, especially photographs, that is ideal for print production purposes.
TS Typescript.
Tablet See *Graphics tablet*.
Tabloid See *Broadsheet*.
Tabulate To arrange type and other elements in regular columns, usually of figures.
Tack The degree of adherence in the *medium/vehicle* of a printing ink or varnish.
Tailband Same as *headband* but at the foot of the *spine* on a *casebound* book.
Thermal printer A computer printing device that images a heat-sensitive paper.
Thermography An imitation of *die stamping*. The finished effect of a similar raised look is achieved by a combination of ink, powder, and heat.

Thick space A space in typesetting that equates to one-third of an *em*.

Thin space A space in typesetting that equates to one-fifth of an *em*.

Thou 1/1000th of an inch. Point **(US)**.

Thread sealing A method of book binding in which the *sections* are 'stabbed' with thread, the loose ends then being sealed with adhesive.

Three-knife trimmer A *guillotine* containing three knives. Used to trim stacks of publications and books. One movement trims the *heads* and *feet*, the second the *fore edge*.

Three piece case (US) See *Half bound*.

Throw-out Usually the extension of a doublepage *spread* where a special *imposition* in the design has asked for an additional page or more to fold out from the *foredge*. Often used for maps. *Foldout* **(US)**.

Thumb index An index where the dividers are cut into the *fore edge* rather than stepped as in a *cut in* or tab index.

Tints Shading in increments from 5% to 90% applied to film or a *plate* to reproduce a degree of a solid ink color. Complex layouts are achieved, usually on a computer or *scanner*, by layering of tints in specific programs to achieve the desired visual effect.

To view The number of pages appearing on one side of a sheet. e.g., 16 pages to view would equal a 32-page *signature*.

Tone The gradation, usually expressed in percentages, from light to dark in ink on paper, contrasted with line work that has no tonal values. Measurable with a *densitometer* instrument.

Tooling (US) See *Blocking*.

Top side See *Right side*.

Track In printing a line from the front edge of a *plate* to the back. Items *imposed* in track will all be subject to the same inking adjustments on the press as they use ink from the same *key* on the press.

Tranny A transparency.

Transpose The condition when two letters or other typeset items were set in error (or design) and need to be swapped to correct.

Trapping The technique of slightly overlapping one limage on an adjacent one thereby preventing unsightly small white gaps appearing between the two colors. A mis-register will only exacerbate the problem by either increasing the gap or overlapping the trap.

Trim To cut a sheet of paper to the required size prior to presswork, or a printed product during *finishing*.

Trim marks (UK) See *Cut marks* **(US)**.

True small caps See *Small caps*.

Turned in The cloth or other material used on the *case* of a book that is turned in round the edges to prevent the board's edges being exposed.

Turner bar On a *web-fed* press the web (paper running through the machine) is sometimes split before folding. The divided webs are then re-aligned to the left or right of the previous direction by pairs of turner bars placed at 45 degrees to the axis which turn the web twice by 45 degrees. Also known as a double parallel fold.

Twin-wire paper (1) A high-quality, even-sided, and usually uncoated paper produced from two *webs* joined together on the *Fourdrinier* machine while still wet, with their respective *wire sides* at the center. **(2)** Publication papers produced form a single web on a machine that has a small supplementary top wire pressing down on the sheet or on a *vertiformer* in which the sheet is formed between two wires as it moves downwards.

Two (or more) set/up To impose a job for printing with multiple images to view, so as to obtain more copies from the sheet when printed, thereby reducing the length of the run and utilizing the available size of the press.

Two-color machine (press) A printing press that prints one side of the sheet in two colors in one pass. Some two-color presses are also *convertible*.

Type area The area on a page determined by the designer to be allocated for the placement of type and illustrations, excludes margins.

Type scale (UK) See *Line gauge* **(US)**.

Typeface classifications Typefaces are classified by their design characteristics and style, or attributable to their historic origins, e.g., Egyptian, Old Style, Cursive, Modern.

Typefounding *Hot metal* type was made by pouring a hot, liquid alloy through a mold into a specially prepared *matrix* for each character. As it cooled and set it took on the shape of the character and was ready for composition.

Typo Abbreviation term for a typographical error.

Typographer A designer of typefaces.

U

UCR See *Undercolor Removal*.

UPC Universal Product Code. See *Bar code*.

USM Un-Sharp Mask. A photographic darkroom process, available in digital form within software such as Photoshop. It uses a blurred positive to create a "mask" of the original image, which, when combined with the negative, creates an illusion of increased sharpness. Like all sharpening techniques, it does not improve poor focus, but creates the perception of sharper detail. Other sharpening techniques increase the contrast between pixels along the edge of an object.

UV (1) Ultraviolet. See *Radiation drying.* **(2)** A coating on top of a previously printed product to enhance the visual effect.

Ultrafan A book binding method utilizing single sheets that are fanned in both directions with the application of cold-set glue to the spine edges. Very strong and often used for library rebinding.

Ultraviolet A wavelength of light outside of the visible spectrum. See *Radiation drying.*

Unbacked A sheet printed only on one side.

Undercolor removal A technique used in the color *separation* process that removes unwanted or excess color, either to reduce the amount of ink to be used on press (for economy but more often to reduce *trapping*), or where these colors cancel each other out in the various *achromatic* systems.

Underline/underscore A typesetting term to indicate a fine rule being placed just below the baseline and used to indicate emphasis.

Unders See *Spoilage.*

Underside The side of a *web* on the wire side of a papermaking machine. Often the "wrong" side from the printer's point of view.

Unit (1) Multicolor printing presses are divided into units printing one or both sides, each one carrying a different *plate* and ink color on the fountain for that unit. **(2)** The division of the *em* of the body size in typesetting. Every character in a *font* has its own 'unit' width. The systems vary from type foundry or manufacturer and are essential to achieve *justification* in composition.

Unix An *operating system* used on certain computer workstations. It facilitates multiple-user computers to run multiple tasks. The kernel of the Linux "open source" operating system was originally based on Unix.

Unjustified setting When lines of type align vertically on one side and are ragged set on the other. The amount of indent on the ragged edge can be specified to prevent an ugly appearance. The word space is usually kept to a constant value to enhance the visual effect.

Unsewn binding See *Adhesive binding.*

Up Used to determine the number of similar sheets that can be reproduced in one pass from a larger sheet, e.g., two-up, eight-up.

Upload When a file is transferred from one computer system to another, often over long distance. Can be achieved via *FTP* or as an email attachment. Contrast with *download.*

Upper case Capital letters (caps). From the portion of the type case that held the capital letters in the days of hot metal typesetting.

V

VDU Visual Display Unit. Now rarely used acronym, referring to a computer monitor.

VOCs Volatile Organic Compounds. Toxic, smog-producing by-products from certain printing/finishing chemicals. Many printers now use soy-based inks that contain no VOCs.

Vacuum frame A device, some of which have a built-in lighting source, used to expose a sheet of film in contact with another film or *plate.* A vacuum pump excludes the air to make sure the *emulsion* to emulsion contact is consistent to reproduce the entire contents.

Vandyke See *Blues.*

Variable data printing When every digitally printed piece varies from its predecessor and successor. Used extensively for direct mailing pieces to target perceived individual preferences in product, but can also be just the name and address.

Variable space The space inserted between words to justify them. This can be controlled with acceptable minimum/maximum amounts of allowed space, defined as being "to the em", as in "5 to the em". See *Hyphenation* and *justification.*

Vector graphic Graphic (drawing) format that uses mathemetical calculations to reproduce lines and curves on screen. When an image is scaled up, the calculations are redone so that the image displays without image degradation. Vector graphics are different to pixel graphics, which degrade or "pixelate" when blown up beyond the resolution and image size they were saved at. Software packages such as Adobe Illustrator are vector drawing packages. To edit a vector illustration within software such as Photoshop, the image first has to be rasterized (turned into a bitmap).

Vehicle See *Medium.*

Vellum The inner side of a calfskin, used for binding limited edition and presentation fine books.

Vellum finish The finish on machine-made paper, smoother than parchment or antique/wove finishes.

Verso A left-hand page.

Vertiformer A *twin-wire* papermaking machine in which the normal horizontal wire of a *Fourdrinier* paper machine is replaced by a pair of vertical wires. The headbox sits at the top and the sheet is formed between the two wires as they move downward.

Viewer A lighted box or booth on/in which reflection art, transparencies, and proofs are viewed and compared under controlled lighting conditions to industry standard—Kelvin 5,000.

Vignette A *halftone* with etched, gently fading edges, as opposed to being *cut out* or squared up.

Virgin pulp Pulp for paper making that does not contain any *PCW* content.

Virus A malicious code which may be transmitted along with a job file, or included in a computer transaction. In varying degrees, depending on the structure of the virus, it may infect one, or a group of computers if networked, and can corrupt, misuse, or destroy content on the receiving computer's hard disk. Viruses often find their way onto systems via email attachments, and have a tendency to be coded to exploit flaws in the Windows operating system and some programs that run on it. Until the adoption of Intel processors, Macs were less prone to virus attack.

Viscosity The fluidity of inks in the printing processes, *letterpress, litho offset,* or *screen printing* where the viscosity is very high, compared to the viscosity in *gravure* and *flexography* inks, which are low.

Visual (UK) See *Comp* **(US)**.

Volume A measure of thickness of papers in relation to their *substance.*

W

WF (1) Wrong font. Proofreading correction mark indicating the incorrect *font* was used. **(2) (UK)** Woodfree, see *Freesheet.* **(US).**

WYSIWYG Pronounced "Whizzywig." The acronym for "What You See Is What You Get," which essentially means that what you see on a computer monitor is, as near as is physically possible, what you will subsequently see output from an *imagesetter,* or other output device. The display of four-color work will be more accurate in the color gamut of the monitor has been *ICC* calibrated to match that of the proofing medium, and even the press.

Waterless offset Offset printing achieved without the use of a damping solution. Requires a special, silicone-based *plate.* See *Dry litho.*

Watermark A design impressed by a *dandy roll* into a newly-formed *web* of paper containing a unique logo or symbol, which is visible when held up to the light. Digital files, such as images, can also be "watermarked" digitally, either invisibly, to trace the route of piracy, or visibly—such as in the widespread use of copyright messages embedded within low-resolution positional images from commercial image libraries, prior to the purchase of, and permission to reproduce, high-resolution versions for print reproduction.

Web (1) Paper running in a continuous roll (web), through a *Fourdrinier* or *cylinder* machine.
(2) Colloquial abbreviation of World Wide Web.

Web break (1) The occurrence of a *web* of paper splitting in the papermaking process as the web is feeding through the drying rollers. **(2)** When the web of paper splits apart during its run through a web-fed litho press.

Web offset Reel-fed *offset litho* printing. There are three systems: *blanket to blanket,* when two *plate* and two *blanket* cylinders on each unit print and *perfect* the *web*; three-cylinder systems, in which plate blanket and *impression* cylinders print one side of the paper only; and satellite or planetary systems in which two-, three-, or four-plate and blanket cylinders are arranged around a common *impression cylinder* printing one side of the web in as many colors as there are plate cylinders.

Web-fed presses Printing presses that operate from paper fed from a roll. Contrast with *sheet-fed* presses.

Wet on wet When multicolor work is being printed and the paper is feeding from one *unit* to the next before the ink has dried from the previous unit. "Wet trapping."

Weight (of type) In any given *font,* light, medium, black, bold, or ultra versions of the same basic typeface, affecting its overall blackness and visual impact on the printed page.

Whole bound See *Full bound*.

Widow A single word, or a short line, appearing at the top of a page.

Windows The *PC* operating system made by Microsoft, available in countless different versions and upgrades for different scenarios—e.g. home, corporate networks, mobile, and so on. The operating system found on well over 90% of the world's desktop and laptop computers.

Wire-O binding A binding method for publications. The pages and covers are punched with rectangular holes and a double-loop wire is then inserted through the holes. The loops are crimped to keep the wire in place. A strong, lay-flat binding. Allow for a deeper spine margin.

Wire side The side of a *web* of paper that was in contact with the paper making machine's wire side.

Wiremark The mark left by the paper making machine's wire on the underside of the *web* of paper.

Woodfree paper (UK) See *Freesheet* (US).

Word break The acceptable break point(s) in a word for hyphenating it to maintain the required *measure* in justified typesetting.

Word spacing The amount of space allowed between words by the typographer's/designer's specifications.

Wordwrap In text entry systems when a word is too long to fit on the screen in use the line will automatically transfer the entire word to the start of the next line as it is being keyboarded by the operator.
Work and back See *Sheet work*.
Work and tumble/turn/twist Work on a press that is printed entirely (and on both sides of the sheet) from one *plate* or *forme* while changing the gripper (tumble), or without changing the gripper edge (turn) or turning the sheet at right angles (twist).
Working A single printing operation imaging one or more colors on one or both sides of the sheet, depending on the type of press being used.
Wove(n) A paper with an even, fine, woven-like surface feel. No *laid* lines.
Wraparound (1) A *plate* that wraps around a plate cylinder. The normal condition in *litho* printing, but not universal in *letterpress*. **(2)** One sheet or *signature* wrapped around another in the binding stage.
Wrappering The addition of a paper or board cover in binding by a strip of glue or stitching at the spine, or to wrap extra pages round a *signature* to make it total the required number of pages, or to add illustrations around text only signatures.
Wrong grain See *Machine direction*.
Wrong reading Film that has been made such that it reads from right to left from the side in question.
Wrong side See *wire side*.

X

XML (Extensible Markup Language) A metadata (data about data) markup language used to code and identify the different elements of text, graphics (and any other digital data) within a file for searching and also for use on the Internet. XML is "platform agnostic," in that any computer device can read it, regardless of the operating system it runs on. Anyone can write their own XML "tags" to describe the format of a piece of data. It is at the heart of the idea of "Web services," the seamless and intuitive creation and flow of online applications and information to and from the user, and is therefore a vital tool in cross-platform publishing.
Xerography Proprietary name for a form of electrostatic printing.
x-height That part of a letter with no *ascender* or *descender*, e.g., an "a" or an "x."

Y

Yapp See *Limp* binding.

Z

Zero make-ready press A *web-fed press* with a unit being prepared with a *plate* and made-ready while another unit is printing. When the active unit completes its run, the second unit immediately commences printing.
Zinco A line *block* **(UK)** *cut* **(US)** for *letterpress* printing.

Paper sizes

There are numerous international standard paper sizes, plus some that are used specifically within the USA and Canada. Here is a guide to the principal ones you need to know about in most forms of print production work.

The "A" series

This is a system for sizing paper and was first used in Germany in 1922 where it is still called "Din A." Each size is derived by halving the size immediately above it. Each size is the same as another geometrically as they are halved using the same diagonal. A0 is the first size and is one square metre (11 square feet, approximately) in area. A series sizes always refer to the trimmed sheet. The untrimmed sizes are referred to as "RA" or "SRA." Many countries have officially adopted the A series system, the USA being the main exception. The "B" series is used when a size in between any two adjacent A sizes is needed. As quoting just the A or B number can cause confusion, both the A or B size and the size in millimeters should be given when specifying paper.

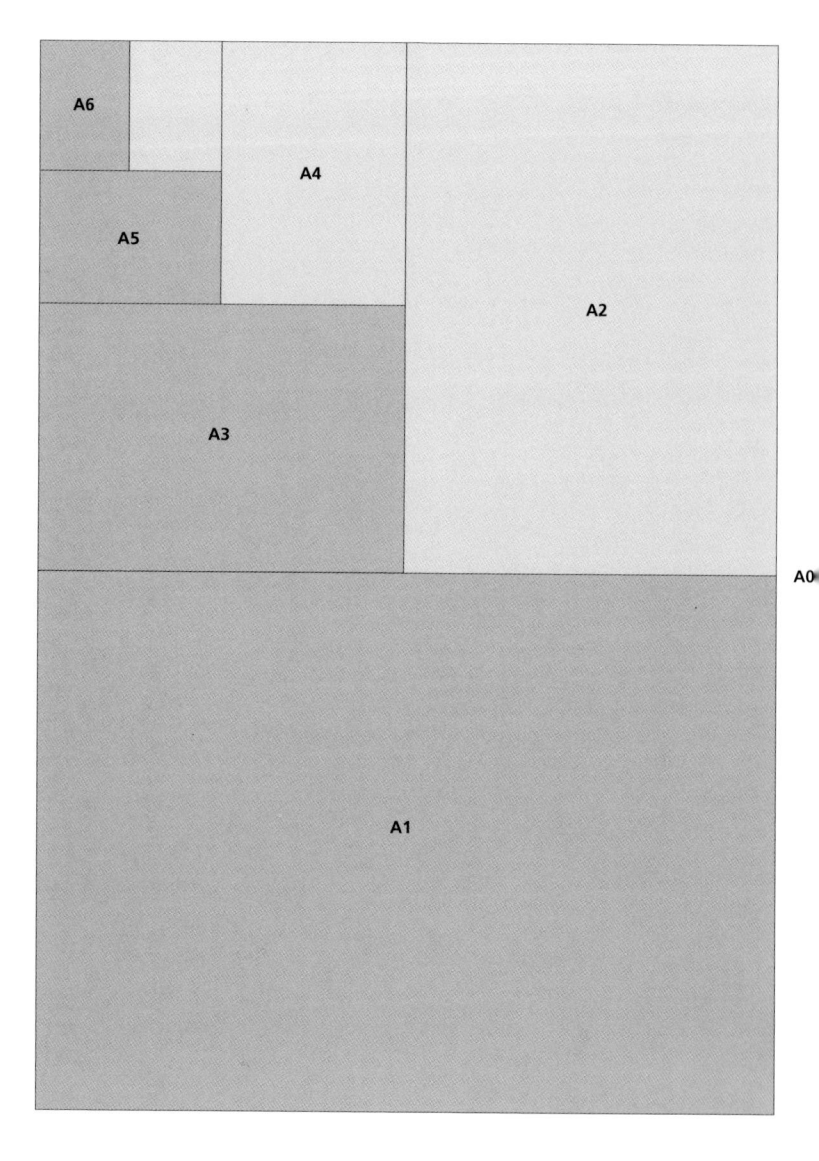

ISO A Series

	mm	inches
A0	841 x 1189	33.11 x 46.81
A1	594 x 841	23.39 x 33.11
A2	420 x 594	16.54 x 23.39
A3	297 x 420	11.69 x 16.54
A4	210 x 297	8.27 x 11.69
A5	148 x 210	5.83 x 8.27
A6	105 x 148	4.13 x 5.83
A7	74 x 105	2.91 x 4.13
A8	52 x 74	2.05 x 2.91
A9	37 x 52	1.46 x 2.05
A10	26 x 37	1.02 x 1.46
RA0	860 x 1220	33.86 x 48.03
RA1	610 x 860	25.02 x 33.86
RA2	430 x 610	16.93 x 24.02
SRA0	980 x 1280	38.58 x 50.39
SRA1	640 x 900	25.20 x 35.43
SRA2	450 x 640	17.72 x 25.20

ISO B Series (untrimmed)

	mm	inches
B0	1000 x 1414	39.37 x 55.67
B1	707 x 1000	27.83 x 39.37
B2	500 x 707	19.68 x 27.83
B3	353 x 500	13.90 x 19.68
B4	250 x 353	9.84 x 13.90
B5	176 x 250	6.93 x 9.84
B6	125 x 176	4.92 x 6.93
B7	88 x 125	3.46 x 4.92
B8	62 x 88	2.44 x 3.46
B9	44 x 62	1.73 x 2.44
B10	31 x 44	1.22 x 1.73

ISO C Series envelopes

	mm	inches
C0	917 x 1297	36.00 x 51.20
C1	648 x 917	25.60 x 36.00
C2	458 x 648	18.00 x 25.60
C3	324 x 458	12.80 x 18.00
C4	229 x 324	9.00 x 12.80
C5	162 x 229	6.40 x 9.00
C6	114 x 162	4.50 x 6.40
C7	81 x 114	3.20 x 4.50
DL	110 x 220	4.33 x 8.66
C7/6	81 xd 162	3.19 x 6.38

ENDMATTER

Paper usage formulae
To calculate the number of sheets of paper required
to print a book or booklet (excluding covers):

$$\frac{\text{Number of copies to be printed} \times \text{Number of pages in book}}{\text{Number of pages printing on both sides of sheet}} = \text{Number of sheets required}$$

To calculate the number of copies obtainable from
a given quantity of paper:

$$\frac{\text{Number of sheets} \times \text{Number of pages printing on both sides of sheet}}{\text{Number of pages in book}} = \text{Number of copies}$$

Bulk calculation for books
In the USA, the bulk of a paper is expressed as a "bulk factor" that is the number of pages of the paper that measure one inch thick. The term for this is PPI (pages per inch). The metric system used elsewhere, describes bulk with a volume figure that gives the thickness in millimeters of 200 pages of a 100 gsm paper. The following formulae are used for metric bulk calculations:

To calculate bulk where the volume of a paper is known:

$$\frac{\text{gsm} \times \text{volume} \times \text{half the number of pages}}{10{,}000} = \text{bulk (mm)}$$

To calculate caliper:

$$\frac{\text{gsm} \times \text{volume}}{10} = \text{caliper in microns}$$

To calculate volume where caliper and substance are known:

$$\frac{\text{caliper in microns} \times 10}{\text{gsm}} = \text{volume}$$

British standard book sizes		
	mm	inches
A format	178 x 111	7.01 x 4.37
B format	198 x 129	7.80 x 5.08

	Quarto		Octavo	
	mm	inches	mm	inches
Crown	246 x 189	9.69 x 7.44	186 x 123	7.32 x 4.84
Large Crown	258 x 201	10.16 x 7.91	198 x 129	7.8 x 5.08
Demy	276 x 219	10.87 x 8.62	216 x 138	8.5 x 5.43
Royal	312 x 237	12.28 x 9.33	234 x 156	9.21 x 6.14

NB With the exception of A and B format, the above sizes are for sewn books. The unsewn sizes are 3mm (1/8in) narrower to allow for the paper cut off in the unsewn binding process.

Commonly used USA paper sizes:

Legal – 8 ½ x 14 inches
Foolscap – 8 ½ x 13 inches
Quarto – 8 ½ x 11 inches

US book sizes				
	mm	inches	mm	inches
	140 x 216	5 ½ x 8 ½	156 x 235	6 ⅛ x 9 ¼
	127 x 187	5 x 7 ⅜	136 x 203	5 ⅜ x 8
	140 x 210	5 ½ x 8 ¼	143 x 213	5 ⅝ x 8 ⅜

Conversion tables USA weights to g/m²

In the USA, basis weight is described as the weight of a ream (500 sheets) of paper in one of several standard sizes, depending on the type of work for which the paper is being used. These are:

25 x 38 inches – book (books and general printing)
24 x 36 inches – tag
20 x 26 inches – cover
17 x 22 inches – bond (stationery and forms)

Cover board is also specified by calliper (thickness) rather than weight. The unit used a "point", which is a thousandth of an inch (0.001 inches), so 10 point stock is 0.010 inches thick. Point is abbreviated to "pt.".

500 sheets 25 x 38 inches		500 sheets 24 x 36 inches		500 sheets 20 x 26 inches		500 sheets 17 x 22 inches	
lb	g/m²	lb	g/m²	lb	g/m²	lb	g/m²
20	30	25	41	50	135	8	30
25	31	30	49	55	149	10	38
30	44	35	57	60	162	12	45
35	52	40	65	65	176	14	53
40	59	45	73	70	189	16	60
45	66	50	82	75	203	18	68
50	74	55	90	80	216	20	75
55	81	60	98	85	230	22	83
60	89	65	105	90	243	24	90
65	96	70	114	95	256	26	98
70	104	75	122	100	270	28	105
75	111	80	130	105	284	30	113
80	118	85	138	110	298		
85	126	90	147	115	310		
90	133	95	155	120	324		
95	140	100	163	125	338		
100	148	125	204	130	352		
105	155	150	244	135	366		
110	162	175	285	140	379		
115	170	200	325	145	392		
120	178	225	365	150	405		
125	185	250	400				
130	193	275	450				
135	200	300	490				
140	208						
145	215						
150	222						

Select bibliography

Bookmaking, Marshall Lee (W. W. Norton, 2004)

Color Management, John T. Drew and Sarah A. Meyer (Rotovision, 2005)

The Effective Editor's Handbook, Barbara Horn (Pira International, 1997)

Five Hundred Years of Printing, S.H.Steinberg revised by John Trevitt
(The British Library and Oak Knoll Press, 1996)

Getting it Printed, Eric Kenly and Mark Beach (F & W Publications, 2004)

Graphic Designer's Digital Printing & Prepress Handbook, Constance Sidles
(Rockport, 2001)

Handbook of Print Media, Helmut Kipphan (Springer-Verlag, 2001)

Notes on Book Design, Derek Birdsall (Yale University Press, 2004)

Picture Credits

1.1 Gutenberg Bible, courtesy of Topfoto/British Library/HIP
1.11 Courtesy of Canon
1.14 iPad, courtesy of Apple
2.2 JDF logo, courtesy of CIP4
2.26 Kodak iQsmart^3 scanner, courtesy of Kodak Graphic Communications Group
2.37 iMac, courtesy of Apple
2.39 Dell Vostro, courtesy of Dell Inc.
2.40 LaCie 324 monitor, courtesy of LaCie
3.6 Dupont Cromalin Blue, courtesy of Dupont
3.11 Viewing booth, courtesy of Verivide Ltd.
3.15 Agfa Avanxis IV, and 3.17 Agfa Avalon platesetter, courtesy of Agfa Graphics
3.18 Agfa Xcalibur platesetter, courtesy of William Clowes Ltd.
3.21 Letterpress forme, courtesy of Ski Harrison/ Whittington Press
3.24 Hell K6 HelioKlischograph, courtesy of Hell Gravure Systems GmbH.
4.7 Heidelberg Printmaster, and 4.8 Heidelberg CD102, courtesy of Heidelberg Druckmaschinen A.G.
4.9 Timson T48, courtesy of Clays Ltd.
4.11 KBA Compacta 215, courtesy of KBA
4.15 Kodak NexPress, copyright Eastman Kodak Company
4.16 Agfa Grand Sherpa 50, courtesy of Agfa Graphics
4.25 Locking up a forme, 4.26 Taking an impression, and 4.27, Letterpress press room, courtesy of Ski Harrison/Whittington Press
5.2 Pine forest, 5.6 Sorting paper for recycling, 5.8 Bales of pulp, 5.12 Jumbo reels, 5.14 Reels, 5.22 Harvesting timber, and 5.23 Planting Eucalyptus, courtesy of Stora Enso
5.3/5.10 Arctic Paper Mill and machines, Munkedals, Sweden, and 5.11 Calendering roller, courtesy of Arctic Paper
5.21 FSC Web site, copyright Forest Stewardship Council A.C.
5.24 Three-roll ink mill, courtesy of Bühler A.G.
6.1 Polar guillotine, courtesy of POLAR
6.5 Stahl folding machine, courtesy of Heidelberger Druckmaschinen A.G.
6.9 ISP BinderyMate, courtesy of ISP Stitching & Bindery Products
6.10 Heidelberger Stitchmaster ST 350, courtesy of Heidelberger Druckmaschinen A.G.
6.12 Book bindery, and 6.13 Perfect binding line, courtesy of Williams Clowes Ltd.
6.23 Gold-foil-stamping, courtesy of Clays Ltd.
7.3 Chinese factory, courtesy of Leo Papers Ltd.
7.4-7.6 Midas Printing, Hong Kong

Index

ablative technology 76
accordion fold 142
accounts 160
accreditation 134
achromatic color removal 43
acid-free paper 126
Acrobat 14, 26, 54, 59, 78
Acrobat Distiller 58, 78
additive primaries 36
additives 136
addressing 156, 175
adhesive 124, 144, 154
adjustment layer 55
Adobe 14, 28, 52, 54, 55, 58, 78
advertising 6, 20, 33, 65–66, 96, 167
after-processing 124, 129
air conditioning 95
airbrushing 12
airfreight 164
aluminium 75, 78
AM (amplitude modulation) 39
Amazon 19
America 8, 114
anilox rollers 110
Antique finish 123, 127, 130
Antique laid paper 127
Apple 14, 33, 44, 56–57
application files 65
apprenticeships 48
Approval 65
archiving 30, 33, 60, 163
Asia 148
asset management 33
atmospherics 95
attachments 60
audio books 20
augustijn 51
authors 163, 178
auto-stereo images 113
automation 12

back-gauge 140
backups 33, 56, 163
bad register 179
bank paper 126
banknotes 113
bas-relief 113
Baskerville 52
Bavaria 88
beating 120
belt presses 80, 108
bespoke printing 158, 161–62
bibles 152
billboards 106
binders 72, 153
binder's board 176
binding 18, 26, 95, 126, 130, 132–33, 140, 142, 144–51, 153, 163, 167, 170, 173, 176, 179
binding lines 12
binding machines 108
biogas 135
bite 108
bitmaps 52, 55, 58–59, 75
black 11, 36, 43, 66, 91
black-and-white printing 30, 34, 46, 56, 62, 66, 91, 96, 110, 127–28, 170, 176
blanket-to-blanket presses 91

bleed 68, 168, 173
blemishes 68
blind stamping 154
blind-embossing 113
blockbusters 154
blocking 108, 148, 154
blocks 80, 108–9
blogging 21
Blu-Ray 14, 33, 60
blues 36, 70, 75–76, 164
board 126, 136, 148, 175–76
bold fonts 52
bond paper 126
book production specifications 176
booklets 142, 152, 173
books 6, 8, 11, 18, 20–21, 28, 34, 40, 70, 80, 88, 92, 96, 108, 114, 119, 126–28, 130–32, 140, 142, 144, 153–54, 161, 167, 170
booksellers 19
bottles 104
box making 152
brass 148, 154
broadband 17, 20, 60
brochures 91–92, 144, 158
broke 118
browsers 60, 78
buckle folds 142
buckram 148
bulk 130–31
bulk after printing 132
bulky mechanical 126
Bullock, William 8
bull's eyes 179
burst binding 144
business cards 91, 113, 152, 181
buying paper 161

CAD (computer-aided design) 152
calendars 147
calendering 123, 126, 128
calibration 17, 46, 57, 65–66, 92
caliper 130
Cameron belt press 108
Canada 134
Canon 16, 98
carbon neutrality 24
carbonless copying papers 129
cartons 62, 128, 152, 154, 156, 175, 180
cartridge papers 126, 128
cased books 126, 144, 154, 176
casemaking 148
cast-coated papers 128
casting off 28
catalogs 92, 95, 100, 126
Caxton, William 8
CCDs (charge-coupled devices) 46
CDs 24, 33, 60, 104
cellophane 110
cellulose acetate 152–53
certification 24
CGS Oris 65
chain of custody 134
chase 108
chemical curing 136
chemical pulp 116, 126
children's books 126, 128, 147, 167
China 8, 114, 167, 182

chlorine-free bleach 135
chokes 43
chromo paper 128
cicero 51
CIF (cost of insurance and freight) 167
CIJ (continuous flow ink-jet) 65
CIP4 26, 92
circulars 113
clamps 140
closed-loop systems 92
Clymer, George 8
CMMs (color-matching modules) 44
CMYK 36, 39–40, 44, 46, 58, 65, 68
co-editions 91, 176
coated papers 17, 124, 128, 133
codes of conduct 24
cold foil stamping 154
collating 98, 108, 152
collotype 110–13
color balance 62, 95
color bar 65–66, 70
color casts 30, 33
color correction 12, 59, 68
color management 44, 56, 65
color photographs 33
color on press 70
color proofs 68
color separation 12, 36
color supplements 100
Color Sync 44
color values 70
color variation 179
Columbian press 8
comics 110
compiling 78
compositors 11, 48
compression 58, 60
Compugraphic 12
computer printers *see* printers
computers 56–57
concertina fold 142
condensed fonts 52
conservation 135
continuous-tone printing 110
contract proofs 65
contracts 180
contrast 30, 33, 103
copper engraving 113
copy fitting 28
copy-dot scanners 46, 75
copy-editors 28
copyright 52
CorelDRAW 30, 54, 59
corrections 163, 180
costs 18, 24, 48, 59, 65, 92, 96, 98–99, 103–4, 109, 139, 147, 160, 167–68, 173, 175–76, 181–82
couriers 17, 60, 156, 164
covers 128, 140, 147, 152–54, 173, 176, 179
craft binders 148
crash 148
creasing 108
Creative Suite 14, 54
Creo Veris 65
Cromalin Blue 65
cropping 54
cross-platform design 23

cross-platform publishing 78
cross-ply boards 148
CRT (cathode ray tube) 57
CTP (computer to plate) 14, 17, 24, 62, 75–76, 78, 80, 164
curl stability 132
currencies 167
Curves 30
customs brokers 167–68
cut-off 87, 95, 100, 103
cutting 140
cutting and creasing 152
cyan 11, 36, 43, 91, 176

dampening 94–95
dandy rolls 123
dashboards 104
DAT tapes 33
databases 18, 20, 48, 96
Daye, Stephen 8
daylight 68
DCS (Desktop Color Separations) 58
deadlines 6, 180
debossing 154
deckles 119
delivery 175
delivery dates 160, 161, 175, 180
delivery instructions 156
Dell 57
Delphax 98
deluxe editions 148
densitometers 66
descreen/rescreen 46
design applications 54–55
desktop publishing 12, 14, 17, 48, 51–52, 56
developing countries 24
DI (Direct Imaging) 94
The Diamond Sutra 8
diaries 152
dichromate 110
dictionaries 152
Didot, Firmin 48, 51
die stamping 113
die-cutting 108, 140, 152
dies 148, 154
digital images 30, 36, 46, 54–55, 58
digital printing 14, 17–18, 20, 24, 80, 88, 94–99, 129, 139, 153, 175
digital proofers 44
digital proofing 65–66, 178
digital proofs 62, 66, 164, 170
digital typesetting 11
discounts 158
distribution 156, 180
doctor blades 100
Docucolor 98
Docutech 98
DOD (drop on demand) 65
door trims 104
dot gain 34, 40, 62, 66, 94
dot-for-dot pickup 46
double-keyboarding 28
double-page spreads 142
doubling effects 113
downloading 20, 60
dpi (dots per inch) 46, 58, 75
dressmaking patterns 104
Dropsend 60

dry back 70
drying 91–92, 100, 103–4, 107, 110, 132, 136, 152
dummies 140, 176
duotones 34
duping 33
duplicate books 108
duplicating 113
Duplo 113
Dupont 65
durability 168
DVDs 14, 24, 33, 60, 104
dye-sublimation 65
dyelines 76

e-auctions 161
email 14, 17, 58, 60, 164, 167, 180–81
EBI (electronic beam imaging) 97
eBooks 6, 20–21
ePub 6
ECF (Elementally Chlorine Free) 135
economics 11, 17–19, 48, 72, 80, 91, 95–96, 106–7, 170, 173, 215
EDI (Electronic Data Interchange) 180
editing 55
editors 163, 168
EFI 65
Egyptians 114
electrographic printing 129
electronic circuits 104
electronic media 6
electrophotography 97
electros 80, 123
electrostatics 65, 97
em 51
embossing 108, 113, 123, 154
encyclopedias 6, 20
endpapers 147, 176
energy conservation 135
energy costs 24
Enfocus Pitstop Professional 59
England 8, 114
English finish 123, 127
engraving 80, 83, 103, 113
envelope making 152
environment 24, 94, 114, 116, 118–19, 134–35, 139
EPS (Encapsulated PostScript) 54–55, 58
errors 6, 12, 14, 26, 28, 59, 68, 178, 180
esparto 116
estimates 160, 175–76, 180–81
etching 11, 80, 83, 110, 113
eucalyptus 116
Europe 8, 17, 44, 48, 51, 65, 114, 148, 164, 167, 173
evaporation 136
export staff 167
exposure control 75
extent 173
external-drum platesetters 75–76
extras 175–76, 182
EXW (Ex-works) 167
eye move 113
EZ-PDF 78

Far East 8, 17, 164, 167
feeders 84
felt 123
Fetch 60
file exchange 60

file formats 58–59
file size 60
film proofs 62, 68
film storage 14
filmsetting 11–12, 48
finishing 12, 18, 26, 91, 98, 132, 139–40, 152–54, 163, 170, 178–79, 181
flaps 147
flat artwork 33, 46
flat back 148
flatbed platesetters 76
flatbed presses 88, 100
flatbed scanners 39, 46, 56
flexography 66, 80, 83, 92, 100, 110, 136, 139, 154
Flightcheck Professional 59
floppy disks 12, 60
FM (frequency modulation) 39–40
FOB (Free On Board) 167
FOGRA 65
foil stamping 108, 148, 154
folding 12, 87, 91, 108, 132, 140, 142, 152, 170
fonts 51–52, 54, 58–59, 65, 76, 78
food 136, 154
forme 80, 108, 152
forms 91, 113, 160–61
foul copy 168
foundries 48
four-color process 11, 36, 40, 43, 46, 62, 83, 96, 110, 139, 142, 173, 176
Fourdrinier brothers 114
Fourdrinier machines 114, 119, 123
Fournier, Pierre 48
FPO (for position only) 46
FrameMaker 54
France 11, 48, 51, 114
freesheet 126
freight forwarding 167–68
french fold 142
Friends of the Earth 134
frog eyes 179
FSC (Forest Stewardship Council) 134
FTP (file transfer protocol) 17, 60, 163–64
fulfillment services 18
fumigation 167

gamut 36
Garamond 52
gathering 152, 170
GCR (gray component replacement) 43
Germany 8, 11, 51
GIF (Graphic Interchange File) 55, 58
glare 66
glass 104
gloss 91, 113, 128, 131, 147, 152–53, 158, 175
glue lines 142, 152
gluing 87, 152
glyphs 52
GMG 65
Google 182
grades 116, 130
grain 33, 130, 133, 142
graphics tablets 56
gravure 66, 83–84, 87–88, 95, 100–103, 109, 113, 136, 139
grayscale 46
green 36
Green Press Initiative 134

Greenpeace 134
greetings cards 152
groundwood pulping 116
growth 92
gsm (grammes per square meter) 130
guards 140
guide proofs 65
guillotines 12, 140
Gutenberg Bible 8
Gutenberg, Johannes 8, 136
gutters 144

H&J (hyphenation and justification) 163
half-sheet work 72
halftones 30, 34, 46, 65, 75, 83, 95, 103, 106–8, 126–28
halos 179
hand binding 148, 173
hand move 113
handbills 158
handheld devices 20
handmade paper 119, 127
hard drives 14, 33, 56
hardbacks 147–51, 154
head box 123
headbands 148
health and beauty products 154
heat setting 136
Heidelberg 95
hexachrome 40, 91
hi-bulk grades 130
Hi-Fi 91
hickies 132, 179
HiFi color 40
highlights 30, 39
hinges 147
history of paper 114
Holland 51
holographic foils 154
hot melt 144
hot metal typesetting 108
house style 28
HP (Hewlett Packard) 56, 98
humidity 95, 132, 153, 176
hydrapulpers 120
hypertext 14

IBM 56, 98
ICC (International Color Consortium) 36, 40, 44, 65, 92, 178
ICG 65
ideographs 8
iDisk 60
iGen 98
illustrations 11, 14, 17, 28, 30, 54, 66, 72, 91, 127–28, 132, 147, 168
Illustrator 14, 30, 36, 54, 59
iMacs 57
imagesetters 14, 39, 72, 75–76
imposition 59, 72–75, 142
imprint pages 176
iPad 20-21
InDesign 14, 17, 28, 43–44, 48, 54, 59, 78, 170
indexes 20, 28
India 28, 48, 167
Indigo 97–98
industry standards 65
ink rub 132
ink-jet printing 98, 104, 106
inks 6, 24, 26, 34, 36, 40, 43, 62, 66, 70, 75, 84, 88, 92, 94–98, 100,

103, 106–10, 113–14, 128, 132, 136–39, 173, 179
inputs 26
inserts 144, 147, 176
instant printers 91, 95
insurance 167, 182
intaglio 83–84, 100, 113
Intel chip 56
intellectual property rights 182
Interarchy 60
internal-drum platesetters 75–76
international suppliers 164–67, 182
Internet 6, 17, 20, 60, 161, 180–82
Intertype Photosetter 12
inventories 96
invitations 108, 113
invoices 161, 167, 175, 182
iPods 21
iRex iLiad 20
ISBN (International Standard Book Number) 19
ISDN (Integrated Services Digital Network) lines 60
ISO standard 44, 65
italic fonts 52
Italy 51, 114

jackets 148, 153–54, 173, 176
Jaz disks 60
JDF (job definition format) 26-27, 54, 59, 78, 181
JMF (Job Messaging Format) 26
job tickets 26, 54, 59, 78
journals 20, 156
JPEG (Joint Photographic Experts Group) files 44, 55, 58, 75
just-in-time arrangements 161

KBA Karat 95
keyboarding 163, 168
Kindle 20-21
knife folds 142
knockout 43, 54
Kodak 65–66, 98
Koenig, Frederick 8
Konica 98
kraft 116, 148

labels 154, 156, 175, 180
laminates 100
laminating 24, 126, 129, 139, 152–54
landscape 33, 133, 173
languages 91, 167, 176
Lanston, Tolbert 11
large formats 98–99
laser engraving 80
laser printing 97
Lasercomp 12
layout grids 72
LCD (liquid crystal display) 57, 97
leaflets 91, 126, 142, 152
LED (light-emitting diodes) 57, 97
legal considerations 176, 180–82
lenticular printing 113
letterheads 88, 113, 119, 154, 181
letterpress 11–12, 80, 84, 88, 100, 108–10, 113, 152
Levels 30
LG (long grain) 130
licenses 52, 58, 78
lighting 57, 66, 68, 70
limited editions 108, 119, 148

line block 11
line images 46
line lengths 51
line originals 30
lines per inch 34
lining 148
Linofilm 12
Linotype 11
Linotype VIP 12
linting 132
liquids 136
lithography 11–12, 14, 62, 66, 72, 75–76, 80, 84, 88–96, 100, 103, 108–10, 113, 129, 136, 139–40
long edge 132
long runs 62, 70, 83, 87, 91–92, 95, 100, 103, 130, 178
loose-leaf binding 153
Lumitype 12

McCain stitching 144
Macintosh 14, 52, 56, 58, 78
macros 163
magazines 12, 20, 28, 30, 34, 65–66, 76, 84, 88, 92, 95–96, 100, 110, 126, 128, 130, 140, 144, 156, 160, 161
magenta 11, 36, 43, 70, 91
magnetography 98
mail-order catalogs 92, 100
Mailbigfile 60
mailing 147, 156
make-ready 18, 70, 84, 87–88, 91–92, 95, 110, 170, 173, 175
manuals 128, 147, 153, 160
manuscripts 12, 168
maps 128
Markzware 59
Matchprint 65
materials 106–7, 110, 148
matt 91, 128, 132, 153, 175
mechanical papers 126
mechanical pulping 116
medium runs 91
Mergenthaler, Ottmar 11
metadata 26, 30, 44
metal 88, 98, 104, 110, 139, 154
metal type 108–9
metameric papers 131
metamerism 68
MF (machine finishing) 126
MG (machine glazing) 126
Microsoft 52, 78
midtones 39
Minolta 98
misregister 43
mistakes *see* errors
mobile phones 20
moiré 39, 46
mold-made paper 119
monitors 17, 36, 44, 52, 57, 66, 92
Monophoto 12
Monotype 11–12
moveable type 8, 136
MP3 players 20–21
mull 148
multinationals 24

negotiation 158, 182
networks 56, 60
New York Herald Tribune 11
newspapers 11–12, 19–20, 65, 76, 80, 92, 110, 114, 119

Nexpress 98
niche publications 18
nipping 147
Nipson press 98
notch binding 144, 147
notepaper 84
novels 91, 154
Nuvera 98

oblong 173
Océ 98
OCR (Optical Character Recognition) 28
off-machine processes 124
Office 78
offset lithography 11–12, 18, 34, 62, 66, 72, 76, 80, 83–84, 88–96, 103, 108–9, 113, 129, 136, 139–40, 154
OmniPage 28
one-ply board 148
opacity 131
OpenType 52
operating systems 56
OPI (Open Prepress Interface) 46
OPP (oriented polypropylene) 153
origination 170
OS X 56
out-of-print books 18–19
outputs 26, 30
outsourcing 160, 163
overprinting 43, 54
overs 180
overtime 160
ownership 182
oxidation 136
ozalids 70, 75–76, 164

packaging 6, 20, 40, 70, 80, 88, 91, 100, 110, 126, 136, 154, 167, 180
packing 156, 167, 175, 180
page geometry 72
page layout 12, 17, 23, 28, 30, 46, 48, 52, 54–55, 58–59, 72, 75, 168, 170
page margins 6
page size 170, 173
PageMaker 14, 59
pagemarkers 148
Palatino 52
pallets 156, 167, 175, 180
pamphlets 142
Pantone 36, 40, 70, 91, 173
paper 6, 8, 17, 24, 26, 28, 34, 40, 62, 65, 84, 87–88, 91–92, 95–96, 98–100, 103–4, 108–9, 113–35, 140, 142, 147, 175–76, 179, 182
paper merchants 161
paper size 130
paper stretch 142
paper testing 131
paperbacks 126, 144–47, 152, 176
papermaking 114, 116, 120, 123, 126, 134–35
papyrus 114
parchment 114
part works 153
Pass4Press 65
PCs (personal computers) 14, 17, 20–21, 54, 56, 78
PDF/X 58
PDFs (Portable Document Format) 14, 17–18, 20, 26, 28, 43, 52, 54, 58–59, 62, 65–66, 72, 75–76, 78, 80, 96, 164, 168, 170

PEFC (Programme for Endorsement of Forest Certification) 134
pen plotters 83
penalty charges 168
penetration 136
perfect binding 144–47, 179
perfecting 91
perforating 87, 108, 140, 144, 152
peripherals 56–57
personalization 96, 99
pharmaceuticals 154
photocomposition 12
photocopying 14, 24, 91, 97, 168
photogelatin 110
photographers 30
photography 66, 83, 103, 106, 147, 170
photogravure 11, 100
photopolymer 75–76, 80
Photoshop 14, 30, 33–34, 36, 39, 44, 54–55, 58–59, 68
photostencils 83
phototypesetting 52
Pi Sheng 8
picas 48, 51
picking 95, 132
PICT 58
pigment 136
pine 116
planographic process 84, 88, 110
plastic papers 128
plastic-comb binding 147
platemaking 18, 58–59, 66, 70, 72–75, 80–84
plates 147
platesetters 39, 72, 75–76, 78
PLC (printed laminated case) 148
plotter proofs 28, 54, 68, 70, 76, 78, 164
plug-ins 54, 78
PMS (Pantone Matching System) 139, 173
PNG 55
POD (Print on Demand) 17–19, 96, 153
podcasting 6, 20
point-of-sale work 104
points 48, 51
politics 182
pollution 135
polyester 75
popup advertisements 6
portrait 33, 173
posters 6, 98, 104, 128, 136
PostScript 14, 51–52, 58–59, 78, 96
power supplies 6
PowerPC 56
PPC (printed paper case) 148
PPI (pages per inch) 131
preflighting 59–60
prepress 14, 18, 26, 43, 66, 78, 80, 92, 103, 139, 163–64, 175, 178
prepress houses 30, 33, 44, 48, 54, 56, 59, 62, 75, 78, 158, 164, 168, 178
presensitizing 75
presets 48
press checks 70
press controls 92, 95
press proofs 62, 66, 170
press-rooms 95
price 158, 161, 163–64, 168, 170, 175–76, 180, 182

price lists 91, 113
primary colors 36, 43
print broking 160
print buying 158–63, 178
print management 160, 161
print orders 180–81
print processes 84–87
print reverse auctions 161
print schedules 70
printers 14, 17, 44, 52, 54, 56, 58, 62, 65, 83
printing plates 84
printouts 60
private presses 108–9
production editors 28
profiles 30, 36, 40, 44, 65, 92, 178
profit 158, 160, 163
promotional items 70, 92, 113, 128, 158, 160, 170
proof correction marks 28
proofing 24, 28, 40, 44, 57, 59, 62, 65, 78, 128, 163, 168, 178, 180
proofs 17, 24, 28, 30, 54, 56, 62, 70, 163–64, 168, 180, 182
PSD files 55, 58
pulp 114, 116, 118–20, 126, 129, 135
punch register system 72
PUR (polyurethane resin) 144
purchase orders 176
PVA (polyvinyl acetate) 144

quadtones 34
quality 158, 164, 167, 178–79
quantity 175, 182
QuarkXPress 14, 17, 28, 43, 48, 54, 59, 170
quotations 158, 160–61, 163, 168, 176, 181–82

Rainforest Alliance 134
raster files 55, 58
RealTimeProof 66
reams 130
recycling 6, 24, 114, 118–19, 128, 135, 139, 148
red 36
reels 84, 91, 98, 100, 123–24, 132
refining 120
reflection copy 33
register 95, 100, 130, 132, 179
relief process 84, 108
remote proofing 44, 62, 66, 164
repalletizing 180
reports 91, 128, 153, 160
reprinting 18, 62, 92, 103, 168, 176
repro houses 33, 36, 39, 44, 46, 54, 56, 60, 62, 66, 68, 70, 75, 78
repro instructions 30
resins 136
resolution 46, 58–59, 68, 78, 168, 170, 178
retouching 55, 75
RGB 36, 39, 44, 46, 68
RH (relative humidity) 132
riga tipografica 51
ring binders 153
RIP (Raster Image Processor) 39, 43, 58–59, 75
ripping 59, 78
Riso 113
Robert, Nicholas Louis 114
roll-coating 123

roll-fed printing 84
roman fonts 52
rotary presses 108, 114
rotary principle 88, 110
rotogravure 100
round cornering 152
rounded and backed 148
royalties 78
run-on rate 175

saddle-stitching 142, 144, 152
salespeople 160
SC (super calendering) 126
scaling 54
Scandinavia 118
scanners 12, 14, 17, 33, 36, 39, 43, 48, 56, 75
scanning 55, 59, 168
scheduling 180–81
scoring 140, 152
scratches 68
screen printing 66, 83, 98, 104–7
sealing 152
second proofs 180
secondary colors 36
security 113
self-ends (self-endpapers) 147
self-publishing 19
Senefelder, Alois 11, 88
serifs 75
servers 33, 56, 60
service 158, 160–61, 164, 167
set width 51
setoff 179
sewing 140, 170
sewn book binding 147
SG (short grain) 130
SGML (Standard Generalized Markup Language) 23
shade 131
shadows 39
sharpness 30
sheet-fed presses 72, 84–87, 91–92, 100, 142, 175
sheeters 91
sheeting 152
shingling 142
shipping 164, 167
short runs 18, 48, 84, 88, 91, 95–96, 104, 106–8, 113, 147, 153, 175
shrink-wrapping 156, 175
side sewing 147
side-stitching 144
Sierra Club 134
signatures 142, 144, 147, 176
signs 104
silkscreen printing 104
Singapore 167
Singer sewing 147
single keystroke 12
six-color presses 91
slot binding 144
sludge 139
slurring 66
slushers 120
small offset 91
smashing 147
Smooth finish 123, 127
smudging 91
soft proofing 66, 164
software crashes 6
Sony Reader 20
Spain 114

spam 6
special colors 40
special instructions 131
specifications 130–31, 139, 158, 161, 168–77, 180
spectrophotometer 65
spectrum 36
spines 130, 133, 140, 142, 144, 147–48, 152–53
spiral binding 147
spoilage 175
spot color 62, 65
spot varnishing 152
spreads 43
spruce 116
square back 148
squash 95, 108
stab stitching 144
stacking 132
stains 68
stamps 129
standby mode 24
Stanhope, Earl of 8
stapling 98, 144
stationery 91, 114, 126, 132, 160–61
stencils 83, 104, 106, 113
stereos 80
stitching 87, 140
stochastic screening 12, 39
storage 14, 17–18, 33, 56, 58, 60
strawboard 176
stripping 72
Stuffit 60
subscription copies 156
substance 130
subtractive primaries 36
surface treatment 123
sustainability 24, 114, 116, 119, 134
swatches 70, 139
SWOP (Specifications for Web Offset Publications) 44, 65
SyQuest cartridges 60
system failures 6

t-shirts 104
tagging 23, 26, 44
tailbands 148
taxation 182
TCF (Totally Chlorine Free) 135
technical papers 129
templates 17, 48, 180–81
tension 92
text files 14, 20
themoplastics 113
thermal platesetters 78
thermal-transfer 65
thermography 113
thread-sealing 147
three-dimensional effects 113
TIFF (Tagged Image File Format) files 44, 46, 55, 58
The Times 8
Times 52
timescales 180
Timson 108
tinplate 11
tints 14, 40, 54, 96
tipping 147
title pages 176
title-verso 176
tonal range 30
toners 96–99, 129, 136–39
tracks 70

trade unions 24
transfer protocols 14
transfers 104
translations 176
Transmit 60
transparencies 33, 46, 68, 168
transport 24, 156, 164
trapping 43, 54, 66, 78
trim marks 68
trimmed page size 170–73
trimming 179
tritones 34
TrueType 51–52
Tsai Lun 114
turnarounds 160
twin-wire papers 123
two shot process 144
two-color printing 173
two-up sections 142
type measurement 48–51
typefaces 8, 28, 52, 54, 108
typesetters 164, 168
typesetting 48–51, 108, 114, 163–64, 167–68
typos 70

UCR (undercolor removal) 43
unders 180
United Kingdom 34, 48, 51, 65, 118, 173
United States 34, 48, 51, 65, 118, 130–31, 134, 164, 167, 173, 176
units 48, 51
unsewn binding 144, 147
upright 173
UV (ultraviolet) 136, 152

vacuum bases 104
validity 175–76
vanity publishing 19
variable data printing 17
varnishing 139, 152
vectors 52, 54, 58–59, 75
vellum 114
viewing booths 68
vignettes 39
viruses 60
Vista 56
vlogging 21
VOIP (voice over Internet protocol) 66
VPNs (virtual private networks) 60

W3C (World Wide Web Consortium) 23
wallpaper 100
warehouses 156, 168, 175, 180
warping 92, 95, 153
wastage 24, 43, 87, 94, 175
wastepaper 118–19, 135
water conservation 135
watercolor paintings 119
waterless offset printing 94
watermarks 119
wavelengths 36
web presses 152
Web publishing 78
websites 6, 19–20, 23, 60, 163
web-fed presses 12, 84–87, 91–92, 95, 100, 103, 108, 110, 130, 142, 175
weight 130
wet proofs 62
wind power 135

Windows 52, 56
WinZip 60
wire-stitching 24, 144, 152
wiro binding 147
woodblocks 8, 11
woodfree 126
Word 28
wordprocessing 28, 48, 54, 58
workflow 14, 26, 30, 43, 58–59, 78, 80, 83, 178, 181
World Wildlife Fund 134
Wove finish 123
wraps 147, 176
WSOP (web sized offset printing) 126

Xeikon 98
xerography 97
Xerox 97–98
XML (eXtensible Markup Language) 23, 26, 78
XPS 78
XTensions 54

yellow 11, 36, 43, 91
Yousendit 60

Zip disks 60

Acknowledgments

Updating this book to bring in the many developments in printing processes in recent years has been a daunting task and only possible with the help of several experts on the various topics. In particular, I would like to thank Tony Crouch, who also wrote the glossary, and John Peacock. Both also checked the whole book. Others who helped me on particular topics are: Martin Bristow; Philip Cohen; Bernard Healy; Geoffrey Hook; Barbara Horn; Richard Keller; Chris Maynard; Jo Rooke; David Sinden; and Teresa Solomon.

Thanks also to Judy Palmer for her help with picture research and to the team at RotoVision who helped get this new edition off the ground—my editor Chris Middleton, who supplied supplementary text on some digital aspects of print production; April Sankey (publisher); Tony Seddon (art director); and Jane Waterhouse (design, layout, additional picture research, and in-house photography).

The publishers would like to thank John Woodcock for the illustrations, and Jon France, for editorial and design support.

About the author

David Bann is a graduate of the London College of Printing (now Communication), and a Fellow of the Institute of Paper, Printing & Publishing. He has spent his career in the production side of book publishing. He has been production director of Penguin and Rainbird and has lectured extensively on book production. He is Michael O'Mara Books' Production Consultant, and also handles production for several smaller publishers.